TOURISM MARKETING

Tourism Marketing

M.A. Khan

ANMOL PUBLICATIONS PVT. LTD.
NEW DELHI - 110 002 (INDIA)

ANMOL PUBLICATIONS PVT. LTD.
4374/4B, Ansari Road, Daryaganj
New Delhi - 110 002
Ph.: 23261597, 23278000
Visit us at: www.anmolpublications.com

First Published, 2005

PRINTED IN INDIA

Published by J.L. Kumar for Anmol Publications Pvt. Ltd., New Delhi - 110 002 and Printed at Mehra Offset Press, Delhi.

Contents

Preface

Tourism and Hotel Industry are the two significant sectors of modern day economy and are complimentary to each other. The new world order has turned the whole mankind into one family or society. Today's world is a global village, where distances have no meaning. Although, tourism and travelling are the two phenomena, as old as the civilized world, yet, tourism evolved into a regular and well-organised industry, during the last century only.

Hotel industry is part and parcel of tourism sector. The tourists are honoured guests and the hotels offer them the demanded hospitality. Hence, the two form a correlated industrial sector, which is growing and flourishing fast, with promises for future.

Extension of education and expansion of knowledge have created a new anxiety, among the members of the new generation, regarding the above said two areas. In fact, the two sectors offer high profile career avenues and good opportunities for aspirants and job-seekers. However, like other disciplines, Tourism and Hotel Management also require proper training for professionals. Hence, a large room for exhaustive and exclusive books on the subject, is there.

This series of comprehensive books has been outlined within the parameters of the syllabi of various universities and institutes, in a broad-based manner, in order to cover all streams of the discipline and for the benefit of students at graduate and post-graduate levels.

The undersigned is confident of a due recognition and proper acknowledgement from concerned circles. Further expectation is that this series of useful books would prove to be practically helpful to the professionals and students equally.

— Editor

1

Introduction

Evolution of the concept of tourism marketing can be associated with the various business and social changes, which have occurred since the introduction of industrialisation. Industrialisation had brought about the need for holiday and travel even in its early stages as the workers felt the need for temporary rest and relaxation after long hours of work. Industrialisation enabled societies especially in western countries, and later on, elsewhere, to produce a range of consumer products in mass quantity. The products were to be sold to the consumers to be consumed. The selling thus became an important business function.

In the early stages the concept of selling was also applied to selling travel and holidays. However, like consumer products, tourism also assumed huge proportions, resulting in a multiplicity of products and sales intermediaries trying to get maximum share of the market. This gave rise to competition industry . Today, tourism is the fastest growing industry in the world and also one of the world's most competitive industry. This competition is constantly growing as more and more destinations seek to attract tourists and more companies and organisations become involved in the highly-skilled business of destination planning, transportation, accommodation and catering for the tourists.

Like any other product, tourism needs to be marketed. Perhaps travel and tourism needs to be marketed more vigorously because it is an industry in which the customer has immense variety of choice as also varied motivations for travel. Marketing concept helps in understanding and identifying the needs and desires of holidaymakers and then satisfying the same. This aspect of marketing is particularly important to the travel and tourism industry.

Marketing and its role today has changed drastically over the years. However, markets and marketing systems were in existence much earlier. It is therefore important to understand how the markets and marketing systems were evolved before discussing marketing in the tourism industry. From the time of simple barters to the present day complex marketing systems, exchanges, have undergone a great change since the advent of the industrialised societies first in the west and, subsequently, all over the world. Most of an industrialised country's production was conducted in small manufacturing units. In the nineteenth century the market for the goods was limited to the areas surrounding the manufacturing unit. It was rare that a particular manufacturer's product found place in other parts of the country. The main cause for products not finding wider markets was the absence of distribution channels and non-availability of products in sufficient quantities as required by these channels. The absence of quality products and the means of transport to carry these goods over to distant areas were other inhibiting factors. A large majority of people during this period had a limited purchasing power as a result of considerable unemployment. The market for goods other than the necessities of life was rather limited. Only a fraction of the population could afford to indulge in the purchase of such luxuries.

Introduction of mass production during the subsequent years in the post-industrialisation period brought about a change. There was an increase in purchasing power of a large number of people. Also, rapid industrial advancement placed at the disposal of the consumer, a large variety of goods of improved quality, and in abundant quantity, from a large number of competing manufacturers. Supply exceeded the demand. The consumer's choice began to be limited as a result of mass production. This fact compelled the manufacturers to give greater consideration to the needs of the consumer.

The growth of communication systems as a result of rapid industrial advancement played an important role in the development of the marketing concept. The advent of the mechanised transport, first the railways, and later road transport systems, made the physical distribution of goods produced possible over much wider areas. This in turn resulted in increased production being disposed of, over a large geographic area, by means of railways and road transport networks. Subsequently, the mass communication channels like telegraphs, telephones and then circulation of newspapers, helped the manufacturers dispose their products in large quantum. All these developments eventually led to the adoption of a new concept, i.e., the marketing concept by the progressive and forward-looking manufacturing organisations.

The Concept

Several attempts have been made to define 'marketing' but so far no universally accepted definition has been devised. This is perhaps due to the fact that 'marketing' as a comprehensive management function is a fairly recent concept which effectively only started to be applied in the early 1950s. Like most innovations, marketing has been gradually adopted by increasing number of enterprises, mainly in the field of consumer products, with diverse ideas developed, as to what it should embrace and how its principles should be implemented. In the last few decades, however, marketing has become an established management process and practice in most industries.

To understand about marketing, it is necessary to distinguish between the familiar word in everyday use and the term as it is used professionally by marketing managers. There are several definitions of the term, marketing. However, the one definition which is universally quoted is by Philip Kotler. Kotler defines the marketing concept as follows :" The marketing concept holds that the key to achieving organisational goals consists in determining the needs and wants of target markets and delivering the desired satisfactions more effectively and efficiently than competitors."

Some other experts in the field have defined the concept as follows :

Philips and Duncan: "marketing includes all the activities necessary to place goods and services in the hands of consumers and industrial users, excluding only such activities as involve a significant change in the form of goods."

Carl Dysinger: "Marketing is finding out what the consumer wants and selling it to him at a profit."

Neville Teller: "as the efficient utilisation of a company's resources to match existing or future consumer demand, and the manipulation and promotion to ensure that the products of these resources are in the right place, at the right time and at the right price to meet that demand."

Colin Mclver: "marketing is concerned essentially with the prediction of people's future behaviour and an attempt to influence their behaviour in some particular way."

Eugene J. Kelly: "as a business discipline, marketing consists of systematic study of the demand generating or consumer motivating forces, the temporal and spatial considerations influencing economic transaction, and the interacting efforts and responses of buyers and sellers in a market."

Dr. William H. Kaven: "Marketing is a business process by which the existing and potential demand for goods and services is determined, cultivated, and then supplied by the seller. The process includes the efforts of all functional areas of the seller working in concert to produce at the right price, time and place the service or product that meets the market's demand and the marketer's profit goals."

All the above definitions emphasise that concept is a customer orientation backed by integrated marketing aimed at generating customer satisfaction. The important aspects of marketing which emerge are :

(i) Identification of customer needs,

(ii) Prediction of customer behaviour,

(iii) Converting customer needs and motivations into effective demand; and

(iv) Moving the product to the final consumer or user so as to achieve the objective set by the organisation.

The American Management Association has defined marketing as - "the indentification or creation of customer needs and thereafter the motivation and coordinated use of all functions within a business that can fill those needs and benefit both the buyer and the seller."

The British Institute of Marketing has formulated the following definition : "Marketing is the management function which organises' and directs all those business activities involved in assessing and converting customer purchasing power into effective demand for a specific product or service and in moving the product or service to the final customer or user so as to achieve the profit target or other objectives set by the company."

The Institute of Marketing has defined Marketing as "the creative management function which promotes trade and employment by assessing consumer needs and initiating research and development to meet them. It coordinates the resources of production and distribution of goods and services; determines and directs the nature and scale of the total effort required to sell profitably the maximum production to the ultimate user."

Application of the marketing concept has certain important benefits. *Firstly*, the management using this concept realise that customer needs are more basic than particular products. This provides a more reliable and enduring base to the operations of such managements. *Secondly*, the focus on the customer needs helps the management to spot new product opportunities more speedily. *Thirdly*, merchandising becomes more effective under this concept. This is because managements view their tasks as that of meeting customer satisfaction rather than creating demand for its products among the customers. The physical product is only a part of the satisfaction sought by the buyer because he wants, in addition, convenience, service and certain other symbolic values. *Fourthly*, the managements are able to create more harmony between their own interests and those of the society because the market orientation under this concept means that the managements build their profits through seeking better ways to satisfy customer needs.

Perception

It is a well-known fact that as long as the inherent sense of curiosity and adventure dwells in the hearts of human beings, the desire to travel, in order to see new sights and experience new things, and to live under different environments, will always grow. It may be presumed that such being the case, marketing in the tourism industry is greatly simplified as part of the process has already been completed by the desire for travel in people . The best example would be that a person may or may not choose a tangible product which has been introduced by a manufacturer in the market, solely depending on his ability to afford it or his likes and dislikes. On the other hand, without exception, all human-beings will always nurture a desire to travel in order to see places. The question then arises that if the desire is ever-present in people to travel and experience new things, why would the tourism industry need marketing efforts at all?

Tourism is a very complex industry because of its multi-faceted activities which together produce the 'tourist product'. It is also complex because of various sub-sectors that are in themselves complete industries, if considered independently (lodging, transport, etc.). Its complexity, furthermore, lies in the fact that tourism promotion in its various forms has to be directed at large numbers of people in various lands of different socio-economic structures, having different needs, tastes, attitudes, expectations and behaviour patterns. It is only efficient marketing strategy that will help understand people's tastes and preferences for travel. And hence the need for marketing in tourism.

The Definition

Tourism marketing is defined in a number of ways. It could be defined as the "systematic and coordinated efforts exerted by the National Tourist Organisations and/or the -tourist enterprises at international, national and local levels to optimise the satisfaction of tourists, groups and individuals, in view of the sustained tourism growth."

According to Krippendorf, J., marketing in tourism means "systematic and coordinated execution of business policy by tourist undertaking whether private or state owned at local, regional, national or international level to achieve the optimal satisfaction of the needs of identifiable consumer groups, and in doing so to achieve an appropriate return."

Tourist Product

Tourism marketing and marketing in general both emphasise consumer orientation and satisfaction. The concept of consumer orientation, however, makes it necessary to understand the components of the tourist product from the point of view of the consumer. The product for the tourist covers the complete experience from the time he leaves home to the time he returns.

Availability of a product is the prerequisite in the marketing function. Unless there is a certain product, be it tangible or intangible or a service, marketing is not possible. A product may be defined as the 'Sum of the physical and psychological satisfactions it provides to the buyer.' 'Marketing' by definition is the development of a product to meet the needs of the consumer and then employing the techniques of direct sales, publicity and advertising to bring this product to the consumer. In the case of tourism product, the basic raw materials would be the country's natural beauty, climate, history, culture and the people. Other aspects would be the existing facilities necessary for comfortable living such as water supply, electricity, roads, transport, communication and other essentials. In other words the tourist product can be seen as a composite product, as the sum-total of a country's tourist attractions, transport, accommodation and entertainment which hopefully result in consumer satisfaction. The tourist product can be entirely a manmade one or nature's creation improved upon by man. Each of these components of a tourist product is supplied by individual providers of services like hotel companies, airlines or other suppliers, and is offered directly to the tourists by them. A consumer can combine these individual tourist products through a large number of ways. There would be many possible destinations, each with a number of hotels, each to be reached by more than one airline. Thus the potential choice facing the consumer is very large. A number of tourist destinations have placed at the disposal of a tourist a large variety of tourist products in abundant quantity from a large number of competing destinations. This, eventually, has led to the adoption of the new concept, i.e., the marketing concept in tourism by various countries promoting tourism. The important point about marketing is that it is applied to situations where the choice can be limited to a relatively small number of brands giving the consumer a reasonable choice. The process of selection thus becomes easier. In the field of tourism this process is taking place by the increasing use of 'package tours'. A package tour is a travel plan which includes most elements of vacation, such as transportation, accommodation, sight-seeing and entertainment. The tourist product is a composite product, whether it is sold as a package or assembled by the individual tourist himself or his travel agent.

Significant Features

Tourism, basically, is an infrastructure based service product. The nature of the service marketed being highly intangible and perishable offers a limited scope for creating and maintaining the distinctive competitive edge. Effective marketing of tourism needs constant gearing up of infrastructure to international standards and presupposes its coordination with the tourism suppliers. In strategic terms, it calls for the action of an integrated approach to management and marketing. In operational terms, it means the implementation of a better defined, better targeted market-driven strategy for realising the defined objectives.

Marketing of tourist product has certain peculiar characteristics. Although general principles of marketing of products of other industries could be applicable to marketing of tourist product, there are certain differences in approach. Among the peculiarities of the tourist product are:

Tourism is an Intangible, Non-material Product : No transfer of ownership of goods is involved as compared to a tangible product, say for example, a motor car. In tourism, instead, certain facilities, installations, items of equipment are made available for a specified time and for a specified use. For instance, a seat in an aeroplane or a train for a journey from one point to another or a booking in a hotel through a travel agent are carried out for a customer or services such as information and advice are provided.

Production and Consumption of Tourist Services are Closely Interrelated : The travel agent or tour operator who sells his product cannot store it. Production can only take place or can only be completed if the customer is actually present. There is a close link between production and consumption of tourist services. Most tourist services cannot be consumed incrementally. In other words, consumption, once begun, cannot be stopped, interrupted or modified at all. As a result, risk and uncertainty for the customer are higher, and his need for reliable pre-purchase information is stronger. The potential customer's decision-risk and dependence on accurate information is further increased because he cannot see, inspect, compare or try out tourist services before deciding to use them.

Multiplicity of Producers : The tourist product cannot be provided by a single enterprise. Each of the components of a tourist product is highly specialised and together make the final product. This is not so in the case of other tangible products where one manufacturer produces a total product. In tourism on the other hand, an airline considers 'seats flown' or passenger miles to be its product; a hotel produces 'guest nights' a travel agent 'bookings', a theatre and museum or an archaeological site measures its production' in number of visitors. In the tourist's view, however, the product he buys covers the complete experience of his visit to a particular place. In other words the tourist product is not an airline or a rail seat, or a hotel bed or a theatre ticket, but rather an amalgam of many components which together make a complete product. Because of these peculiar characteristics, coordination in marketing efforts, is very crucial.

Highly Unstable Demand : The demand is influenced by factors such as seasonal, economic, political, etc. The seasonal changes greatly affect the demand. Seasonality means that tourism plant is frequently used for a limited part of the year and therefore uneconomic. Many tourist areas have a short season - often as little as three months. A corollary of this seasonal usage is the seasonal unemployment, which is a serious problem. Some of the developing countries which have recently established tourist industries suffer particularly from seasonality. Seasonality also places strains on the transport system and other services. Thus seasonality presents a problem not only in relation to employment but also in relation to investment. On the other hand political unrest and economic instability caused by currency fluctuations and inflation, etc., greatly affect tourism demand.

Dominant Role of Intermediaries : In most industries, manufacturers have predominant control over product design; distribution and promotion and pricing. On the other hand in tourism, sales intermediaries like tour operators, travel agents, reservation services and hotel brokers play a very dominant role and enjoy superior marketing strength. From the standpoint of tourism marketing, this strong position of the travel trade has significant implications. The travel trade determines to a large extent which services will be sold and to whom. The type of services to be offered as well as the pricing policies and promotion strategies to be adopted by tourist enterprises, are, therefore, determined not only by the needs and preferences of the customers but also by those expressed by travel sales intermediaries.

Diverse Motivations : It is comparatively simple to determine why people buy a certain make of refrigerator, smoke certain brands of cigarettes, use certain brands of toothpaste or prefer a certain type of packaged food. The subjective and objective reasons, expectations and desires which influence tourists' choice for a certain holiday destination, type of accommodation and vacation activities are far less evident. Very often two people make exactly the same choices for entirely different and sometimes even mutually exclusive reasons. Travel motivations unlike motivations for buying a tangible article like a refrigerator, are heterogeneous - composed of diverse elements.

Marketing in tourism, due to the various factors mentioned above, as compared to marketing in other industries therefore needs a somewhat different approach. Tourism marketing to a considerable extent depends on various market factors mentioned above. Unlike the normal consumer product or service, the tourist product is marketed at two levels.

(i) The national or regional tourist organisation will be engage in a marketing campaign to persuade the potential tourist to visit the country or region for which it is responsible. In view of the fragmentation of supply, the complementarity of tourist services, the predominance of many small and medium sized enterprises and importance of tourism to an economy, the official tourist organisations have important functions in tourism marketing. The official tourist organisation will however not sell a tourist product directly to customers. It will have two major objectives. In the first place, it will seek to create knowledge of its country in tourist-generating markets and persuade visitors in these markets to visit that country. Secondly, it will seek to create an image of its country's tourist attractions in the best possible manner in tourist-generating markets so that the potential visitors are attracted

(ii) The various individual firms providing tourist services can market their own components of the total tourist product after the national tourist organisations have launched marketing campaigns to persuade the potential tourist to visit the country or region for which it is responsible.

Major Functions

Marketing Function : It is basically customer-oriented, backed by integrated marketing aimed at customer satisfaction. The focus of marketing therefore centres around a customer. Professor Kotler in his definition has also emphasised this fact and stated that achievement of organisational goals depends on determining the needs of target markets (customers) and delivering the desired satisfaction more effectively and efficiently.

From the above it follows that organisations, before achieving their desired goals, have to go through series of marketing functions; and specific understanding of both marketing functions and specific marketing tasks becomes very crucial to grasp the subject of marketing. The marketing function can be considered as a system where interaction occurs between an organisation and a customer.

The main marketing functions and the tasks these functions set for themselves are as follows :

(a) Market Research

(b) Product formulation and development

(c) Analysis and selection of target markets (segmentation)

(d) Distribution networks

(e) Product Promotion

Research and Surveys

Identifying the customer needs especially in a tourism industry which has very high service base content is very important. This is possible only through systematic market research and analysis. This is basic for successful marketing. It relates to providing answers to various questions pertaining to the marketing activities. Market research can be defined as the "Systematic collection of information relating to supply and demand for a product or a proposed product in such a way that the information may be used by the organisation to formulate informed decisions about its policies and its objectives." The marketing process in fact starts by finding out answers to questions like who are the potential tourists, where do they come from, what axe their likes and dislikes, etc. In order to formulate any marketing strategy it is very essential for a national tourist organisation and others engaged in marketing a tourist product to know the answers to the following questions:

(i) Who are the persons who engage in tourism and where do they live?

(ii) Who are the potential customers and where do they come from?

(iii) What are their likes and dislikes?

(iv) What are their travel preferences and interest?

(v) What do they buy and where do they stay?

(vi) What mode of transport do they use?

(vii) What are their entertainment preferences?

(viii) What are the trends in competition?

(ix) What type of marketing programmes would be needed?

Answers to all the above questions are obtainable only through research. A tourist-organisation promotion effort, without appropriate answers to the above questions, will go waste. To make the overall marketing efforts effective and successful, the tourist organisation has to be totally aware of the trends in the travel habits, vacation habits and most important of all, the reasons attributed to the better success of a competing destination. A marketing manager cannot visualise successful marketing strategy without having an uptodate knowledge of their markets in general. It is very important to have detailed information on all the aspects of a market. Results of such research will work as guidelines for launching a successful marketing programme.

Various Techniques

Market research is a continuous process. Among the variety of methods used, some seem to be widely resorted to because of their advantages over others. Research techniques can be grouped as:

(i) Desk research
(ii) Field research
(iii) Sample surveys
(iv) Motivation research

Desk research includes the collection and analysis of all available data, statistics and published information on tourist trends and markets. In tourism much of the basic information about tourist trends and markets is available from existing sources. There are a number of international organisations like United Nations, WTO, EC, OECD, IATA, WTTC, ICAO, etc., which publish certain statistical information. Other data and statistics may be obtained from national tourist organisations, trade associations, carriers, hotel companies, etc. This information proves very useful in helping national tourist organisations to identify their markets and determine the objectives. This published information is of particular use to those countries which do not possess resources enough to undertake independent market research.

Field research, on the other hand, is the research work carried out in the tourist-generating markets itself. The special investigations in the field are to be carried out with a view to know more details of the market situation. Field research includes many methods among which the most common are the sample surveys and the motivation research.

Sample survey could be defined as the study of a given population through only a part or a fraction thereof. Much marketing information is obtained through the use of samples. In this method the population or 'Universe' for which information is required is defined, for example, all households in a country might be the universe or population under investigation. Then, a statistically valid sample of the population is drawn and information is obtained from the sample. Sampling techniques consist of personal interviews of tourists, travel agents, carriers and hotel managers, etc., by way of personal interviews with the help of prepared, questionnaires, by mailing questionnaires or through telephone contacts. There are certain advantages of this method. Lower cost is the major reason why data are collected by sampling in place of complete enumerations. The actual obtaining of information from the sample units (i.e., households in this case) is done by way of use of interviews and questionnaires. The questionnaire is administered to the sample population and various data obtained. The sampling place could be anywhere. Interviews may take place at homes or offices, at the place of arrival departure or temporary stay. In many countries there are a number of specialised firms which carry out sample survey enquiries, as well as government agencies similarly equipped.

The survey investigation can be classified by reference to the kind of information they seek to provide. There are surveys of market behaviour which record the holiday habits of the population, cross analysed by socio-economic, and other characteristics. The trends in holiday-making over many years may be seen and inferences made about the motives of holidaymakers. Furthermore, surveys may be undertaken to monitor the conduct of marketing campaigns.

Motivation research on the other hand attempts to describe and forecast the motives of the population under investigation, by use of techniques originally used in psychology. Assuming that every individual knows what he wants, motivation research is oriented to discover the needs of potential tourists in order to adopt the tourist supply accordingly and thus be able to satisfy them. In other words motivation research is the investigation into the motives behind travel. It concerns itself to answering the 'why' of human behaviour in contrast to answering the 'how' which is subject to sampling surveys. It analyses rather than describes the attitudes of both actual and potential tourists to travelling in general and to the tourist product offered in particular. Motivation research provides answers to very important questions. Research in the past has shown that people from some countries, are traditional good travellers (the French, the Germans, the American and the British), while others have become a nation of travellers only recently.

The most important techniques used in motivation research is the depth interview method. The questionnaire to be used for this method needs to be carefully designed, as motivation research aims at discovering the deep, subconscious and even unconscious of human beings. An ill-designed questionnaire is likely to reach no deeper than the conscious level where rational factors prevail. Other techniques used are the projective methods like word association tests, sentence completion test and pictorial tests, etc. and observations. Means have been devised to record the reactions of a person and to understand his motives.

Production and Growth

Having identified the consumers and the markets through the method of market research, the next step is the product formulation and development. The concept of consumer orientation makes it necessary to understand the various components of the tourist product from the point of view of the consumer. In the tourism industry product is what gives the consumer the various benefits they are seeking and its production and delivery. The formulation and development of a product involves factors like service, quality, range of different products offered in the market, the features and benefits it offers, and the brand name.

Availability of a 'product' is the prerequisite in the marketing function. Unless there is a certain 'product', be it tangible or intangible or a service, marketing is not possible. A 'product' may be defined as the 'Sum of the physical and psychological satisfactions it provides to the buyer. 'Marketing' by definition is the development of a product to meet the needs of the consumer and then employing the techniques of direct sales, publicity and advertising to bring this product to the consumer.

In the case of tourism product, the basic raw materials would be the country's natural beauty climate, history, culture and the people. Other aspects would be the existing facilities necessary for comfortable living such as water supply, electricity, roads, transport, communication and other essentials. In other words the tourist product can be seen as a composite product, the sum-total of a country's tourist attractions, transport, accommodation and entertainment which hopefully result in consumer satisfaction. The tourist product can be entirely a manmade one or nature's creation improved upon by man. Each of these components of a tourist product is supplied by individual providers of services like retail travel agents, tour operators, hotel companies, airlines or other suppliers, and is offered directly to the tourist by them. A consumer can combine these individual tourist products through a large number of ways. There would be many possible destinations, each with a number of hotels, each to be reached by more than one airline. Thus the potential choice facing the consumer is very large. A number of enterprises have placed at the disposal of a tourist a large variety of tourist products in abundant quantity from a large number of competing destinations. This eventually has led to the adoption of the new concept, i.e., the marketing concept in tourism by various enterprises marketing tourism. The important point about marketing is that it applies to situations where the choice can be limited to a relatively small number of brands giving the consumer a reasonable choice. The process of selection thus becomes easier. In the field of tourism this process is taking place by the increasing use of package tours. A package tour is a travel plan which includes most elements of vacation, such as transportation, accommodation, sight-seeing and entertainment. The tourist product is a composite product, whether it is sold as a package or assembled by the individual tourist himself or his travel agent. The tourist product can, therefore, be analysed in terms of;

(i) Attractions; (ii) Facilities; (iii) Accessibility.

Tourist attraction is a very important element. Unless these are there, the tourists will not be motivated to go to a particular place. Attractions are those elements in the tourist product which determine the choice of a particular tourist to visit one particular destination rather than another. The attractions could be cultural like sites and areas of archaeological interest, historical buildings and monuments or scenic like flora and fauna, beach resorts, mountains, national parks or events like trade fairs, exhibitions, arts and music festivals, games, etc. Facilities are those elements in the tourist product which are a necessary aid to the tourist centre. *The facilities* complement the attractions. These include accommodations, various types of entertainments, picnic sites, recreation and so on. These are indeed important for every tourist centre. *Accessibility* is another important component in the tourist product. It is a means by which a tourist can reach the area where attractions are located. Tourist attractions of whatever type would be of little importance if their locations are inaccessible by the normal means of transport. If the tourist attractions are located at places where no means of transport can reach, or where there are inadequate transport facilities, these become of little value. The tourist attractions which are located near to the tourist-generating markets and are linked by a network of efficient transport, receive the maximum number of tourists.

Segmentation : Market segmentation is one of the important functions of marketing. The technique of market segmentation has been used by organisations to effectively target selected groups in the market with specially designed products and services. Market segmentation can be defined as "the process whereby producers organise their knowledge of current and potential customer groups and select for particular attention those whose needs and wants they are best able to supply with their products. According to Dibb, Simkin, Pride and Ferrell Market Segmentation is defined as :

> "The process of dividing a total market into groups of people with relatively similar product needs, for the purpose of designing a marketing mix (or mixes) that precisely match the needs of individuals in a selected segment (or segments)."

From the above definition it emerges that the market segmentation is the process of identifying groups of buyers of a total market with different buying desires or requirements. It identifies and analyses the socio-economic, life styles and motivational characteristics of potential buyers into useful categories and thereby launching advertising and promotional campaigns for these selected groups. The identification of segment of a total market is therefore of crucial importance. Due to manpower and financial constraints, it is not possible for an organisation to reach the entire market. Segmentation of the market in therefore made in order to achieve the most efficient use of marketing resources. The main objectives of the market segmentation, therefore, are :

(a) Developing new markets for product variations or new products;

(b) Developing defence against competitors by differentiating one's own product from theirs and matching it more closely to the requirements of a particular segment of the marker;

(c) Achieving maximum effects for given expenditure on marketing activities, particularly communication activities;

(d) Developing marketing programmes and budgets on the basis of a clearer idea of the response characteristic of specific segments.

The following information on the tourist markets will assists in segmentation :

(i) Income distribution of overseas travellers and particularly correlations between income and distance travelled and travel expenditure;

(ii) Travel expenditure data, i.e., distribution of per head expenditure on travel;

(iii) Discretionary income of households, correlated with other characteristics enabling targets to be identified closely;

(iv) Historical trends in travel in different socio-economic categories;

(v) Survey data on attitudes to and motivations for overseas travel;

(vi) Geographical dispersion of potential customers within the market;

(vii) Membership of clubs and associations associated with other characteristics which identify particular groups as potential customers;

(viii) Influence of intermediaries (travel agents, tour operators, wholesalers, carriers etc.) on destination choice in particular markets;

(ix) Relative importance of different intermediaries in particular markets (e.g., is all relevant type of travel business concentrated among relatively few intermediaries or it is dispersed throughout the market?).

The segmentation process divides the markets on the basis of several factors. The most important and commonly used market segmentation include the following:

A. Geographic segmentation

B. Demographic segmentation

C. Socio-economic segmentation

D. Psychological segmentation

E. Behavioural segmentation

F. Product-Based segmentation

Under each of the above principal variables, there are several areas which are considered while segmenting the travel markets. These are as follows:

Geographical : Operational areas, e.g., sales regions. Sales Districts such as provinces, cities, Political administrative zones.

Demographic : Age groups Sex differences Ethnic origin Marital status Religious affiliations.

Socio-economic : Income Levels Types of occupation Social class. Educational level of economic activity.

Psychological : Individual life-styles Personality types Perceptual differences Motivational differences.

Behavioural

Patterns of purchase.

Loyalty to fashions.

Levels of brand loyalty.

Benefits/recognition sought.

Product-based

Travel purposes.

Type of holiday.

Average length of stay.

Type of accommodation.

Mode of travel.

Arrangements for travel.

Individual / group travel.

In tourism, market segmentation is very important. The strategy of market segmentation in tourism recognises that a few vacation areas are universally acceptable and desired. Therefore, rather than waste promotional resources trying to please all travellers, the best market strategy is to isolate those segments of the entire market which are likely prospects and aim at the promotional efforts specifically to the needs of these selected groups. Thus, one of the early steps in marketing tourism is to divide the present and potential market on the basis of meaningful characteristics and then concentrate on promotion, supply and pricing efforts on serving these most prominent sections of the market - the target markets. Usually as stated earlier, the market segmentation for tourists is in terms of the following criteria: demographic, geographic, psychographic, social and economic.

For example, market for particular area might be largely archaeologists in their middle years who have an income of over $100,000 per year and who live in mid-eastern United States, or it might be largely businessmen in the age group of say 40-60 years who have an income of over $150,000 per year and who live in southern parts of West Germany. In tourism marketing, the total tourism market can be divided into the above major segments. A further segmentation, however, is possible within each of the above major segments for practical marketing purposes, and includes:

The Vacation Tourist : The vacation or the holiday tourist is the most common and popular tourist. He is immensely affected by changes in price, and is easily influenced by skilled and aggressive marketing effort. This type of tourist is resort-oriented (Rome, Bombay, New York, London, Paris are resorts as much as Venice, Goa, Pattaya, Miami). The vacation tourist market has been regarded as highly seasonal.

The Business Tourist : In recent years the market for this type of tourist has increased greatly. The choice of destination of a business tourist is generally determined by the nature of his business. The marketing efforts will not influence much the choice of the business tourist. As in the case of the vacation tourist who has proved to be very sensitive to price changes, the demand for business tourism is relatively price-inelastic. The demand will tend to be big-city oriented. The visits are of shorter duration and relatively frequent. The trade fairs, conventions, exhibitions, conferences and similar other events attract this kind of tourism.

The Common Interest Tourist : This segment comprises visits to relatives and friends, and visits for the purpose of education, for pilgrimages, etc. Demand for this type of tourism will be relatively price-elastic. The common interest tourist will not be easily influenced by the promotional efforts. The average length of stay of this type of tourist will be relatively longer. Because of his friends and relatives, he will not be a significant user of hotel and other such types of accommodation. The visits will not be frequent and expenditure relatively little on his stay as compared with other two groups.

Market segmentation in tourism has developed from the realisation that there is no such thing as a homogenous tourist market. Tourist market is composed of several homogenous sub groups having same wants, desires and behaviour etc. It is therefore advantageous for an organisation/company to serve one or more of these segments.

Marketing Segmentation

1. Delineation of the segment and identifying its potential.
2. Target market selection matching the characteristics of those segments with what you have to offer.
3. After matching the two, preparing a marketing plan or programme based on marketing mix.
4. Implementation and control or monitoring.

The Strategy

a. When the total market is diffused demographically, geographically and psychologically.

b. When the organisation has been in business for several year already.

c. When there are several competitors.

d. When most competitors employ a segmentation strategy.

It may however be mentioned here that the market segmentation in itself is not sufficient. The identification and location of potential buyers of a tourism product or service does not ensure that purchases will be effected. Market segmentation is merely the first initial step in the development of a total marketing strategy of a firm or an enterprise. It helps in the process of converting as many as possible of the potential buyers into actual buyers.

Marketing Mix

The most important objective of a tourist enterprise is to achieve the best results. This to a larger extent depends on a properly conceived marketing plan through which a strategy is to be developed to achieve the best results. Through the segmentation process appropriate targets are identified and analysed. The marketing strategy thus developed would now attempt to penetrate and persuade the target markets through a variety of tools mainly promotion and advertising. In addition, the marketing strategy will also look into the crucial question of pricing and distribution. The various tools are to be mixed in such a way that the enterprise obtains the optimal use of financial and manpower resources available at its disposal.

The mixture of various marketing tools is called the 'marketing mix'. Marketing mix is a mixture of elements which interact and complement each other to achieve targeted results. The term was first introduced by Professor Neil Bordes in the year 1953 when he got the cue from a study of Management of Marketing costs which described the marketing executive as a mixer of ingredients. Professor Philip Kotler, has defined the 'marketing mix' as the set of marketing tools that the firm uses to pursue its marketing objectives in the target market.

Tourist Marketing Mix : Tourist 'marketing mix' is largely a complex group of several factors intervening to achieve the marketing 'end product' which is increased effectiveness in demand output in relation to supply and marketing investment by tourist enterprises. Marketing mix helps the marketing manager of an enterprise whether individual or firm or an official tourism organisation to understand where marketing action can be initiated to improve the acceptability of a tourist product and stimulate the demand within the market. A tourist enterprise with a combination of specific activities can achieve the best possible results. It can decide *which* specific activity to use, *how* it is to be used, *when* and *where* to use and what resources to be allocated to them. A judicial mixture of activities at the appropriate time would give the enterprise to achieve its set marketing objectives.

The different components or elements of the mix may be seen as cooperating with or replacing each other as complements or substitutes. An example would be a policy of price reduction by an enterprise to tourist services or facilities which could be substituted by enhancing/increasing available facilities and services for the same price or by strengthening various promotion activities in view of competition offered by competitors and thereby increasing the sales output. A strategy to combine both reduction of prices and at the same time offering extra facilities or extra advertising and promotion may or may not however always be efficient or result oriented. It is therefore essential that the target markets must be clearly defined for the success of marketing mix strategy.

Main Variables : Marketing mix incorporates four core variables. The four variables or four Ps as originally used to describe marketing mix by McCarthy in the year 1960 are :

- Product
- Price
- Promotion
- Place

Each of the above variables includes within it many sub-elements. Cowell in the year 1993 however revised the marketing mix variables for service industry including the travel and tourism.

According to Cowell in addition to four original elements of product, price, promotion and place, there are three more which are :

People

Physical Evidence

Process (Customer involvement variables)

The three revised variables as introduced by Cowell in 1993 are to be used for travel and tourism since being a service industry it has certain special features. The use of marketing mix in travel and tourism has both short as well as long term aspects. The short term aspects relate to meeting the immediate initiatives of the competitors and include aspects like :

a. Price reduction
b. Aggressive promotion
c. Introduction of a new product
d. Special offers
e. Incentives

Long term aspects relate to meeting the objectives set aside for future long duration plans. These are based on longer range plans and are derived from the study of all kinds of trends in the market like natural, economic, social environmental and technological. The four variables or Ps have been illustrated below with illustrations taken from a well known and a branded tourist product. 'Palace on Wheels' is a famous train with historic charm and modern conveniences. For one week it is possible to roll back the pages of Indian History. The royal train takes the tourist on a royal Odyssey bringing alive the luxury of princely travel of the bygone age of the Raj. The train has been designed to offer all the modern comforts. The journey offers a complete package and covers nine well known historic cities in north India. Most of the travelling is done during night and the days are left free for discovering the various attractions.

Palace-an-Wheels

- Various special features and characteristics of the product
- Size and facilities offered

- Service elements of the product
- Benefits it offers
- Image, reputation
- Branding
- Positioning - upmarket / down market

Price

- Normal
- Promotional
- Corporate
- Discounted
- Wholesaler
- Seasonal

Promotion

- Advertising
- Sales promotion
- Press and public relations
- Brochure / Folder
- Personal selling
- Direct mail
- Outdoor
- Sponsorship
- Point-of-sale material

Place (Distribution)

- Travel agents
- Tour operators
- Airlines
- Reservation system
- Direct from producers
- Trade fairs and exhibitions
- Clubs
- General sales agents (GSA)

2

Tourism through the Ages

In recorded history there have been instances whereby one is able to know that man has been travelling throughout the ages. From the very early historical period, travel has had a fascination for mankind. Much of the travel in the beginning was largely unconscious and a simple affair. People travelled by foot over paths, open fields and also through forests. Movement across the landscape was a tough adventure requiring great skills and endurance. There were no travel procedures and formalities as there were no frontiers. All human activity focussed upon day to day survival. The early hunters were keeping themselves busy in search of basic necessities like food, water and shelter. This often meant difficult and dangerous travel for entire communities. Although travel in the pre-historic times was rigorous and unsafe, but it could not stop early people from migrating all over the globe.

It was however, in the Neolithic age that several innovations were made which changed the nature of travel. Around 4000 B.C. sailing vessels were built in Egypt. It was also during this period that animals were domesticated and trained to carry and transport community members, tools and agriculture supplies. Invention of the wheel during this period was also an important landmark which made movement of people to distant lands possible. The Sumerians invented the wheel around 3500 B.C. Invention of the wheel had considerably reduced the burdens of travel as also distance. It was now possible to travel hundreds of miles to new lands in search of fortune.

Most early travel, however was not undertaken for the purposes of pleasure since the motive was not to seek any holiday from the work situation. The primary motive for which the travel was undertaken was related to trade, exchange of goods, commerce and the activities associated with it. The traveller in the ancient past was thus a trader and a merchant looking for merchandise and engaging in trade and commerce. There was, however, another type of traveller, whose motive was other than engaging in trade and commerce. This traveller was a pilgrim, a scholar in search of ancient texts, and a curious wayfarer looking forward to new and exciting experiences. Seeking knowledge was his primary purpose for undertaking travel.

Commercial Travels

Most early travel was associated with trade and commerce. Throughout history, traders and merchants have travelled to far-off lands in order to trade with other regions and communities. Travellers from distant lands started moving about in large numbers and visited many places for the purposes of commerce. With the gradual opening of the trade routes, travel became easier as well as regulated. At the market-places, travellers made contacts with each other, resulting in increased flow of trade and commerce. Trade relations gradually matured into cultural relations and better understanding of each others way of life. This was a favourable development towards increase in travel activity during this period. Some of the earliest travellers probably were the Phoenicians. They were probably the first real travellers in the modern sense. These were also the people who were credited with the invention of money. The medium of money was being used in various business and commercial dealings. Many traders could now pay for their travel to different centres of trade and commerce as also for the accommodation they required. The invention of money and the development of trade and commerce beginning about 3000 B.C. perhaps can be said to be the most significant development of the time which paved the way for the development and organisation of travel.

Early travel in the orient, particularly in India and in China, was also largely based on trade and commerce. Travel to India in particular was undertaken by travellers from all over the ancient world. Both India and China enjoyed the reputation of being countries of fabulous wealth where trade and commerce flourished. It is on record that long before the Christian era, travellers visited India in search of fortune. This trend continued and became more marked in course of time with Europeans heading towards Indian shores for the sole purpose of trade and commerce.

The Exploration

The urge to explore new lands and to seek new knowledge in ancient and distant lands was yet another motive of travellers in subsequent periods. Although trade and commerce continued to be the strong force for many travellers to undertake journeys to distant lands, seeking new knowledge and exploring the unexplored lands was becoming a strong urge in ancient times. Homer's great work 'Odyssey' records the wanderlust of the ancient Greeks and Romans. There are innumerable references to great explorers who spent many formidable years of their lives in search of knowledge. These great explorers can, perhaps, be credited with the distinction of being the pioneers who subsequently paved the way for modern day travel.

Religious Tours

Travel for religious purposes assumed a significant importance during middle ages and became a well established custom in many parts of the world. By the end of the Middle Ages, a large number of pilgrims were travelling to the main shrines in Europe and elsewhere. The adoption and spread of Christianity subsequently led to numerous pilgrims making their way to the holy land. So deep and strong was the hold of faith that the ritual of pilgrimage flourished over the centuries. It became a great unifying force and the pilgrimages strengthened religious bonds. The pilgrimages also provided the necessary impetus for a 'stay-at-home' agrarian society to break out of its narrow geographical confines and visit places associated with religion. It also served as a powerful means of forging unity and understanding between peoples from widely different regions.

Pilgrim travel assumed a great importance in India. Emperor Ashoka travelled a great deal in his eagerness to spread doctrines of Buddha. Ashoka and his entourage first travelled to Nepal starting from Patliputra and then ventured to Lumbini Gardens, the land of Buddha's birth, on to Kapilavastu, the place where Buddha spent his childhood. From here, he went to Sarnath, where Buddha spent many years of his life and finally to Gaya, where Buddha got enlightenment. Through his travels, Emperor Ashoka had special memorials set up at each spot and also rest houses where travellers could rest. Harsha was another emperor who was greatly influenced by the Buddhist scriptures. He built institutions and Dharamshalas for the travellers. Rest houses were built in towns and villages, Numerous monasteries and temples were also built for the pilgrims. The powerful influences of a crusading religion that slowly penetrated a foreign land, such as Christianity in Europe and later in America and Buddhism, Islam and Hinduism in Asia allowed an assimilation and perpetuation of very distinctive languages, literature, art, architecture, philosophy and forms of government. Religion thus played and continues to play a crucial part in travel.

Perhaps the earliest travellers from distant lands to the Indian soil were the trading Persians. Evidence of caravans of Persians visiting India lies engraved in the inscriptions dating to the Persian king Darius. During the rule of the Guptas, there was free access to the ports along the Western Coast, seaborne commerce with Europe through Egypt was yet another reason for travel in and around the country. There are also references of many known Persians, who visited the Indian soil for commerce and trade. There is also a mention of cultural exchanges between Persia and India. Reference has also been made to the influence of Persian customs in the court of Chandragupta Maurya. Great travellers from various far away lands visited India. Probably the greatest traveller remembered from the distant past is Hieun-tsang. A devout Chinese Buddhist, he made the perilous journey to India around A.D. 633. His main mission was to collect and translate ancient Buddhist scriptures. Some other travellers whose names need special mention are Alexander the Great, Marco Polo, Benjamin of Tudela, Ibn Batutah, Francisco Friar, Alfonso D' Albuquerque and Mark Twain.

One of the important developments during this period was the emergence of some sort of communication system and accommodation. Development of trade and commerce necessitated this development. Shulgi, the ruler of ancient Babylonia, claimed to have built roads and rest houses at various places for wayfarers. With trade and commerce forming a link in development, it was inevitable that some sort of communication system connecting the centres of trade, commerce and learning were found to be in good shape. When Alexander the Great, during his journeys, reached India, he found well maintained roads covered with shady trees. Along one royal highway, 1,920 kilometres long and about 19 metres wide, people travelled in chariots, palanquins, bullock carts, on horses, camels and elephants.

Adventurous Travels

The great travellers who ventured to explore distant lands had fascinating accounts of their travels. Even if we go back just a few hundred years to the third century A.D., since the first exploration of Alexander the Great, or only about seven hundred years since Marco Polo, and their amazing explorations crossing many land we get fascinating accounts of the travels of these great persons. The first medieval traveller to reach the orient was probably Benjamin of Tudela, a Jewish scholar, who left Saragossa in the year A.D. 1160. He wrote a detailed account of his thirteen-year long journey through Europe, Persia and India, giving information on the Jewish communities, and the geography of various places he had visited. Yet another famous traveller who recorded interesting accounts of his travel experiences was Ibn Batutah. Ibn Batutah wrote a detailed diary of his travel experiences. He was born at Tangier in A.D. 1304. In the year A.D. 1325, he left his home and passing through various countries in Africa and West Asia, crossed the Sindhu in A.D. 1333. His travel took him to places as far as Indonesia and China. Out of a total of more than 17,000 miles, he covered more than 14,000 miles in the course of his travels through India, the Maldives and Ceylon.

Marco Polo, the fearless traveller, spent almost twenty five years in Asia during the latter part of the 13th century. His wanderlust could well have been inherited from his father. Young

Marco Polo left Venice in the year 1271 with his father and uncle. The three together travelled through Persia and Afghanistan to the "roof of the world", the then unknown Pamir Plateau. After crossing the wind-swept Gobi desert, they reached Kublai Khan's palace and remained in China for over twenty years. On his way back home, he stopped in Sumatra, Java, India and Ceylon.

Marco Polo's description of a place Zipangu (the present day Japan) in his memoirs, set the course for Columbus on his historic journey in 1492. Two of Columbus's contemporaries who also became famous and wrote excellent accounts were Vasco da Gama : who opened the sea route from Western Europe to India in 1498, and Ferdinand Magellan whose ship sailed around the world. Francisco Friar, John of Monte Corvino also visited India on their way to and back from China during the decade of the thirteenth century. Mention may also be made of the famous Portuguese chronicle, the Commentaries of the Great Alfonso D'Albuquerque.

In the sixteenth and seventeenth centuries more European monks, travellers and adventurers visited India and many other places in search of knowledge. The first great sailor to do a westward circumnavigation of the world was Francis Drake who was knighted by Queen Elizabeth I in the year 1581. From 1768 to 1779 Captain James Cook made three long voyages to the Pacific in search of a non-existent southern continent mentioned by Ptolemy who, earlier in the 2nd century A.D., had travelled widely and who wrote an eight-volume work on geography.

Pleasure Travel : The concept of pleasure travel as it existed in the west can be associated with the Roman empire. Romans probably were the first pleasure travellers. Travel received a great stimulus from the good communication system and security of the Roman empire. There existed a fine network of roads and new roads were built increasingly wherever the Romans went. Travel literature was published extensively giving routes, the names of the roads, distances between places and time required in travelling to them. The Romans were able to travel over a hundred miles in a day using relays of horses. They journeyed primarily to see famous temples in the Mediterranean areas, particularly the monuments and the famous pyramids of Egypt. The Roman travelled during holiday occasions, particularly the famous Olympic Games. Spas and seaside resorts which developed during this period may be associated with pleasure travel. Medicinal baths and seaside resorts which later were named as spas were popular with the Romans. The inland spa had its origin in a belief in the efficacy of its mineral waters for medicinal purposes, either by drinking the water or by immersing in it. The patients using the spas would require certain diversions, and gradually, the spa resorts added facilities for pleasure and entertainment to medical facilities. The visitors now not only enjoyed medicinal baths but also various forms of entertainments. Theatrical productions, athletic competitions, festivals and other forms of entertainments and amusement were often provided at the sites where spas were located. The spas had become extremely popular with travellers.

Subsequent development of spas, after their original use for recreational purposes by the Romans, played a big role in the development of pleasure travel in many countries in Europe. Development of various seaside resorts is also linked with the latter half of the eighteenth century, when people started realising the possible curative effects of sea water. Sea bathing also became very popular and many believed that bathing in sea water was more beneficial than inland spas. The seaside resorts began to appear as an alternative to the original inland spa. By the year 1865, there were major seaside resorts in Britain, France, Italy and a few more countries of Central Europe. This development was a result of a demand for vacation travel. However, the use of these resorts was still confined to those with considerable means. Nevertheless, both the spas and the seaside resorts paved the way for the modern pleasure travel all over the world where millions of people visited various seaside resorts each year. The fall of the Roman empire in the fifth century was a great setback for pleasure travel in Europe. During the Dark Ages only the very adventurous and brave persons would travel. A trip in this period in history was considered dangerous. No one would associate travel with pleasure. Also with the decline of the Roman empire came a sharp decline in trade and commerce. In the absence of a prosperous community with the incentive to travel for pleasure, travelling ceased to exist for its own sake.

Next Stage

The Renaissance marked the next important stage in the history of travel. The reappearance of tourism in Europe follows the Italian Renaissance and the development of a full scale urban system and network of roads. By the end of the fifteenth century Italy itself became the object of attention. At this time Italy was Europe's economic and cultural leader. It was, however, totally disunited politically. Wars were fought on Italian soil. These wars played an important part in the dissemination of the Renaissance and the subsequent development of the 'grand tour'. Although it declined materially, Italy was still the 'intellectual' capital of Europe. For the aristocracy and intelligentsia of north-west Europe it represented both the classical heritage and all the latest ideas and inventions. A growing number of young noblemen were being sent abroad to complete their education in France and Italy.

The development of the Grand tourism followed a shift in the focus of culture and of economic and political power. The wealthy and educated, of states whose position of dominance in the world was comparatively new, visited countries that had passed their peak of prestige but were still venerated for historical and cultural reasons. Thus Romans visited Greece and the eastern Mediterranean; the English, from sixteenth century onwards, visited Italy. The Grand tourist respected the learning, antiquities and social refinements of the world. The eighteenth century is conventionally considered, the golden age of the Grand Tour, especially the thirty years between 1763 and 1793. With the new wealth of the English bourgeoisie the number of tourists had multiplied. The Grand Tour was no longer an aristocratic preserve. It had been invaded by the bourgeoisie. During this period a great many poets, authors and intellectuals visited Italy and other countries nearby with a view to broaden their knowledge and learn new arts and crafts. The Grand tourists paved the way for the popular tourism of the nineteenth and twentieth centuries.

Concept of Annual Holiday : The introduction of Annual Holiday in Europe was yet another important landmark which enabled many people to undertake travel in large numbers during the eighteenth century. The annual holiday was the forerunner to the 'paid holiday' which later on was responsible for an extraordinary growth of tourism during the twentieth century. The term holiday derives from holy days associated with religious observances. In the present day parlance it is used generally in a secular sense meaning a respite from the routine of daily workday life and a time for leisure, recreation and amusement.

A feature of ancient Rome, public holidays were among the most enjoyable events of the period. The most important and enjoyable public holiday was known as "Saturnalia" - the feast of Saturn - celebrated in the month of December, where everybody high or low in status indulged in feasting and frolic. Also in Europe certain days commemorating religious festivals and saints' days became holy days on which there was holiday from work. In the year 1552 in England an act was passed during the reign of Edward VI "for the keeping of holidays and fasting days." This act still continues to be on the Statute Book. Subsequently, public and semiofficial offices in England frequently closed on certain saints' days. There were, however, no general public holidays until the time of the Industrial Revolution. The concept of modern annual paid holiday is very largely an outcome of the post Industrial Revolution.

The so called 'travel bug' of modern parlance had its seeds in the ancient past. Although the purpose and motives for travels in the subsequent periods underwent a great change, the urge to travel has always been there. The growth and development of travel has been closely linked with the growth and development of society as a whole. The travellers of the ancient past were in fact the explorers in search of knowledge of different lands, of people, their cultures and their traditions. They were also traders interested in development of trade and commerce. In fact, these very developments paved the way for development of travel in the subsequent periods.

Rail Transport : Nineteenth century witnessed a great technological development, first in England, and later on in Europe and America. This development had a profound effect on transport which resulted in the growth of travel in general. This great technological development led to the advent of the railway. The introduction of railways in the nineteenth century was a crucial landmark in history.

The first rail link between Liverpool and Manchester was started in the year 1830. The newly completed railway track in England featured special provisions for carrying passengers in addition to freight. Later on, an extensive programme of construction of railroads to provide trunk lines between major centres of population and commerce and industry was taken up in England. Although the railway network in the beginning was responsible for carrying goods from industrial centres to the centres of trade and commerce, it had, however, initiated the process of carrying the passengers which later on was to become a mass movement. Railways provided the necessary vehicle for the movement of the people from the place of their residence to newly formed and expanding pleasure spots like seaside resorts. These resorts for the first time were within the reach of many people who but for the introduction of railways, would otherwise not have been able to reach them.

The newly formed railway companies in England, however, were slow to take advantage of the various opportunities available to them for the expansion of the pleasure travel and thereby the passenger travel. These companies were concentrating in meeting the demands of trade and commerce as a result of their expansion. Gradually, the railway companies started to concentrate on carrying more passengers which resulted in the development of short day trips. This trend was later to be followed by railways by way of organising excursion for the public. These excursions were offered to the public at special fares.

Organised Rail Travel : The birth of the organised rail travel, however, came in the year 1841. A baptist preacher of Derbyshire on his way to a temperance meeting in Leicester was inspired with the idea of engaging a special train to carry the 'friends of temperance society' from Leicester to Loughborough and back to attend a quarterly delegate meeting. The man behind this idea was none other than Thomas Cook who later on came to be known as one of the greatest travel organisers of the times and, in fact, a pioneer. Thomas Cook broached the idea to his friend and a few weeks later the idea culminated into collecting as many as 570 passengers who made a journey by the Midland Counties Railway at a specially reduced return fare of one shilling per passenger.

Encouraged by the success of this venture, Thomas Cook arranged similar such ventures by chartering trains to places which were now becoming popular with the excursionists. In the year 1843, nearly 3,000 school children were taken on a trip from Leicester to Derby. Many more excursion trips were arranged by Thomas Cook on a fully commercial basis. From the year 1848 to 1863, Cook conducted circular tours of Scotland with almost 5,000 travellers a season. By the year 1855, Thomas Cook had extended his field of operations to other countries in the continent, organising the first all inclusive tours to the Paris Exhibition in that year.

Another important development which can also be associated with Thomas Cook is the spurt in pleasure travel. The large scale movement of people to various pleasure spots like resorts and spas was a result of organised conducted excursion trips by Thomas Cook. It was however, the introduction of the railways which made all this possible for Thomas Cook to achieve and become a pioneer in organised travel.

The news about introduction of the Liverpool and Manchester railway reached the neighbouring countries in Europe. Encouraged by this development many other countries in Europe opened the railway lines. Railway tracks were laid in France, Austria and Switzerland. Across the Atlantic the tracks were laid in America which ushered in the spurt of travel to and from places where tracks were laid. This great revolution in rail transport technology produced an immediate expansion in European travel. It was estimated that in the year 1881, the railways carried over 600 million passengers over the lines operated by over one hundred odd companies. All of them, however, were not excursionists. With the phenomenal success, the railways were now keen to stimulate travel further and also to improve the system. There was also now an element of competition and the various railway companies tried to make travel as comfortable as possible.

In America, the first class railway travel was introduced in the early 1870s, by an American named G.M. Pullman, who developed the Pullman coaches with their luxury furnishings and dining facilities. The longer distances in America necessitated the ensuring of greater passenger comfort. Long-distance travel could now be undertaken in comfort and with pleasure. The Pullman coaches manufactured in America were being imported by some railway companies in England and other countries in Europe. By the year 1872 the Pullman company had over 700 coaches working over 30,000 miles of railway track under contract with over 150 different railway companies.

East was not far behind in catching up with the leaders in the area of rail-road construction. India took up the construction of railways in the same century. Soon after its introduction in England, the business community there was pressing the East India Company to introduce railways in the subcontinent of India. After prolonged negotiations with British rail-road companies, the GIP Railway Company could be incorporated in an Act of Parliament in 1849 and a contract signed between East India Company and the GIP Railway Company requesting them to raise the requisite capital required for the construction work. The contract for the actual construction was awarded to an English company, Messrs Faviel and Fowler. It was on April 16, 1853 that the first train in the east took off from Boribunder in Bombay to Thana, covering a distance of 33 kilometres. Four hundred guests selected from various segments were invited to travel by the first train in India. From a small beginning on April 16, 1853, when the first train steamed off from Victoria Terminus for Thane, 33 kilometres away, the Railway System in India has grown into the world's second largest system under one management, second only to Russia.

Sea Transport : Like the railways, shipping made a significant contribution to travel during the nineteenth century. While railways were responsible for inland travel, especially in Europe, the steamship crossed the boundaries and made strides in intercontinental travel. The shipping technology made a number of innovations in the nineteenth century. In America a number of sailing ships were built which were considered to be superior to those built in England or elsewhere. The English felt a great need for improved communications across the Atlantic with America for the purpose of trade and commerce and passenger transportation. As a result of this there were great strides in the development of deep-sea shipping. The history of the Cunard Steamship Company in England demonstrates important features in the growth of North Atlantic Shipping. A subsidy in the form of the award of mail contract represented a recurring theme in the development of passenger transportation. With the passage of time toward the last quarter of the nineteenth century, emigrant traffic became an important factor in North Atlantic travel. America was considered at that time the 'new world', full of opportunities and fortunes for people in Europe. A great number of people from the continent started going to America in search of fortunes. First, Great Britain and later Germany, along with other countries, became the principal generators of emigrants to the 'new world'. Many also travelled to see the new world.

Use of the ships in the cruising fashion for the charter and operation of cruises on a limited scale dates from the mid-nineteenth century. One of the earliest cruises perhaps was described by Mark Twain in his first book, *The Innocents Abroad*, published in the year 1869. The year 1869 also brought about the possibility of a much shortened route between the West and the East as a result of opening of the Suez Canal. This in turn stimulated the introduction of better steamship carriage to the Far East. The worldwide growth of shipping companies towards the end of the nineteenth century led to the formation of shipping conferences which developed cartel-like agreements. These agreements were on fare-structure applicable to the carriage of passenger traffic and cargo to various territories to which the vessels of these companies operated.

Industrial Societies : The second half of the nineteenth century, in fact, witnessed the growth of travel as a result of development of industrial societies. These societies which developed in Western Europe and North America greatly felt the urge to travel purely for the purpose of rest and relaxation. This trend certainly gave way to what came to be known as the tourism phenomenon in the latter part of the century and in the twentieth century. It will not be out of place to mention that the concept of modern-day tourism had its seeds in the development of industrialised societies of Western Europe and North America. Though an accurate analysis of the measurement of tourism can be traced back to only about half a century ago, the scattered figures published from 1855 onwards point to the direct relationship between the development of industrial societies and the expansion of tourist movements. This has also been supplemented by various official statements, observations by travel writers, and the various travel guides and other literature on sale from time to time. The emergence of the industrialised societies was a direct result of the industrial revolution in the West, initially beginning in England. In its wake the industrial revolution brought about tremendous changes in the society and the tempo of change was quite fast and took a big jump.

The Industrial Revolution was responsible for changes both in the economic as well as social systems prevailing at that time. A large number of factory towns, both big and small, sprang up which in turn necessitated large-scale migrations from the countryside to towns and cities. The Industrial Revolution was responsible for the emergence of the working class which was needed to run factories. In the beginning the working class was burdened with long working hours and poor working and living conditions and lower wages. The sudden concentration of population in towns and cities made matters worse.

Development of Seaside Resorts **:** As the industrial momentum gathered and the cities and their populations increased at an enormous rate, the need for some relief was acute. Escape from the routine of work began to be felt in greater intensity. The prosperous and well-to-do who could afford the escape, proceeded to various resorts for rest and recreation. By this time a large number of such resorts had been developed around the English coast and in nearby countries. A number of large scale pleasure zones were developed at some considerable distance from the large cities and towns of central Europe. The French Riviera with Nice, Cannes and Monte Carlo were some of these pleasure zones. The problems were, however, for the not so-well-to-do who could not afford such a luxury and they were in large numbers.

Gradually the industrialisation brought in better working conditions and increase in material wealth for a large number of workers. The simultaneous improvements in transport and communication systems during the second half of the nineteenth century enabled a large number of industrial workers, not only in England, but elsewhere as well to avail of holidays for rest, relaxation and pleasure. Thus the need to develop more holiday resorts was felt. The substantial increase in workers' purchasing power and disposable income for travel were two important factors which helped the growth of pleasure zones. By the end of the century the Riviera was unmistakably the most popular pleasure zone. Its development became possible when escape to the South had become a major feature of pleasure travel in Europe. Many resorts were developed to cater to the increasing needs of people who could afford a holiday. In the late nineteenth century the Italian Riviera also began to be popular with the English and the French.

Twentieth Century

By the turn of the twentieth century all the main characteristics of modern tourism were evident in embryo. Changes in mental attitudes towards pleasure seeking, the recognised value of travel for education, increase in material wealth coupled with social prestige, a growing need to find relief from working routine, improvements in passenger transport systems—all these factors produced a fertile ground for the development of excursion traffic on a large scale.

Pleasure travel continued to expand in the beginning of the century. However, up to the first quarter of the twentieth century travel including pleasure travel was essentially a luxury commodity within the reach of privileged sections of the society having both free time and considerable purchasing power. The pleasure tourism had by now assumed a class and a charm of its own associated as it was with elegant luxurious hotels, Pullman coaches, prestigious nostalgic long distance trains, such as the 'Orient Express' and the 'Blue Riband' and transatlantic liners like the 'Queen Mary'. However, as stated earlier, only the few privileged could manage to indulge and afford such luxury. During this time also there appeared a number of associations, which enrolled members from among the embryonic middle and working classes and organised excursions, holiday camps, family rest and holiday homes for them. This class of people had emerged as a result of increasing prosperity due to industrialisation and urbanisation.

Not many people, however, benefited from such activities at that time.

World War I was responsible for a temporary halt to tourist movements. Tourism has always flourished in peace as it is a peacetime activity. As such the war saw a considerable decline in tourist travel not only within Europe but also all over the world. However, soon after the war, travel soon reached pre-war peak levels, and within the next three to five years, greatly exceeded them. Early post-war period also brought in its wake prosperity coupled with large scale migration, and this period increased the demand for international travel. Gradual development of the mass communication system like the radio and the press played an important role in increasing travel by way of widening knowledge and interest of a large number of people about other countries. The post-war period also brought about attitudinal changes which were destined to influence the volume and nature of tourism. For example, the war was responsible for breaking down international barriers, resulting in the fostering of an ideal optimistic, peaceful internationalism - just the climate in which tourism is likely to flourish the most.

Post-war era also saw a rise in the standard of living of working and middle classes in America and certain other countries in Europe. Soon after the war tourists began to appear in countries where tourism had been practically unknown a few years earlier. The major tourist countries enjoyed an unprecedented boom in the twenties. In the year 1929 there were nearly one and a half million visitors to Switzerland, over one million to Italy and about two million to Austria. France, Spain and Great Britain also received a considerable number of visitors.

Motor Car : The unprecedented boom in tourist movements in the twenties, especially in Europe and America, can be directly linked to the introduction of the private motor car. The motorised private and public road transport and the improved road conditions led to a tremendous growth of travel. The invention of the private motor car and coach received its first great impetus in the ten years which preceded World War I. The motor car revolutionalised holiday habits of the Europeans and Americans. It became increasingly important in the pursuit of leisure and tourism. The provision of good motor roads and the road services were important factors in the development of both domestic and international tourism.

Paid Holidays : The concept of modern tourism emerged along with the introduction of holiday with pay. It was in the last quarter of the nineteenth century that increasing attention was paid to the desirability of holiday with pay and at least of cheap holidays for working class people. This group had still largely failed to benefit from the new opportunities offered by rail travel. During this period a few factories gave paid holidays to their workers in some countries in the West. The introduction of annual paid holidays is very largely of English origin and this had important repercussions on the development of mass tourism. The annual paid holiday was established during the inter-war years as a reality for a considerable part of the working population. By the year 1939, in UK, some eleven million people were covered by the Holidays with Pay Act (1938). Introduction of paid holiday had led to great mobility of the population, created new industries, resulted in the creation and growth of many towns of distinctive function and broadened the horizons of millions of people. In fact, the introduction of paid holidays can truly be associated with the development of modern mass tourism.

Modern tourism really got under way in the year 1936 when, at the instigation of its trade union representatives, the International Labour Organisation (ILO) adopted the first convention that was to support serious movements to promote paid holidays and, in turn, tourism. That convention on paid holidays was an innovation well ahead of time, when only fourteen countries, mostly European, had enacted general legislation on paid holidays. Soon afterwards tourism experienced an extraordinary growth. Paid holidays are now established all over the world, and in most countries a minimum duration of one to three weeks is specified either by law or by collective agreements, between the employer and the workers.

The right to paid holidays has universal recognition now. The trend is to grant longer holiday periods. The employers have realised that the paid holidays have not adversely affected industrial production. The legal minimum in many countries at present is three weeks. Some countries have even gone beyond this and grant four weeks of paid holiday. Today it is recognised that in Western Europe the fifth week, even from the standpoint of output, may also be regarded as a productive investment. Sweden has recently enacted legislation introducing this additional week of paid holidays. Worldwide, more than 500 million wage-earners are entitled to paid holidays. Out of this number roughly half are in Europe, little less than 30 per cent in the America, and the rest in Asia and the Pacific. Presently the main potential for tourism markets is made up of wage-earners and their families. As a result of economic and social changes due to further industrialisation the world over and the rationalisation of the tertiary sector, the number of wage earners in the world is bound to grow at a much faster rate than before. This concept of paid holidays which originated with the advent of industrialisation in the West has given modern tourism a tremendous boost.

The encouraging trend in tourism witnessed during the post-First World War period however, received a great setback as the Second World War intervened. As stated earlier, tourism and holiday-making on global as well as national scale is a manifestation of prosperity and peace. It can occur on a large scale where a great majority of people enjoy prosperity and security. It is quite sensitive to world economic and political conditions. The Second World War, like World War I, brought in economic destruction and political instability —the two major deterrents to the growth of travel and tourism.

Post-second World War Period : The post-Second World War period brought in a rapid development of tourism. As the world began to settle down after the years of readjustments immediately after the war ended in the year 1945, there was a remarkably rapid increase in both domestic as well as international tourism. The United Nations reported that in the ten-year period between 1955 and 1965, the number of tourist arrivals in some sixty five countries increased threefold from 51 million to over 157 million. This trend in the growth of international tourism continued till the mid-

1960s. It continued to be determined by the living standards in the developed countries. The widespread introduction of the holiday with pay to a large majority of people during this period was yet another important factor responsible for growth of tourist traffic. In the year 1976, there were nearly 220 million international tourist arrivals in the world. This was an increase of more than 90 per cent over the year 1965. This was a period of intensive economic and technological development in most industrialised countries which had earlier suffered a great deal as a result of war. Most of the developing countries during this period were also able to benefit from the growing trend in the developed countries to engage in tourism.

Tourism and its development are closely interrelated to consumer's purchasing power on the one hand and peace and prosperity on the other. Any domestic or international economic fluctuations or political disturbances result in a temporary setback. Tourism received a setback in the year 1974, when the world economy was seriously affected by the great energy crisis which occured at the end of 1973. As a result of the energy crisis there occurred inflation which was responsible for lower purchasing power which in its wake had brought in a steep fall in tourist movements. Tourism like all other sectors of production and consumption, suffered the economic consequences of that crisis. As a result of efforts made by governments of industrialised-and developing countries to keep inflation within acceptable limits, the tourism activity received a boost once again in the principal generating countries. As a consequence, there was a resumption of international travel. Total international tourist arrivals in the year 1975 amounted to about 213 million. The international tourist arrivals in 1976 were estimated at between 218 and 222 million. According to most recent estimates produced by the Secretariat General, World Tourism Organisation, international tourist arrivals in 2000 were estimated at 710 million. The principal generating as well as receiving areas for international tourism continues to be Europe and North America accounting for 70 per cent and 20 per cent respectively of international tourist arrivals.

Air Transport : The late twentieth century period can thus be termed as a period which is responsible for introducing a phenomenon called 'mass tourism'. Although the enormous expansion of tourism has taken place primarily in the advanced industrialised countries, where tourism has become a part of the life-style and consumption pattern, it has also shown its might in the developing countries as well. The key role of air transport has been a major factor in the growth of international tourism, especially in respect of long distance and inter-continental travel. Although commercial travel was introduced even before the Second World-War, air transport for the masses has essentially been a post-Second World War phenomenon. The principal period of growth, however, has been post '1950'. With the tremendous increase in speed, safety and comfort provided by the new civil aircrafts like Douglas DC-6s and DC-7s and Super-constellations, there was a noticeable increase in the long distance international as well as intra-regional tourism. In the year 1952 the two-class travel introduced was made possible by the larger capacity of new aircrafts. The increase in the aircraft capacity was also responsible for lower air fares. The steady fall in the cost of flying also resulted in the increased traffic across the Atlantic. This period also saw the first attempt to introduce a 'package holiday' around air transport which subsequently became the model for most of the present day's global tourism.

Jet Travel : The most dramatic event which introduced an entirely new dimension of speed, comfort and efficiency to air transport and brought mass travel to its present level was the advent of the jet travel in the year 1958. As a result of the entry of advanced jet aircraft in the civil aviation industry, air travel from the year 1960 onwards grew tremendously. Great advances have been made in the aircraft jet technology with the introduction of newer and sophisticated planes with emphasis on comfort, luxury, speed and safety. New wide-body jets such as Boeing 747, the McDonnell -Douglas DC 10, the Airbus A 300, the Lockheed Tristar L-1011 and the latest all-computerised 'fly by wire' Airbus A 320 are all part of the response to the requirements of the ever-growing travel market. Added to all this, the technical brilliance of the supersonic aircraft like the Concorde and the Tupolev 144 have added glamour to the passenger aircraft industry. It will not be out of place to mention here that the international tourism as we know it today, has been largely shaped by air travel. Introduction of 'inclusive tours' is yet another decisive development during this period responsible for mass tourism. In all 'inclusive tours' travellers are carried on charter flights at rates substantially below those of normal scheduled services.

The principal causes of the rapid growth of demand for tourism in the highly developed industrialised countries in the course of recent decades can be summed up as economic, social and technological in nature. Rising per capita incomes, coupled with increasing prosperity, had given higher purchasing power and an increase in discretionary incomes to a large majority of people. As a result this has made tourism and travel accessible to many. A larger proportion of people can now afford an 'annual holiday'. In fact, many can even afford to take a 'second holiday' for a shorter or a longer duration. The economic prosperity has also resulted in many more people owning a private motor car. Increased mobility as a result of use of motor car for travel, therefore, is yet another important economic factor which is responsible for growth in tourism in Europe and North America.

The social causes of the rapid growth of tourism on the other hand can be linked with new attitudes towards travel and leisure. Traditionally considered a luxury, travel now is considered to be a normal activity and an indispensable part of life-styles and consumption patterns of a large majority of people enjoying a higher standard of living. The present day tourist, having a different kind of background than a traveller of the past, is much more informed. His ideas about travel are quite different and he comes from a wider social background. His tastes and desires are much more varied. A large number of people are now going abroad to participate in more exciting, challenging and exotic activities like mountaineering, water skiing, trekking, winter sports, underwater swimming and the like.

The technological causes of the rapid growth of tourism can

be associated with the advancements made in modernising transport and communication systems. The impact of the modern transport technology, specially in the aviation field has brought about a completely new meaning to travel and tourism. Travel to even remote destinations has now become a reality. The technological developments have now made it possible for an increasing number of people to travel to far away places which only a few decades ago were regarded as being almost inaccessible. The gradual evolution of the originally homogeneous air travel market into two separate and distinct segments — charters and schedule air travel has greatly increased the demand. Added to this, the newer marketing methods like the 'package tour' is a major contributing factor to the growth of tourism. Opening up of new travel destinations, particularly in the developing countries, creation of new facilities to receive a larger flow of tourists and increasing tourism promotion and marketing efforts by the tourist service enterprises have greatly increased the tourist flows.

3

Evolution and Development

In any sphere of economic development, careful planning and implementation is required. This is essential in order to achieve the overall objectives of the development. Planning is a general term which signifies a proposed method of action or procedure to achieve a pre-determined goal or an objective. There are certain basic factors which are to be taken into consideration in the overall planning process in order to achieve goals. First of all, there must be an objective which must be clearly understood and accepted by all those who are to be involved in the planning process. Secondly, there must be a well-defined programme leading to the objective. Thirdly, there must be properly devised mechanisms to measure the progress *vis-a-vis* objectives set.

The key factors, therefore, for a successful planning are the objectives, programme and the measurement of the objective. The preparation of a plan pre-supposes two very important planning principles. Firstly, the plan must be comprehensive in nature. In other words, all major internal and external factors influencing the pattern and magnitude of development must be considered, understood and fully analysed in establishing policy and direction for growth. Secondly, in preparation of any plan, it is essential to follow a planned process which implies an orderly sequence of tasks or actions.

The need for planning arises whenever some rational thinking is required to arrive at a choice among a set of limited means so that certain ends are satisfied, especially when the means are substitutable among themselves. In other words, planning essentially attempts to allocate scarce resources between different competing uses with a view to maximising output, income and employment and, to ensure the balanced growth of different sectors. Such planning may be at an individual level or at a firm level or an industry level, or for the economy as a whole. There are broadly two economic systems prevailing in the economy: Planned economy and Market economy. Planned economy is one in which each production unit (or a firm) uses only the resources of men, material and equipment allocated to it by quota and disposes of its products to persons or firms indicated to it by simple order. On the other hand a market economy is controlled by the forces of the market, like demand, supply, prices, transport, etc. Planning can be applied to any type of economic system, whether centrally structured or built up of many units of purely market economy character. The different institutional frameworks will lead to compulsory planning under the first system and to indicative planning under the second.

The Planning

In the field of tourism, the need for planned development is of paramount importance. Many countries in the world, especially the developing countries, have lately realised the importance of tourism and the benefits which it brings out. The use of macro-economic planning techniques for tourism sector are however relatively new. The planning methods for national economic development which have been largely utilised since early fifties do not always cover tourism development as a particular field. The increasing significance of tourism as a source of income, employment generation, regional development and as a major factor in the balance of payments for many countries has been attracting increasing attention on the part of many governments as well as others with an interest in economic development. Thus, tourism development became more and more a particular field of research in the economic planning undertaken by many countries.

Tourism planning is the process leading to tourism development as it is through the planning process that the set developmental goals are achieved. Tourism planning is also a tool for addressing the various choices associated with tourism development. It fosters the achievements of tourism objectives and goals and also the assessment of tourism benefits and costs. Tourism development on the other hand is a broader term which incorporates the planning, tourist infrastructure, management of tourist attractions and facilities and accommodation and transport services. Tourism planning is a continuous and long term process of preparing a destination for receiving tourists and also continuously upgrading and improving a destinations attractiveness for the tourists.

Community involvement in the entire process of tourism planning and development is crucial. In fact communities are the basic element of tourism. In recent times, communities have become conscious of their participation in the developmental process and have realized the need to be more proactive and responsive in their approach to tourism. Tourism depends heavily upon the goodwill and acceptance of the local host communities. It is therefore necessary that planning must consider the desires and preferences of the local community whose participation is vital in tourism planning.

UN Conference : The United Nations conference on International Travel and Tourism held in Rome in 1963 emphasised the need for planning in tourism and made several recommendations. Some of these were as follows:

(i) that the governments of developing countries should give high priority to projects concerning the development of tourism in their respective countries;

(ii) that the governments of developing countries should consider the possibility of seeking the assistance of the United Nations Special Fund for Regional and Sub-regional Surveys of existing and potential tourist traffic estimates and forecasts, with a view to the establishment of short-term and long-term plans for the development of tourist facilities and plant.

The conference endorsed the relevant comments of the Groups of Experts who had pointed out that tourism was expanding swiftly as world economy improved and more and more travellers sought new places to visit. It further stated, that, to the extent permitted by its economic resources, a country should see a steady growth in the number of new tourist resorts developed. Existing possibilities of attracting tourists for mountaineering, winter sports, fishing, hunting, beaches, spas, national parks, game sanctuaries, national monument sites and shrines, folk traditions and customs, pilgrimages, festivals and sporting events should likewise be developed and protected.

Emphasis was laid on the importance of ensuring protection, not only for monuments, archaeological remains and buildings of historical, cultural or architectural importance, but also for the customs, traditions, art and folklore of indigenous people. The conference also agreed that a developing country which proposed to set up a national tourist organisation should consider obtaining a preliminary survey in order to assess clearly what positive tourist attractions the country already had, what potential tourist attractions existed, and how they could most effectively be developed within the limits of the funds available.

The conference recommendations had far-reaching implications as far as planned development of tourism was concerned. All member states and the specialised agencies of the United Nations were called upon to consider and implement as appropriate the recommendations contained in the report of the conference. These were of particular interest to those countries which were just beginning to develop tourism. Until quite recently tourism was principally a feature of, and was largely confined to the developed countries. Many of the developing countries saw the possibilities in tourism development. Encouraged by the conference recommendations, many developing countries introduced tourism development programmes.

The United Nations Conference on Trade and Development (UNCTAD) in the year 1965 also emphasised the promise which tourism held out for the developing countries. For some countries, tourism offers a major opportunity since it provides employment for many, stimulates investment and is an important source of foreign exchange. The third International Union of Official Travel Organisations (IUOTO) Travel Research Seminar held in Prague, Czechoslovakia, in 1964, examined in great detail the many problems involved in the development of the tourist industry and concluded that planning, whether at national, regional or local level, was indispensable and that all tourist planning should be based on two types of preliminary surveys: (i) detailed survey of the characteristics of the area being considered for development and, in particular, of its tourist resources; (ii) studies of future customers based on surveys and forecasts.

Careful planning is a prerequisite for complete success of any programme. The haphazard development in many countries had made the planners aware of the need for planning of tourism development based on scientific research, Any country, whether it already has an active flourishing tourist industry or is thinking of developing a tourist industry, has to decide on many crucial issues before launching tourism development. The official government agencies, especially in the developing countries, have to be extra-cautious as they cannot afford to waste scarce resources on development plans which do not bring benefits. The governments in these countries have to decide on the following issues:

(i) Rate of growth of the tourism sector, whether it wishes to encourage mass tourism or develop it more slowly, gradually and selectively;

(ii) The importance of the tourism sector to the national economy and how its development and growth are to fit in with the plans for national, regional and local development;

(iii) The respective roles which it assigns to public and private sectors in the development of the industry;

(iv) The respective roles to be played by domestic and foreign capital. Whether the foreign investments are to be encouraged in case the country's financial resources are limited;

(v) Decision as to whether the tourist industry should be treated in the same way as other industries or whether the peculiar character of the industry warrants it being given special treatment;

(vi) Decision as to whether tourist industry is to be developed on a continuous long-term basis or only as a short-term arrangement to overcome the trade deficit.

The Organisation for Economic Cooperation and Development (OECD) in a seminar held at Estoril, focussed its attention on all the above issues. According to the report "much of the discussion turned on the fact that tourism is by its nature somewhat different from other sectors of the economy, since it is an industry based on movement of people rather than goods. For this reason it is particularly susceptible to subjective considerations quite apart from the play of the economic forces. Political and social pressures, psychological attitudes, changes of fashion, may all influence the course of tourism development markedly and unpredictably. It is essential therefore that tourism industry should be as flexible as possible to be able to adapt to changing conditions and requirements. The discussions at the OECD seminar also drew attention to the fact that tourism involves several considerations which are essentially of a non-economic nature. The report of the seminar stated: "Tourism often has significant cultural implications (for example, the restoration of ancient monuments); and political (the improvement of international understanding)."

The fact that tourism is by its nature somewhat different from other sectors of the economy makes it more necessary that there should be careful planning. This is much more important for the developing countries which cannot afford to waste scarce resources. The various issues involved in the planning and development of tourism especially in the developing countries show how necessary it is for these countries to adopt a monetary policy, a policy of agriculture, of public works, of health, of transport, etc. as different elements of its national economic plan, and it should on the same grounds, adopt a specific policy of tourism development.

Coordinated Planning : The peculiar characteristics of tourism make it particularly beneficial in terms of general economic development. From this follows the necessity of adopting a policy, which will take into account all the country's economic sectors which have a direct or indirect interest in its expansion. On the other hand, tourism, as an integral part or specific sector of the general plan of economic development, can only prosper within the context of the country's overall progress even though it calls for its own particular policy.

Tourism like other economic activities flourishes best when it fits into a context of general economic policies and programmes designed to lead to the optimum growth of the economy of a country as a whole. This calls for coordination. Coordination between tourism planning and the general plan must, therefore, be based on coordination of effort in all the sectors concerned. Tourism policy must therefore be a global policy of development, taking into account the important implications, affecting the progress of this activity. In addition, the overall tourism development plan must take into account the social and cultural components of the phenomenon, as these also acquire prominence in the development process.

The planning of tourism, whether at the national or the regional level, must be regarded as an integral, and, therefore, coordinated part of the country's general economic and social planning. This coordinated approach has a direct bearing on the success of the tourism industry, more so in a developing country. It is also to be remembered that tourism is not one business but involves many industries and a whole range of complex processes. A plan for tourism can only survive and serve its stated purposes, if there is coordination among all the processes. A first requisite is the need to ensure that the government organs specifically responsible for the tourist sector play their important role, which is that of cooperating with all those governmental departments responsible for other branches concerned with the expansion of tourism.

The principal aim of the tourist plan is to arrive at a balanced growth of demand and supply. In other words to arrive at an optimum harmonisation of the inter-relations between the two poles of market, while avoiding the creation of serious economic, territorial or social imbalances. Hence, the basis of planning in a sector must be viewed globally and mutually arranged with the country's economic and social development and with the overall policy of planning, for the territory in which the location of tourist centres assume primary importance.

Process of Planning

A process for tourism planning or the subjects of analysis of a plan of tourism development must be correlated with all the elements noted above, in order that they can achieve an optimum level of expansion without creating serious imbalances of various kinds. If a country, region or an area possesses attractions and provides some hospitality for prospective tourists, tourism will probably develop. If this tourism development is to benefit the host area, formal forward-looking planning is essential. If tourism planning is to happen in a specific area, someone or some entity must stimulate and enunciate the original idea. This basic inspiration must be shared by some entity which holds controlling interests and responsibility for the resources to be utilised by the tourism industry. This principle holds true for planning a programme of any scope or dimension. For instance, there may be an existing resort, hotel or industry in a region. The stimulus may be the realisation that there is potential for growth if only existing facilities can be expanded or new ones generated. At the other extreme, an area may have potential but underdeveloped resources. No matter what the situation, for effective tourism planning, there must be active involvement and participation by persons or entities controlling the essential resources.

There are several processes or analysis of a plan for tourism development. It is very important that these processes are properly adhered to. The description of these planning processes as given here can only be briefly indicative and limited to mere suggestions of the topics or steps without entering into detailed analysis. Any plan must take into account these processes if it is to attain objectives in a given period of time. The main steps or phases in the planning process are as follows:

(a) assessment of tourist demand and supply; (b) establishing objectives; (c) territorial planning; (d) basic infrastructure; (e) financial planning; (f) human resource planning; (g) administrative structure; (h) marketing and promotion; (i) monitoring progress; and (j) time factor.

Demand and Supply

One of the early steps in planning is gathering information on the things the way they are and on the potential available for desirable growth. One of the main problems in investigating the potential of tourism can be the simple lack of information. Recording of information and the development of statistics is, therefore, of utmost importance. The important initial steps in evaluating a potential for tourism development lies in determining present status. An analysis of the present structure of demand and supply in tourism is a precondition of any other estimate. This information base is a prerequisite for initiating tourism planning programme. In the first place there must be a survey of the tourist attractions of various types which the country has to offer. Without a full study of the attractions a country possesses, it is not possible to plan for future expansion. It is, therefore, of fundamental importance that a very careful assessment be made of all attractions — physical, cultural, historical - that a country possesses.

Peters lays down a number of principles on which assessment should be based. *First,* it is highly desirable that the attractions should be developed progressively throughout the entire country so that tourism is spread as widely as possible. In this way the benefits which accrue from the industry are also widely spread and most arts of the country benefit. *Secondly,* areas and attractions which are singled out for special development should appeal to the widest possible cross section of tourists over the longest possible season. By adhering to this principle, overdependence upon a particular season of the year will be avoided. *Thirdly,* priority should be given to those attractions which can be most easily and most successfully developed viz. those which can be based upon the existing infrastructural services and would require less finance. *Fourthly,* since it is very difficult, rather impossible, to develop all the potential attractions at the same time, it is important that similar or competing attractions should not be embarked upon until the volume of visitors can justify them. Finally, it is important to know that the tourist is usually looking for something new, he desires new experiences, different environments, new thrills, etc. Any country possessing attractions which are unique or out of the ordinary should attempt to capitalise on these for they are likely to have a great drawing power.

Demand must then be estimated, for both national and foreign tourists. Both internal and external data on tourism activities affecting the area under consideration should be assembled. This task should use to publish statistics on travel and tourism which are readily available from international and regional organisations. In addition travel and accommodation statistics can be assembled from the region under study. Next the tourist supply must include all the different types of facilities additional to various types of accommodation establishments. Special attention must be given to the seasonal factor, i.e., the annual fluctuations in the demand as related to the country's tourist attractions.

Aims and Objectives

The initial data or the information thus gathered should develop a composite picture of what tourism can do for and to a particular area. In order to relate these projected results to a decision on whether to proceed with tourism development, there must be a basis for comparison. This basis is the cumulative set of objectives which should be developed concurrently. Basically, objectives for tourism should be a sub-set of the overall objectives (either implicit or documented) for the nation, its economy, people and the social structure within an area. There are, however, no hard or set rules as to what the objectives should be. In general, however, tourism objectives should deal with growth leading to increased standard of living, employment levels, opportunities for intellectual growth, enhancement of the investment potential in an area or country. Cumulatively, tourism objective should describe the set of conditions under which a favourable decision should be made.

If the data indicate that reasonable objectives for tourism development can be met, this will generally lead to a decision to proceed with a conceptual planning study. As a first step towards preparation of conceptual plan for tourism development, a market study begins with a determination of the type of tourism business which exists and can be expected. Market study provides the basis for conceptual planning. The conceptual plan provides a general view of the future tourism development programme and the steps necessary to achieve targeted results. The various steps involved in conceptual planning, once the market survey has been performed, include:

(i) Statement of objectives; (ii) Selection of site; (iii) Requirements of various facilities; (iv) Supplementary attractions; (v) Land use allocation and control; (vi) Budgets, and (vii) Legislative requirements.

Preparation of master plan is another important step in planning. Master Planning is a process for completing and detailing additional work on the portions of the conceptual plan which are approved for further development. The differences between conceptual and master planning lie largely in the level of details involved. Where conceptual planning, for example, might indicate the need to expand airport runways and terminal facilities, master planning would go into specifics on land and construction.

Planning Territory Wise

The need will arise for locating each pole of tourism development so as to fit in with the general policy of territorial planning. Particular attention must be given here to natural and cultural assets of the country, while avoiding the damage which results from an unbalanced exploitation of their economic value. The need for tourist territorial planning must be reconciled with the limits in place of industrialisation and urbanisation which, even though complementary to tourism, can constitute a serious danger to it. It will also be necessary to plan further tourism development in the selected zones in order to avoid excessive concentration in one area.

The Infrastructure

If a tourism development programme is to succeed, it is necessary to provide life support through a number of infrastructural facilities and services. Infrastructure elements comprise the system of services and utilities which are necessary to the operation of a tourism destination. The estimation of the basic infrastructure required for tourist expansion accordingly becomes a key economic factor in proceeding to the active phase of implementation. This infrastructure will be either specifically touristic in nature, e.g., transport, or more general, such as energy producing units, and will in any case relate with the type of tourism envisaged. The requirements for infrastructure will vary for different areas. The requirements, for example, will be different for a mountain resort and for a tourist pole adjacent to some cultural attraction. The requirements will be for both tourists and local residents. As various agencies are responsible for the development of infrastructural services, coordination is very essential. Without coordination, different elements of infrastructure may infringe upon others resulting in wasteful expenditure. Specific areas of infrastructure are power, water, communication, sewage and drainage, roads and highways, parks, recreation and health care facilities.

Fiscal Aspects

Financial planning is very essential for a successful tourism development plan. Before any major attraction facility of a destination gets into full swing, considerable expenses are involved. There follows the study of a vital element in tourist development, that is, the financing of both infrastructure and superstructure. Assessing the cost of the project is relatively easy when compared to assessing benefits. There may be a choice of locations or a choice of techniques. Estimates must be made for each choice within a feasible range. Each proposal must be assessed separately to establish its feasibility, cost benefit and degree of priority in making a plan. Agencies concerned with the development of an optional national investment programme should compare investments in tourism facilities and related infrastructure with alternative investment opportunities in other sectors. In World Bank Group Operations, this comparison is attempted on the basis of economic rates of return for well defined investment proposals. In evaluating tourism investments, the World Bank Group pays very close attention to the projected financial results. In general, tourism projects financed by the World Bank Group are justified in terms of both their economic impact and their financial viability.

In the case of the countries which already possess an active tourist industry or have a potential for increased tourism development, finances for investment will usually be available readily. However, in the case of developing countries, which are anxious to develop tourism, due to financial constraints, the provision of adequate resources of capital may be difficult. The development of tourism sector will be only one of the number of options for development before a government, since government resources will inevitably be inadequate for all the competing claims upon them. In view of this the proposed investment in tourism must be justified in terms of its anticipated contribution, to the economic development of the country.

Except in centrally planned economies, such as in countries like CIS, Poland, Yugoslavia, public investment will be supported by private investment as happens in mixed economies like France, Italy and India. The government may take the initiative in project development, but it will expect private investment support. If the government is anxious to develop and promote an active tourist industry it will help the private investor to the maximum extent. This can be done first, by creating a favourable climate for investment and, second, by assisting private investor to consider tourism development as an attractive investment proposition. This could be done by way of offering special financial incentives such as subsidies, tax concessions, preferential rates of interests, credits, special facilities for purchase of land, etc. All these investment incentives in some form or the other encourage private investment in tourism sector.

In addition to public and private finance, foreign capital also plays an important role in tourism development programmes. Attention will have to be given to financial means and facilities designed to attract foreign capital. A basic obligation at this stage will be the calculation of the output capital ratio, which will depend for the most part on the external economies which can be achieved. Foreign investment is usually welcomed by many developing countries, largely because of their own acute shortage of capital resources.

Human Resource Development

Efficient and professional management is an obvious prerequisite of successful tourism development. Of equal importance, however, is the quality of staff training, which is often relatively neglected during the early stages of tourism sector development. Tourism basically being a service business, a developing destination must take the necessary steps to build a pool of efficiently trained manpower to fill various jobs which will be created subsequently. A variety of jobs will have to be created to look after and manage various tourist services. Special attention, therefore, will have to be given to needs in manpower and personnel to be trained and rendered qualified for the various tourism professions. Special care has to be taken to ensure that there will be no shortage of trained manpower in case there is expansion of facilities and services. In the case of a developing country, it will also be appropriate to study at this stage the volume of manpower required for activities complementary to accommodation industry, in particular in the commercial sector.

In planning for human resources development, programmes should be established to screen and train prospective employees so that they could acquire both attitudinal as well as technical skills. Attitudinal characteristics contribute to an employee's success in tourism position and include pride, flexibility, adaptability and judgement. Technical skills required include facility and equipment operation and maintenance, financial management, food and beverage production and service, personnel management and administration and system analysis and design. In order to determine the need for various personnel required, a staff planning exercise may be done. This involves a series of steps which include job analysis, preparing job descriptions, job specifications and preparing staff forecasts. This sequence of activities leads to a detailed forecast of exactly what types of persons, with which specific qualifications and skills will be required at all major facilities within the tourist destination. All this helps in determining the development of requisite education and training programmes within the country for local residents. This will also help in determining whether there is a need for trained personnel from other countries and also whether local people are to be sent for training elsewhere.

Management Factors

Next comes the necessity of setting up an adequate administrative organisation to look after various aspects. If a tourism programme is to succeed, the responsibility of success must be assumed by some entity in the form of an organisation. This organisation should have a charter and resources appropriate to carry out various functions. Many countries have established special departments or agencies to manage and coordinate tourism programmes. Depending upon the economic, social and political structure in the country, the tourism organisation may be a governmental department, a semi-government agency in the form of corporation supported by government but operating outside its organisational structure. It may also be a private sector organisation with government support and recognition. Whatever form the tourism organisation takes, it needs to exercise its authority and responsibility in the sphere of tourism development. The administrative organisation looks after both the legal aspects, i.e., the preparation of the legislation required for the installation of the various tourism services, dealing with such matters as the classification of hotels or the control of travel agencies, etc. It has various departments for planning, marketing, research, training, legal and administrative service.

Promotion of Business

The final stage of the plan is concerned with the preparation of promotional activities aimed at launching the new tourist industry both within and outside the country. The main concern of tourists is having an enjoyable and pleasant experience rather than details associated with planning their journeys. Most of the tourists leave these details to travel professionals and intermediaries who look after all the details of the travel plans. Contacts with and support of travel professionals and intermediaries are among the most important factors for successful marketing and promotion of tourist destination. Facilities and specialities of travel professionals include national tourist offices, regional travel promotion organisation, airlines including other carriers, tour wholesalers, tour operators, travel agents, travel clubs and convention and conference organisers. The various channels of communication used to inform and stimulate include tourist literature in the form of catalogues, brochures and folders, direct mail, advertising, public relations and publicity. All these media are selected and organised into promotional campaigns aimed at selling to consumers and travel professionals and intermediaries. The media campaigns are timed in such a way that these correspond with the selling effort supporting a destination. It is very important to ensure that these activities match the level of tourist development to be achieved.

Monitoring Progress : Monitoring the progress periodically is very crucial to get the best results. Preparation of a plan document is not an end in itself. The task of the planner does not end when a plan for three years, five years or seven years has been prepared. A system of constant revision and monitoring of the plan progress should be a part of the exercise of the planning. Targets must be revised continually in the light of changing resources and other circumstances. To use a more elegant vocabulary, a plan is static and planning must be dynamic. Plans are interesting mathematical or literary or technical exercises that can be formulated with a great variety of methods and degrees of perfection. Planning on the other hand is a diffuse but coherent process of making and revising decisions that must be closely attuned to the implementation of planned action. What is needed is a system of monitoring progress and mechanisms for constantly and rapidly adjusting to the changing conditions and circumstances.

Time Factor : Time factor is a very important element. The main purpose of developmental planning is to move towards self-sustaining growth; that is, to create a cadre of trained manpower, to increase knowledge of natural resources and their effective utilisation and to create institutions for enterprising investment. All this takes time. The plan could be for 25 years, 10 years, 7 years or 5 years duration. Many planners are of the view that the first development plan should be a 10-year plan, as it requires an assessment of long term perspective. Time is a fundamental factor in the preparation of the plan and in the identification of the objectives to be attained upon its termination. The medium-term plan ranges between three and seven years with five years as the most popular choice. The long-term ranges upwards from 10 years to 25 years.

The short-term plan on the other hand is an annual plan which is the controlling plan, as it is the authorised document to check its possible achievements being matched by available resources year by year. It is governed by the medium-or long-term plan, which sets its direction. The annual plan is the operative document, while long-term or medium-term plans are merely a set of intentions. Thus the need for orienting the short-term plan budgets with the long-term or medium-term plan budgets is the core of planning process. Time factor is the main element in the planning including planning tourism in any nation. It is vital to the prospect of achieving the economic and social expansion which is linked with tourism.

Tourism is receiving ever-increasing attention from national governments and from international developmental agencies. It can generate the much needed foreign exchange for financing other sectors of the economy of a developing country and also for bridging the trade gap. In its broadest sense, tourism can do more to develop understanding among people, generate employment and raise the living standards than any other economic force known. There is unlimited potential for tourism development. If properly conceived and executed such development will prove not only to be financially viable but will also prove to be of immense benefit to a country. Inadequate planning and development on the other hand, can increase probabilities of failure resulting in great loss.

It is perhaps much easier to have planned development in countries where there is a potential which is only just beginning to be realised. However even in these countries with a long established and a highly developed tourist industry some measure of planning is essential. Planning is essential for three main reasons: *first,* most countries, to a lesser or greater degree have planned economies and if tourism development is to be part and parcel of national economic development, then this sector of economy also should be subjected to planning. *Secondly,* the success of tourism development depends very largely upon appropriate facilities being available in the right place and at the right time and these can only be provided by adequate research into national tourist assets and markets. Research-has a very important part to play in the future planning of tourism development. *Thirdly,* planning is required to ensure that the natural and man-made assets are conserved and protected to maintain tourist appeal, for lack of care and coordinated development may impair and even ruin those assets upon which the tourist industry is founded.

Ecological Dimensions

A high quality of environment is basic for tourism development. When hundreds of thousands of tourists visit a destination, their impact is bound to be felt on the host areas. The environment has to be examined in terms of its physical characteristics - vegetation, climate, soil, fauna and flora and the dynamics of the relationships between these. The key elements of environmental change connected with tourism development mainly focus on issues of land and landscape both in man-made or built and natural environment. These physical impacts tend to be most visually apparent because tourism development, like any other development activity, will certainly have impact on physical location to a certain extent wherever that location exists. Mass movement of tourists may be responsible for both protecting as well as destroying the environment of a destination area.

A destination's environment in all its forms is a major motivating factor for the initial visitor interest in an host area. If there is any deterioration in the environment of a host area or if the quality of the environment is threatened by visitors or by tourist development itself, the very reason for tourism development may be defeated.

There has been a growing concern over the years regarding environmental protection and conservation. A growing concern for the protection of the environment and the individual's quality of life is being felt. It is within this context that the relationship between tourism and the environment has been receiving a growing level of attention from both the public and private sector organisations in various countries in the world. Various international bodies have cooperated in the preparation of a host of studies, plans, programmes and activities on tourism and environment. At every leading platform where tourism is discussed, environmental protection receives attention.

The concern for environmental protection in the field of tourism can, however, be traced back to much earlier. The

International Union of Official Travel Organisations (IUOTO), the predecessor of World Tourism Organisation (WTO), was one of the first organisations to come to the defence of environmental protection as early as 1950 having, as one of its main objectives, the study and development of natural tourist resources. In the year 1954, the study of environmental questions became institutionalised in the activities of IUOTO and the protection of tourist heritage was included on the agenda of each IUOTO Assembly.

The tourism boom which characterised the 1960s as a result of the introduction of jet travel was also responsible for the advancements in the development of statistical measurements and evaluation of tourism. More and more governments realising the importance of tourism to their country's economies started collecting and compiling the basic tourist statistics to determine the benefits and also to plan for future developments. Some evaluation studies of qualitative aspects of tourist movements were also undertaken. Various surveys conducted showed that natural tourist resources were the primary factor that attracted tourists even in countries rich in cultural heritage. There were large movements from urban areas to beaches, mountains and other natural resources for rest and recreation.

This impact of mass movement of tourists to various tourist resorts was, however, not healthy. The great increase in number of visitors to these areas resulted in rapid, unplanned construction of hotels and other dwellings for use of tourists and for migratory service employees. This unplanned growth threatened to destroy the very environment that was the tourist attraction in the first place. There appeared an environmental threat both aesthetic and ecological from overcrowding of particularly attractive areas.

The need for what began to be described as an 'integrated approach' to the tourism development was felt by both governments, international agencies and the public in general. Increased interest began to be generated in what was termed as the 'ecological impact' of tourism. Awareness and also the recognition of 'ecological threat' led IUOTO to recommend to world governments that they implement a resolution adopted in 1960 by its Fifteenth General Assembly in the following terms: "The General

Assembly, considering that nature in its most noble and unchanging aspects constitutes and will continue increasingly in the future to constitute one of the essential elements of the national or world tourist heritage:

> "Believes that the time has come for it to deal with the problems raised by the dangers threatening certain aspects of nature....
>
> "Decides consequently to recommend to all IUOTO member countries to exercise increased vigilance regarding the attacks made on their natural tourist resources."

Environmental Policy : Implementation of the above resolution required the adoption of a tourist environmental policy. A policy was set forth by IUOTO in a research paper entitled "Study on Human Environment" which was submitted to the Twenty-Second General Assembly held at Ankara, Turkey, in the year 1971. The Tourist Environmental policy had the following highlights:

(a) Recognition that protection of the environment, which is at the very basis of the development of tourism, has often been neglected in physical planning policies. This entailed promoting an awareness that the real interests of tourism did not lie in the immediate profitability of plan but in a rational utilisation of tourist natural resources which, far from damaging them, would contribute to their development. Accordingly, it was seen as essential to base development policies on long term prospects and on the basic needs of tourists;

(b) Recognition that as tourism was largely international in nature offering the natural resources to individuals of another country for their cultural enrichment and well being; the protection of the tourist capital was in the interest of everyone and must be dealt with at world level. Underlying this recommendation was an awareness that close international cooperation was necessary so that no region would be at a disadvantage as a result of having adopted high-quality environmental protection measures;

(c) Recognition of a lack of uniformity in the way in which

environmental protection was handled at national level. In many cases there were no provisions to ensure that tourism interests were represented within bodies with responsibility for the environment and physical planning. It was therefore seen as necessary to establish or strengthen collaboration between all bodies dealing with the problems of nature protection. The need was also seen to set up a special body at national level responsible for coordinating steps to protect nature, a proposal that was subsequently to be adopted by the United Nations Conference on the Human Environment at Stockholm;

Central to such a policy was seen to be the establishment of an inventory of natural tourist resources with a view to identifying in particular:

(i) Protected areas or natural reserves where attempts at the very least should be made to conserve or re-establish the natural balance (national parks, forest reserves, etc.);

(ii) Areas reserved primarily for tourism because of their natural attractions and from which industries would be excluded (beaches, mountain resorts, etc.);

(iii) Mixed natural areas in which the establishment of industry must be so planned as to safeguard the main tourist resources.

Implicit in the above policy directives was the concept of classification or zoning, whereby areas with a particularly sensitive or fragile environment would not be developed for tourism or at least where tourism access would be 'severely restricted'. In areas where tourism development was to be permitted on a larger scale, planning measures were seen as essential if the growth of tourism itself were not to produce adverse environmental effects; the pollution of bathing water, for example. Legislation was seen as playing a key role in the implementation to the tourist environmental policy. It was needed not only in national parks or nature reserves but also in tourist areas in general so as to prevent anarchic construction of dwellings, dirty camping grounds or beaches, forest fires or the proliferation of advertising hoardings outside of towns.

The Guidelines : The establishment of guidelines for the development of new tourist resorts was a key feature of the new tourist environment policy. It suggested that new developments should conform to a definite plan drawn up by a multidisciplinary team of experts in legislation, tourism and ecology. According to these guidelines, if the conception of the plan was the responsibility of regional or local authorities, account should be taken of the developments in neighbouring areas or localities so as to achieve coordination of measures necessary to protect natural surroundings. It was also considered desirable to establish suitable reception capacity at the resort in order to plan the communication and transport infrastructure and the distribution of areas for building a recreational plant thus avoiding traffic problems, air pollution and noise congestion, etc. Finally, architecture and the general aspect of buildings and the location of sports facilities or camping sites should be so designed as to ensure harmony with natural surroundings and vegetation.

For planning parks, forests or even the countryside, the competent authorities should also ensure that ecological principles were applied and prevent the destruction of trees, flora and fauna by determining the areas to be set aside for the construction of buildings and by creating paths and other means of access which were not harmful to the beauty of the sites. The pollution of water and beaches was recognised as a serious threat to main tourist areas and it was recommended that specific measures be taken to limit or prevent these effects.

UN Conference : The United Nations some years back organised a conference in Stockholm on Human Environment. This conference symbolised the growing importance that the people of the world attach to maintaining and improving the quality of human life and to enrich the human environment. It is a fact that, all over the world, man has been using natural resources without any thought of the future. It is the wrong use of these resources which causes problems. Today environmental pollution poses a serious threat to life on earth and this is true not only of the areas where there is a great concentration of industries, but also where there is a great concentration of tourists.

The negative impacts of haphazard and unplanned

development of tourism are well illustrated by many areas in North America and Western Europe and also to a greater or lesser extent throughout large parts of Asia's tourism circuit. Yugoslavia's Adriatic coast and the Seychelles are other examples. Many of the beaches of North America and Western Europe bear a mute testimony to the havoc that can be wrought by uncontrolled development of tourism. Destinations once noted for their particular character are reduced to unattractive show pieces as many countries endeavour to keep pace with the visitor inflow. Despite a measure of governmental control during the development, the great increase in number of visitors to these areas resulted in rapid, unplanned construction of hotels and dwellings for tourists and for migratory service employees. These expansions threatened to destroy the very environment that is the tourist attraction. A prominent leader in the Seychelles objected to seeing his country become a "nation of maitres d'hotel". These examples underline environmental threat, both aesthetic and biological, from overcrowding of particularly attractive areas.

Tourism development brings in special ecological problems not encountered in other types of economic activity. The environmental resources 'exploited' for tourism attract tourists because of their outstanding beauty, recreational possibilities or educational and cultural interest. The modern tourism's most paradoxical trait is its capacity to destroy those attributes which attracted the visitor in the first place. The well known economic analyst and futurologist, Herman Kahn, described the rapidly expanding tourism as "...next only to atomic power in its potential for environmental destruction...." Mass tourism has brought in its wake certain ecological and environmental pollution problems.

The environmental amenities which attract tourists have tended to be taken for granted. Preservation of their quality has only recently begun to concern tourism development planner. For tourism the quality of the environment is the basis for attracting visitors and needs to be conserved. Tourism development can become a positive factor for improving the environment, if certain amount of intelligent basic planning is done. In fact the quality of the tourism product depends upon a high quality natural environment.

It has been seen that major social benefits accrue to tourists themselves. But tourism also has valuable spillover benefits for tourist receiving countries. Notable among these is the contribution of tourism to the preservation of historic sites and cultural values. Careful cleaning and beautifying ancient monuments, clearing the areas around the monuments and improving them, for tourism purposes is a case in point. Through tourism development, the environment is not degraded but in fact can be improved. So great has been the national and international demand for tourism and recreational facilities that governments have increasingly to face up to the choice between extending public access and availability of sites, and conservation and protection against over-development.

Governments are increasingly aware that future growth of the industry will necessitate careful management and avoiding over-development of regions of natural beauty. Moreover, saturation in principal destination areas will require a more active policy of diversification and redistribution of tourist flows.

Regional Factors

The potential of a region for tourism may be so great that its development will be central to economic goals and plans. However, regional planning for tourism more often will be considered as a separate and distinct planning effort, aimed primarily at determining the best location of facilities like hotels, resort facilities and transportation networks. Such planning views tourism primarily as a source of foreign exchange earnings. This approach would recommend development to accommodate maximum possible number of projected visitors and to design facilities to generate the maximum possible spending by the tourists. However, this approach of profit maximising in tourism development can result in deterioration of fragile environment and attractive landscapes through over-building and excessive number of visitors. The aim is conserving the environment amenities of a region and advancing regional development through interdependence. The more the local people benefit from tourism the more they will benefit from a commitment to preserve the environmental features which attract tourism. Consideration of the regions ecological characteristics are essential to providing adequate criteria for the development of facilities and viable plans for the use and management of resources for tourism.

Carrying Capacity and Sustainability : Both carrying capacity and sustainability are closely linked with environment. Every tourist region has a carrying capacity for tourists as well as for any other type of use. This capacity varies with the fragility of the area concerned and the nature of the tourist activity contemplated. For example, an island rainforest is a very fragile environment which could be easily endangered by excessive number of tourists using it. By contrast, a recreational beach is not easily damaged by large number of tourists. Planning facilities for tourist development in the case of the island rainforest would require limitations on hotel and similar other installations in order not to encourage excessive number of tourists. In the second case that of recreational beach, high density accommodation and other installations for tourism might well be tolerated.

Carrying capacity of a place or a region may however alter or change over time. Technological advances for instance may increase the amount of sewage which may be treated properly, thereby increasing the carrying capacity. Similarly improvements in infrastructure designs and developments, modes of transports etc. may also increase carrying capacity over time. An important point to recognise, however, is that the overall carrying capacity of a destination is often determined by just one factor. This one factor becomes the limiting factor beyond which carrying capacity can not be altered or changed. For example, there may be enough hotel rooms to cater for, say, 10,000 tourists per night, but if the sewage system is meant to cope with only 5000 tourists per night, in that case carrying capacity will be 5000 tourists.

"Carrying capacity can be defined as the maximum number of people who can use a site without an unacceptable alteration in the physical environment and without an unacceptable decline in the quality of experience gained by visitors." Mathieson and Wall, *Tourism : Economic, Physical and Social Impact,* "The concept of maintaining a level of development and use that will not result in serious environmental deterioration, socio-cultural or economic problems, or be perceived by tourists as depreciating their enjoyment and appreciation of the area." WTO, *National and*

Regional Tourism Planning. "That level of tourist presence which creates impacts on the host community, environment and economy that are acceptable to both tourists and hosts, and sustainable over future time periods." *Cooper et al, Tourism Principles and Practice.*

Types of Carrying Capacity : Physical, economic, socio-cultural, infrastructure, psychological, ecological.

Physical/Ecological

- Acceptable levels of visual impact and congestion
- Point at which ecological systems are maintained before damage occurs
- Conservation of wildlife and natural vegetation of both the land and marine environments
- Acceptable levels of air; water and noise pollution

Economic

- Extent of tourism that provides optimum overall economic benefits without economic distortions or inflation
- Level of tourism employment suited to the local community

Socio-cultural

- Extent of tourism development that can be absorbed without detriment to the life styles and activities of the local community
- Level of tourism that will help maintain historic and cultural monuments, arts, crafts, belief systems, customs and traditions without detrimental effects

Infrastructure

- Adequate availability of transportation facilities and services
- Adequate availability of utility facilities and services of water supply, electric power, sewage and solid waste disposal and telecommuications
- Adequate availability of other community facilities ' and services such as those related to health, and safety, and of housing for employees in tourism sector

Psychological

- Crowding and the psychological impact of being with too many other people for comfort/enjoyment.

Factors Affecting Carrying Capacity : A wide variety of factors will affect the carrying capacity. These range from the level of technological development to the type of tourist. Any factors which influence the aspects listed under will affect carrying capacity.

Major Factors Usually Include : Alien Factors

- The volume and characteristics of the tourist: mass tourism will have a greater impact than independent/explorer type tourism
- The length of stay
- Geographical concentration of visitors
- The degree of seasonality
- The types of tourism activity:
- Educational level, purpose of visit, age of visitor, etc will all affect the impact. This is very closely linked to the volume and characteristics of the tourists.
- The degree of exposure to other forces of technological, social and economic change e.g. the effect of television, may have a greater impact than tourism.

Local Factors

- The fragility of the local environment: sand dunes, marine environments etc. are more fragile than Trafalgar Square in London or Wall Street in New York.
- The social structure of the host economy: the more developed a country is, the less vulnerable to the influence of the tourist.
- The economic structure: developing countries are less likely to be able to reap the same benefits as a developed country due to the fact that they are likely to have to import more goods to cater for the needs of the tourist because these are not produced locally. They may also be dependent on foreign investment for development - the profits generated

from these developments will be repatriated (or at least some will be).

- The political structure: governments may encourage or discourage tourism. This will be reflected in the resources and support made available to cope with the impact of tourism.
- Availability of local resources: the greater the local resources, the lower will be the need for imports and the greater the benefit for the local community. Natural resources will also serve as an attraction for tourists.
- The policies adopted with regard to tourist dispersal.

Combination of Factors

- The difference between the tourist and host: the greater the difference the greater the impact. This applies to both differences in wealth and differences in culture.
- The amount of contact: fleeting contact will be less likely to allow hosts/tourists to learn about the other's culture. Segregation of the tourist reduces what is called the 'demonstration effect'.

The Sustainability

The term sustainability is linked very closely to carrying capacity. Both are related to the concept of maintaining a level of tourism which does not cause irreversible damage and which allows tourism in a given destination to continue into the future. What has happened in a lot of cases, and the south coast of Spain is a good example, is that tourism grew too fast and growth was uncontrolled. Resorts became too crowded. They became less popular/fashionable and the number of tourists had fallen off.

According to the WTO the term sustainability may be defined as:

> "The underlying approach now applied to tourism planning, as well as to other types of development, is that of achieving sustainable development. The sustainable development approach implies that the natural, cultural and other resources of tourism are

conserved for continuous use in the future, while still bringing benefits to the present society. The concept of sustainable development has received much emphasis internationally since the early 1980s, although tourism plans prepared even before that period often were concerned with conservation to tourism resources.

"The sustainable development approach to planning tourism is acutely important because most tourism development depends on attractions and activities related to the natural environment, historic heritage and cultural patterns of areas. If these resources are degraded or destroyed, then the tourism areas cannot attract tourists and tourism will not be successful. More generally, most tourists seek destinations that have a high level of environmental quality - they like to visit places that are attractive, clean and neither polluted nor congested. It is also essential that residents of the tourism area should not have to suffer from a deteriorated environment and social problems."

Coordinated Approach : Because of the nature of the tourism industry, i.e. it is fragmented with many players, problems have arisen because of conflicting interests. Venice is a good example of where coordinated overall planning has proved difficult. There is no one government department that has responsibility for planning and conflicts have arisen between the needs of the locals and the needs of the tourists. Every one should take responsibility for achieving sustainable development. Government is usually involved, for instance in terms of granting planning permission. Developers are involved, but do not always have long-term objectives, particularly if they come from outside the community in which the development is taking place. The local community have a vested interest in ensuring that their "home" is not spoilt, but often there are conflicts between hotel owners (or any who benefit from tourism) and those who only "suffer" the tourists (e.g.. traffic jams etc). Tour operators and travel agents have started to take a more responsible stance - in their brochures they try and "educate" the tourists to be more aware of local customs involved.

According to WTO two approaches to responsible planning

for sustainable development are possible a top down approach, with plans prepared by a central authority, (central or regional, government), or a bottom-up approach, driven by the community. Often a combination of the two approaches achieves the best results.

In order to achieve sustainability certain steps both at macro and micro level need to be taken.

Macro Level

- Creation or development of popular resorts in one area, as a way to relieve pressure from another area of a more sensitive nature.
- *Dispersion Policy:* the use of resorts may cause the depletion of resources in one area, and the exclusion of the rest of the population of an area from the financial benefits of tourism. To prevent this,. a policy of dispersing tourist resorts across a region or country may be adopted. In West Indies each region has been allowed to develop one beach resort - thereby spreading the benefits across the island.
- *Zoning:* This is the division or categorisation of land - permitting only certain kinds of use on it. This may also be applied to lakes e.g. some lakes may be zoned for water skiing or fishing.
- *The Encouragement of Green Policies:* This is when green policies are adopted to protect and restore the environment or offset an environmental problem, and at the same time indirectly improve recreational resources. An example of this is the growth of urban forests by the City Authorities which could in turn lead to these sites being used for recreation.
- *The Provision of Urban Tourist Facilities:* If there is provision of tourist or recreational facilities like urban farms, water splash parks or access to existing facilities like rivers and lakes, it removes pressure from ecologically sensitive areas as the impact of tourism in urban areas is less. It fulfils the need of the tourists by finding a use for their leisure time and also benefits the local community by retaining

income that would have been spent elsewhere. It also reduces the social and environmental cost of travelling to and from a tourist destination and also in a way substantially removes the desire for a holiday by reducing the demand for travel.

- *Create Environmental Awareness:* Making people aware of the effects of tourism. Providing tourists with information on scarcity of natural resources can do this. Information relating to cultural differences and advice regarding acceptable behaviour may also be considered.
- *Restrictive Entry:* this is where access is controlled by the use of various means ,
- Barriers across entrance points.
- Quotas for visitors during the year.
- *Use of Price Mechanism* : to reduce the number of tourists high prices may be charged. This will create an image of "exclusivity" which in turn helps to justify the high price.
- *Site Management Signposting :* by providing visitors with information and by the creation of signposted walks, behaviour may be modified and tourists may be kept away from sensitive areas. Signposting can be used in conjunction with information provision.
- *Protecting Footpaths :* the sustained use of footpaths can lead to problems such as soil erosion or the widening of paths. In order to prevent this, care has to be taken in planning footpaths and also consideration of what materials should be used in order to create a state of naturalness which also sustains high levels of pedestrian flow.
- *Control of Access Points:* similar to the first point. The location and size of car parks, roads or hotels in relation to areas of a sensitive nature can reduce the number and impact of tourists.

International tourism by definition draws persons from diverse cultures. Regional resource inventories and evaluation for the development of tourism should, therefore, attempt to take into account diverse recreational preferences. The travel preferences of tourists from different cultures should also be considered in the layout and design of tourist facilities. Particular attention is needed for cultural preferences in the total environment destined for tourism use. Such considerations will again assist in assigning specific values to different landscapes and natural resources.

Tourism has the greatest need to protect the environment of the places of natural and cultural importance be it a monument, a beach resort, national park, recreational area or a wildlife sanctuary. The planners must consider the environmental process wherever large investments are made in tourism development. The tourist has a strong desire to see and experience places of wonder and beauty in areas where nature remains essentially unspoiled. Destinations noted for their particular character and beauty should not be reduced to innocuous urban jungles in order to keep pace with the visitor inflow. Wildlife which is deteriorating and vanishing so rapidly can be safeguarded. The environment in which various animals live can be properly preserved. Similarly, many other tourist areas can be safeguarded against forces which are responsible for their degeneration. Tourism must be used as a positive factor in environmental improvement.

Area development and physical planning are therefore very essential for environmental improvement. Tourism development can become a positive factor for improving the environment if a certain amount of basic planning and aesthetics are applied in the entire process. Whenever there is any major tourism development, environmental planning should be made part of that development. Any development without some controls, without any thought given to the environmental factors can, in fact, prove to be disastrous and ultimately will be counter- productive for tourism itself.

As many agencies are involved in tourism development, coordination is therefore very necessary among various segments responsible for environmental development and improvement. With a view to preserving the unique character, atmosphere and natural setting of monuments and other places of tourist interest, a coordinated approach needs to be evolved to exercise environmental control of tourist centres. In countries where there are Town and Country Planning Acts, these should be made effective enough and their provisions should cover legal protection to control environmental balance in tourist development areas. In order to ensure that the Act is properly enforced, it would be desirable to involve all those agencies which are responsible for tourism development. In countries having a federal set-up, the authorities responsible for governing should carefully study the impact that the opening of a new area to tourists is likely to have on the cultural and social environment of the area. A Master Plan or Area Development Plans should be formulated before permitting the tourists access to these areas. Concerned local authorities should be consulted at the time of working out of the proposals for area development with tourist potential. In order to ensure the implementation of the environmental control, it may be desirable for various regions to appoint coordinating committees consisting of various interests and departments to implement effectively environmental policies.

Policy of Conservation

The United Nations Conference on the Human Environment, held a few years back in Stockholm recommended evolving a conservation policy within the framework of the resolution of the 'World Cultural Heritage'. There was a unanimity of opinion that something radical had to be done to save the quality of human life and to enrich human environment. The conference was of the opinion that any development scheme of the particular area should be determined by the absorption capacity of the area, otherwise the environment would deteriorate and may in the long run create more complications than actually serve the purpose. This is true in the case of development of monuments, new tourist areas and resort towns.

A concept of conservation is that of science and ecology. The premise is that of man-environment balance. The only way of striking this balance is to define conservation as protection of natural resources. Conservation means the exercise of rigid controls to prevent habitat destruction, habitat homogenisation, reduction of species and natural resource pollution. Conservation, in the sense of preservation of the cultural heritage is popularly supported today. Many man-made artifacts have a scarcity value that becomes as important to society's well-being as do the natural resources.

Therefore, conservation means their protection, restoration and interpretation.

The relationship between tourism and the environment has been receiving a growing level of attention from both public and private sector organisations all over the world. During the last decade various international bodies have cooperated in the production of a great number of studies, programmes, plans and activities on tourism and environment. The degree of importance of the relationship between tourism and environment is cited in the Manila Declaration during World Tourism Conference held in Manila in October 1980. The Declaration states:

> "Tourism resources available in various countries consist, at the same time, of space, facilities and values. These are resources whose use cannot be left uncontrolled without running the risk of their deterioration, or even destruction. The satisfaction of tourism requirements must not be prejudicial to the social and economic interests of the population in tourist areas, to the fundamental attraction of tourism, and historical and cultural sites. All tourism resources are part of the natural heritage of mankind. National communities and the entire international community must take the necessary steps to ensure their preservation. The conservation of historical, cultural and religious sites represents at all times, and notably in time of conflict, one of the fundamental responsibilities of states". The importance of the relationship between tourism and the environment is also stressed in the letters of agreement exchanged between the United Nations Environment Programme (UNEP) and the World Tourism Organisation. The letters of agreement state: "The protection, development and improvement of the various constituents of the environment of man are among the basic conditions for the harmonious development of tourism. Similarly, intelligent tourism management can contribute in large measure to the protection and development of the physical environment and cultural heritage of

mankind as well as the improvement of the quality of human life. It is, therefore, advisable that tourism development and sound environmental management should be integral concerns of national development policies.

WTO Environmental Committee : The growing importance of this subject of tourism's impact on the environment led the WTO Executive Council to form the Environment Committee. This committee in its first meeting at Madrid attempted to define the relationship between tourism and the environment, and formulate guidelines and activities to be implemented by the World Tourism Organisation in the future in the areas of the environment. Much of the discussion of the Environment Committee Meeting centered on the theme "Tourism Development and its Effects on the Environment."

Tourism development can bring positive results to the countries that succeed in establishing an effective programme. It is important that the damage which can be done to the environment through a misuse of natural and cultural resources be avoided through the implementation of proper policies. Possible negative effects could then be checked such as: ecological deterioration in areas of good environmental quality, especially in mountain and coastal regions and in areas surrounding places of historical, architectural or artistic interest; speculative pressure on special sectors with the ensuing destruction of the landscape and wastage of natural environment, destruction of the traditional values of the domestic architecture and deterioration in the latter when the human dimensions of existing localities are exceeded; saturation and overcrowding of the urban microcosm with consequent deterioration in the quality of the environment in these areas. Various positive steps have been taken with a view to preserve the natural environments. In the national and regional tourism plans compiled by World Tourism Organisation there is evidence of one or more of the following aspects receiving attention:

(a) Creation of natural reserves and national parks;

(b) Preservation of historical towns;

(c) Alignment of roads and highways so as to minimise environmental nuisance;

(d) Restrictions on the encroachment of the town into the countryside;

(e) Zoning of industry;

(f) Restrictions on dumping at sea, in land and in fresh water of household or industrial residues.

The formation of the Environment Committee by WTO Executive Council is the step in the right direction. The Environment Committee has adopted the following goals:

(a) To identify clusters of closely related touristic environmental issues including carrying capacity, ecosystem solvency, protection of cultural elements, protection of the built environment;

(b) To systematise field information;

(c) To define ways to involve tourists in the preservation of the environment;

(d) To develop and disseminate guidelines for use by governments in assessing, controlling and minimising adverse environmental effects in tourist activities.

In order to achieve the above-mentioned goals, the Environment Committee recommended a programme of work that includes the evaluation and updating of existing studies and methodology and the general understanding of touristic environmental problems, cooperation between public and private institutions at the national and international levels aimed at developing touristic environmental guidelines and standards and finally, action by WTO and other international organisations to apply guidelines. All the above steps would minimise the negative impact of tourism on the environment of the destination for both visitors and hosts as also suppliers of services. The destination should manage to enhance its physical environment as also visitor satisfaction.

4

Scope and Sphere

You have inherited a big world—vast, beautiful, green and full of fascinating human beings, animals, birds, oceans, grasslands, forests and deserts.

Only thirty per cent of its surface is land, where you live, while the rest of the earth is water.

Scientists tell you that our earth was formed some five thousand million years ago. There was no evidence of life for several million years. There was evidence of bacteria three thousand million years ago. Primitive land, plants and animals appeared a thousand million years ago. Primitive man came on to the scene only two million years ago—but he was no different from the other animals existing then, except that he had a superior brain. He walked on his two legs but did not go too far away from his cave dwellings and hide-outs.

Historical Backdrop

Ten thousand years ago, man invented the wheel and started travelling long distances. Later, he fixed wheels to his cart or chariot and used animals to pull this vehicle. This gave him speed and comfort. He also discovered that horses could be harnessed to carry him on their backs for long distances. Kings and merchants travelled by comfortable chariots while the kings' men rode on the horses. Only the rich and the powerful travelled while the common people stayed at home.

Some enterprising men travelled in search of God and to discover how this universe came into being. One such great man and a great traveller was Gautam or Prince Siddhartha. He was born at a small place called Lumbini, in India, two thousand five hundred years ago. Due to later changes in political borders, Lumbini is now located a few kilometres across the Indian border in Nepal.

Gautam, the Buddha, was the son of a king and would have been a king if he had not left his home. But the young prince did not have any interest in the material things of life. Even his marriage to a pretty princess and the birth of a son, did not attract him to a worldly-life. He renounced the world and walked hundreds of miles in search of a *Guru* who could teach him the true meaning of life. In the course of his travels, he reached the banks of a small river near Bodh Gaya in Bihar. While meditating under a tree, the meaning of his search for truth was revealed to him. He was at peace for he had learnt the Truth. Prince Gautam was now the 'Buddha'—'the Enlightened One'.

Buddha decided to share the Truth which he had discovered, with the people of the world. So he travelled to Varanasi. On the banks of the Ganges in Varanasi, he delivered his first sermon, to five disciples at Sarnath, which is now an important place of Buddhist pilgrimage.

Thereafter, Buddhism spread all over India—'*the Dharma*' which Buddha preached. Lord Buddha travelled from one place to another, spreading his wisdom, till he died at the age of eighty, at Kushinagar in Uttar Pradesh. Lord Buddha left a large number of disciples who travelled all over the world. His most famous disciple was Emperor Ashoka, who sent preachers to many countries. It was due to Ashoka's efforts that Buddhism spread to almost all parts of Asia.

There were other well-known travellers in the history of the world. Alexander the Great, was one of them. Born in Greece, he travelled to conquer the whole world. He wanted to see the place from where the sun rose.

He came right up to India but met tough resistance near the river Indus. He was tired and exhausted. He decided to go back without finding the source from where the sun rose. But Alexander died on his way home at the young age of thirty.

At different times, there have been large movements of populations. Sometimes, the climate changed and an area could not retain the population, and people moved to greener areas where they could find food for themselves and fodder for their animals. The Aryans used to live in Central Asia. Due to climatic changes, some of their groups moved to Europe and others came to India via Persia (Iran). These mass movements of the past were due to social, political or economic reasons. But some wise men always travelled in the quest of knowledge. They had a lust for travel and an unbounded curiosity. Some of them have left a record of their wanderings for us to read—this is called history.

Much of India's early history is based on the travel accounts left by such visitors. One of them, a historian who came with Alexander the Great, was surprised to see that Indians grew wool on trees. He was referring to the cotton that was grown in India, at a time when people in Greece wore clothes made of animal wool or animal hides. There were two well-known Chinese travellers who came to ancient India—Fa-hien and Hieun Tsang. They wrote about the facilities of travels available in India several hundred years ago. India had good roads with shady trees planted on both sides of the routes. There were *'panthshalas'* for the accommodation of travellers and wells for drinking water. Later, travellers like Ibn Batuta and Al-Beruni wrote about the Indians' love for travel. All foreign travellers found India to be a peaceful country, inhabited by hospitable people, who honoured their guests—there was no bias against the foreigners.

A thousand years ago, a Hindu seer, Adi Shankara travelled from a remote corner of India, in Kerala, to spread the gospel of Hinduism. He set up four *dhams* which devout Hindus are expected to visit once during their lifetime—Badrinath in the northern Himalayas, Dwarka on the west coast in Gujarat, Puri on the eastern coast of Orissa and Rameswaram in the south, in the state of Tamil Nadu. Millions of Indians have, over the centuries, travelled to these four remote corners of India on pilgrimage. And, their enthusiasm is still unabated. Even today, millions of Indians travel to these sacred shrines every year. Their number is increasing due to better transport and improved facilities.

This was travel no doubt, but it was not tourism as we understand it today.

Tourism Today

The concept of modern tourism, as we understand it today, is relatively new—not more than sixty years old. Our world has become small. Every place on our earth is now known and shown on the maps. No new America or India remain to be discovered. The barriers of distance have been broken in the last two centuries, by the invention of steamships, railways, motor cars and the latest in the line, aeroplanes. A man can now have breakfast in London, lunch in New York and dinner in Tokyo.

A lot of good things have happened to the human race. Industrialisation has made the life of man easy. He does not have to work as hard as he did a hundred years ago. He gets holidays from work—in some countries people work only four days in a week and the remaining three days are holidays. Some companies allow their employees to choose their working hours. Besides, there are paid holidays every year. Several companies encourage their employees to go for a holiday once in a year and subsidises their travel. The result is a travel boom all over the world.

It has been estimated that five thousand million people take holidays, worldwide, every year. Of these, six hundred and ninety-eight million travelled internationally or to foreign countries, in the year 2000—a growth of 7.4 per cent over 1999. International travellers spent US$476 billion on travel—a growth of 4.5 per cent over the previous year—receipts per arrival were US$700 (Statistics WTO-2001). World Tourism Organisation (WTO) also estimates that international tourist arrivals will exceed one thousand six hundred million by the year 2020.

This is called tourism—people travelling for pleasure or on business, staying in hotels and spending their hard-earned money at places where they do not normally reside or make a living. It is a new economic phenomenon, a new business, a new industry of vast dimensions and magnitude.

The expenditure incurred by such people in areas other than their own place of residence, brings about prosperity in the areas receiving the visitor, and creates new jobs for the local population. As a result of tourism, the people of the world are coming closer to each other. It must be remembered that tourism can flourish only if there is peace on earth. Any disturbance of peace hurts tourism, as we witnessed during the Gulf War in January 1991—it affected tourism all over the world. Or, America's war on Afghanistan in 2001. International travel was disrupted badly. And, India mobilising its forces on Indo-Pak border in early 2002. The Tourism was the first casualty.

An Industry

Tourism—both domestic and international—is taking place on such a large-scale that it has become a major economic activity in the world. Tourism is also called an 'Industry'—we often term it as a smokeless industry, or, an industry without chimneys. An industry is that which provides jobs to the people. So does tourism; tourism provides more jobs than any other industry because it is essentially a service industry. Worldwide it provides more jobs than any other industry except agriculture, especially in the developed countries like USA, UK, France and Italy. It is highly labour-intensive as it is essentially a service industry, which requires personnel at every level.

Role in Economy

The World Tourism and Travel Council (WTTC), based in London, is a world body carrying on research in tourism matters. It estimates that tourism currently employs 17.7 million people—some five per cent of the total employment in the country. If India maintains its growth—another ten million jobs will be added by the year 2010.

The employment multiplier figure in tourism sector is 2.36, i.e., direct employment of one person in tourism sector creates jobs for 1.36 persons in other sectors of the economy.

The labour capital ratio of one million rupees of investment (in 1986 - 87) prices in hotel and restaurant sector is eighty-nine jobs as against forty-four in agriculture and twelve in manufacturing industries. In Indian exports, tourism ranks third after gems and jewellery and the garments industry.

A significant feature of tourism industry is that it employs a large number of educated men and women. Women, in fact, outnumber men in hotels, airlines, travel agencies, handicrafts and cultural activities.

Foreign Exchange Earner

There are some countries in the world which earn more foreign exchange from international tourism than any other major export. India is one such country. Tourism earns more foreign exchange for India than many other exports, i.e., tea, coffee, engineering goods, jewellery, etc. (Rs 14,200 crore or US $3283 million in the year 2000; Source: Department of Tourism, New Delhi). Gems and jewellery may be earning more foreign exchange, but to earn that amount we have to import gems and raw diamonds from other countries for which again foreign exchange has to be spent. In tourism, there are no visible exports. We do not have to import much for our tourism industry in India—only some items like liquor or food which foreign visitors prefer. Another good thing about tourism as an export, is that we do not really send to other countries any of our tangible products. That is why tourism is called an invisible export. A foreign tourist pays for the services people provide in India. There is no major investment involved. God and our ancestors have given us this beautiful country to live in and its great monuments like Ajanta, Ellora the Taj Mahal, the Himalayas or the three seas around our coast. These are the attractions which people want to see. Experts often call them the 'Tourism Resources' or 'Tourism Assets' of a country.

Competitive Marketing

Tourism has become so important and competitive that many countries—some one hundred and fifty of them—have set up National Tourist Administrations (NTAs) to attract foreign tourists to their country and to encourage their own people to travel within their own country or overseas. Every country wants to earn more tourist revenue than its neighbour, because this money helps them to improve the economic conditions of their own people. In India, this organisation is called the Department of Tourism, under the charge of the Ministry of Tourism. The Indian Government welcomes foreign tourists, both for friendship and for the income and jobs they generate. India's first Prime Minister, Jawaharlal Nehru, who was very keen on promoting tourism, once gave a message to the people of India—"Welcome a Tourist—and send back a friend". Indira Gandhi and Rajiv Gandhi too were great supporters of tourism. So, if you happen to meet a foreign visitor, be nice, kind and polite to him for he is our guest, in our country. If he goes back happy, he will motivate and encourage many of his friends to visit our country. More tourism is generated by the friendliness and courtesy of the local people than by all the advertisements. This is called publicity by word of mouth, which is a very effective medium. No one wants to visit a country where the people are rude and cold.

Perception of Tourist

You may well ask, how do we distinguish between a traveller and a tourist? To count the number of foreign tourists in a country, there is a standard definition which all countries of the world accept. A foreign tourist must spend a minimum of twenty-four hours and a maximum of six months in a country other than his own, living in hotels or other commercial accommodations where he pays in his own currency. A foreigner who comes and works in a country to make a living, or to study in its universities, is not counted as a tourist. This definition has been developed by WTO and accepted by about a hundred and ten member countries. India is one of them.

Inland Tourism

Similarly, a domestic tourist is one who travels more than fifty kilometres away from home and spends at least a night in a hotel, or some place where he has to pay. If a man goes to another city and stays with his uncle, he is not counted as a tourist. That is how we count domestic tourists in India. The definition of a domestic tourist varies from country to country. There is no standard definition acceptable to all countries, as in the case of international tourists. India limits the distance to fifty kilometres and the USA to hundred miles.

Each State Tourism Department in India maintains a statistical cell to compile statistics on tourism.

The Assessment

Statistics pertaining to foreign tourist arrivals are compiled by the NTA of each country, on the basis of information collected from immigration cards at international airports. It is the Department of Tourism, in India.

Information on expenditure, length of stay, etc., is often compiled on the basis of sample surveys conducted from time to time, by the NTA of each country.

Worldwide tourism statistics, are developed by the WTO in Madrid, on the basis of information received from the various NTAs. World Travel and Tourism Council (WTTC), too, carries on research in tourism matters.

Statistical information is essential for developing tourism plans and to avoid making mistakes in planning.

It will, therefore, be understood that tourism is a very big industry. As more and more people have money and leisure, there will be more travel. The money saved for travel and other similar expenditures is called disposable income. Tourism expands as the standard of living of people improves, as also their education. The standard of living of the people in India has been steadily improving. We have in India some two hundred million people, who are clubbed into the 'middle class'—more than the entire population of Japan. Many of them can afford to travel within their own country and some even abroad. The Indian Government is, therefore, trying to help—build all kinds of budget accommodation to suit rich foreigners and Indians as well as for low-income domestic tourists. The Government provides good transport and trained tourist guides and has opened many tourist offices to give information to travellers. State Governments, too, have evinced keen interest. They have opened tourist offices to serve domestic tourists. They have built budget accommodations for domestic travellers.

One finds tourist information offices in all major cities of the world, set up by the local governments or municipal corporations. The objective of opening these offices is to facilitate the movement of tourists. A satisfied visitor is the best publicity agent of a city or a country.

In order to motivate foreigners to travel to their countries, India and many other nations have opened their tourist offices in countries where the people can afford to travel overseas. India had sixteen tourist offices in major cities of the world like Tokyo, New York, Los Angeles, London, Toronto, Sydney, Paris, Frankfurt and Moscow—reduced to eleven recently.

Governments build and encourage private sectors to put up tourist infrastructure. Tourist infrastructure consist of roads, hotels, telecommunication network, transport and entertainment facilities. Attempts are being made to develop infrastructure in a planned manner so as to avoid congestion, overcrowding and damage to the environment. That is where the role of the Government is important.

Development, the World Over

International tourism has grown steadily since 1950, as also tourism expenditure. Revenue from tourism means a lot to the host country, as it is contributed by foreign visitors in foreign exchange, which the host country can use for its economic development. An idea of the growth of tourism and tourism expenditure in India can be had from the following table:

Gradual Growth—1950 - 2000

Year	International Tourist Arrivals (millions)	
		(US$)
1950	25.3	2100
1960	69.2	6,867
1970	160	17,900
1980	285	102, 363
1985	326	108,091
1990	458	249,000
1995	565	405,000
1996	596	435,000

Contd...

Year	International Tourist Arrivals (millions)	
1997	610	436,000
1998	625	445,000
1999	650	455,000
2000	698	476,000

Source: WTO

It is evident that tourism is a growth-oriented industry. It has never looked back since it started in the early fifties.

In 2000, the following fifteen countries were the world's top tourism destinations and spenders.

Top Fifteen Tourism Destinations

Rank	*International Tourist Arrivals (million)* 1999	2000*	*% Change 2000*/1999*	*Market Share 2000**
1 France	73.0	74.5	2.0	10.7
2 United States	48.5	52.7	8.7	7.5
3 Spain	46.8	48.5	3.7	6.9
4 Italy	36.5	41.2	12.8	5.9
5 China	27.0	31.2	15.5	4.5
6 United Kingdom	25.4	24.9	-1.9	3.6
7 Canada	19.5	20.4	4.9	2.9
8 Mexico	19.0	20.0	5.0	2.9
9 Germany	17.1	18.9	10.5	2.7
10 Russian Fed	18.5	-	-	-
11 Poland	18.0	-	-	-
12 Austria	17.5	17.8	2.0	2.6
13 Hungary	14.4	15.6	8.1	2.2
14 Hong Kong (China)	11.3	13.1	15.3	1.9
15 Greece	12.2	12.5	2.8	1.8

Source: WTO* Data as collected in WTO database, January 2001

Tourism in India

India's share in world tourism is not significant—just 0.38 per cent—not even half per cent. Share in receipts is 0.62 per cent.

The international tourist arrivals in India were only sixteen thousand, eight hundred and twenty in 1951. Arrivals jumped to about 1.3 millions or thirteen lakhs in 1990—not including the citizens of Bangladesh and Pakistan. Visitors from Pakistan and Bangladesh were another four lakh. International arrivals in India were 26,41,000 in the year 2000 and foreign exchange earnings were US$3246 million or Rs 13042 crores.

Why is it that India does not get a larger share of international traffic? There are several economic, political and geographical reasons. Important among these are:

- International tourism traffic often flows from developed to developed countries. Therefore, most of the international tourism (three-fourths) is between North America and Europe, Australia, Japan and other developed countries. The developing countries' share is not more than twelve per cent of the world tourism and the percentage is not changing for the better.
- The pattern of international tourist flow reveals a heavy geographical concentration of tourist arrivals. The ten leading destinations, in fact, account for about fifty per cent of the world volume of tourism flow.

  The past few years however, have witnessed a gradual diversification of tourist markets with the emergence of new destinations, especially in the East Asia and the Pacific region, such as China which ranked among the five top destinations in the world. Hong Kong ranked fourteenth and Thailand twenty-first. The same phenomenon is observed in central and eastern Europe where such destinations as Poland and Czech Republic have all choked up sizeable gains in the world ranking. The Russian Federation rose to the tenth ranking. France remained on top of all destinations, followed by Spain and USA.

- Since there is a very large volume of traffic between North America and Europe, airfares on these routes are relatively low. Airlines make money on the volume of traffic. As traffic to distant countries like India is not large, the airfares too are relatively high due to lesser volume, discouraging due to increased cost.
- If a country has rich neighbours as in Europe, regional traffic is very high. In the ASEAN region (Thailand, Singapore, Malaysia, the Philippines and Indonesia) regional traffic is over fifty per cent of overall total arrivals. India does not have rich neighbours. The majority of the citizens of our neighbouring countries do not have sufficient disposable income to travel to India. We also have political and economic problems with some of them. India, therefore, has insignificant regional tourism traffic.
- Geographically, India is located far away from the prosperous countries. The cost of travel to India is, therefore, high. However, these are not excuses to justify the low level of international traffic to India. India should have larger numbers of tourists and the Government of India is making efforts to improve the situation. The promotion of 1991 as a *Visit India Year* was one example, although it misfired due to riots. The Millennium Year too misfired due to poor planning.

Top Earners—2000

If countries are classified according to their tourism receipts, the same pattern emerges as for arrivals. The twenty countries with the highest tourism receipts account for a little over seventy per cent of world receipts. The ten leading countries alone represent forty-eight per cent of the world's total tourism receipts earnings. The United States leads the world in tourism receipts. Italy overtakes France and Spain for the first time, at the second position. The countries in East Asia and the Pacific, in particular China, Australia, Thailand, Singapore and South Korea represented significant growth rates. (Based on 2000 statistics)

Top Fifteen Earners

Rank	*International Tourism Receipts (US$ billion)* 1999	2000*	*% Change* 2000V1999	*Market Share* 2000*
1. United States	74.9	83.8	11.9	17.6
2. Spain	32.5	-	-	-
3. France	31.5	-	-	-
4. Italy	28.4	27.7	-2.5	5.8
5. United Kingdom	20.2	19.3	-4.7	4.0
6. Germany	16.7	-	-	-
7. China	14.1	16.2	15.1	3.4
8. Austria	12.5	11.5	-8.6	2.4
9. Canada	10.2	10.8	5.9	2.3
10. Greece	8.8	9.3	5.8	2.0
11. Mexico	7.2	8.0	10.8	1.7
12. Hong Kong (China)	7.2	8.0	10.7	1.7
13. Thailand	6.7	7.5	12.5	1.6
14. Australia	7.5	-	-	-
15. Russian Fed.	7.5	-	-	-

Source: WTO *Data as collected in WTO database January 2001

Top Fifteen Spenders

Rank	*International Tourism Expenditure (US$ billion)* 1999	2000*	*% Change* 2000*/1999	*Market Share* 1999
1. United States	59.4	67.0	13.0	13.0
2. Germany	48.5	-	-	10.6
3. United Kingdom	35.6	-	-	7.8
4. Japan	32.8	-	-	7.2
5. France	18.6	-	-	4.1

Contd..

Rank	*International Tourism Expenditure (US$ billion)* 1999	2000*	*% Change* 2000*/1999	*Market Share* 1999
6. Italy	16.9	15.5	-8.5	3.7
7. Canada	11.3	12.4	9.4	2.5
8. Netherlands	11.4	11.8	4.0	2.5
9. China	10.9	–	–	2.4
10. Belgium/ Luxembourg	10.1	-	-	2.2
11. Austria	9.8	9.1	-6.9	2.2
12. Sweden	7.6	–	—	1.7
13. Russian Fed.	7.4	-	-	1.6
14. Switzerland	6.8	6.3	-7.8	1.5
15. Australia	5.8	-	-	1.3

Source: WTO*Data as collected in WTO database January 2001

India and South Asian Neighbours—2000

Rank	*International Tourist Arrivals (1000) (US$ million)*	*Tourism Receipts*
1. South Asia	6,299	5,085
2. Afghanistan	-	-
3. Bangladesh	200	295
4. Bhutan	6	9
5. India	2,641	3,296
6. Iran	1,700	850
7. Maldives	467	344
8. Nepal	451	170
9. Pakistan	543	86
10. Sri Lanka	400	253

Source: WTO

India and East Asian Neighbours

Rank	*2000 Arrivals (Million)*	*Tourism Receipts US$ Millions*
1. China	31.2	14,098
2. Hong Kong (SAR)	13.39	7,886
3. Thailand	9.5	7,535
4. Malaysia	10.2	4,947
5. Singapore	6.4	5,974
6. Indonesia	5.0	5,046
7. Japan	4.7	3,600

The following region-wise distribution of world tourism gives a proper global picture (2000).

International Arrivals

	(million)		Growth rate (%)		Market share (%)	
	1999	2000*	1999/1998	2000/1999	1999	2000
World	**650.0**	**698.3**	**3.8**	**7.4**	**100**	**100**
Africa	26.5	26.9	6.1	1.5	4.1	3.8
America	122.3	130.2	2.3	6.5	18.8	18.6
East Asia/ Pacific	97.6	111.7	10.8	14.5	15.0	16.0
Europe	379.8	403.3	1.7	6.2	58.4	57.8
Middle East	18.1	20.0	18.1	10.2	2.8	2.9
South Asia	5.8	6.3	10.7	9.0	0.9	0.9

Source: WTO*Date as collected in WTO database January 2001

Benefits from Euro

The switch to a single currency, Euro, in many nations of the European Union in 1998, had its impact on tourism by making prices more transparent and increasing competition. "It represents a plus for European tourism though not a revolution", said WTO Secretary General, Mr Francesco Frangialli.

The Euro has allowed tourism business such as tour operation, hoteliers and car rental companies to operate in a broader market with more openings and transparent pricing-expanding business.

The advantage to travellers and trade is that they do not have to change money when they travel, or do business in euro countries. The Euro zone includes Austria, Belgium, Finland, France, Germany, Ireland, Italy, Luxembourg, the Netherlands, Portugal and Spain. UK has not yet joined.

The Euro zone is a large territory of two hundred and eighty-eight million population, compared to two hundred and fifty-five million in the USA. Tourist arrivals are eighty-eight million, fourteen per cent of world arrivals while the USA has forty-six million with 7.7 per cent of the world arrivals. Inhabitants of Euro zone annually take seventy-two million outbound trips.

The tourism industry is the accumulation of many products and services, which are consumed by international business and pleasure-travellers as well as the residents of a country. At the core of the industry are accommodation, transportation, food and beverage, travel and financial services, plus attractions and traveller-oriented retail products. These products and services are complemented by many others, such as car rentals, taxis, service stations, telecommunications, retail stores and industry suppliers. Many other industries rely to some extent on tourism. For example, beverages, automobile and clothing manufacturers, construction, real estate and agricultural sectors.

According to an analysis by the Canadian Government, their tourism industry consists of somes "60,000 businesses" which derive all or a substantial portion of their revenue from tourism. They developed the following illustration to give an idea of the businesses partly or wholly dependent on tourism.

Economic Multiplier Effect : Tourism—both international and domestic—according to economists, has a multiplier effect much larger than any other industry.

Every industry has a multiplier effect, but tourism, particularly international tourism, helps the economy of a country by a number of multiples of the tourists' original dollar.

In simple terms, the multiplier concept means that every unit of tourist expenditure goes through several rounds of income creation and expenditure, before its effect is exhausted.

The money spent by a tourist on hotel accommodation, food, beverages, shopping, entertainment and transportation does not stagnate but provides an income to hotel staff, taxi owners, shopkeepers and suppliers of goods and services. They, in turn, spend part of this income on their requirements of goods and services. The second round of recipients once again spend it to meet their needs. Thus, tourist money percolates through numerous segments of the economy. It is just not a few hoteliers and travel agents who benefit from the tourism sector. How many rounds the money would make, depends on the economy. One good calculation for the Indian economy is a figure of a little over three of the original receipts. This is the conclusion derived by the Indian Institute of Applied Economic Research, in the cost-benefit study of Indian tourism (1976). In other Words, in the Indian context, a tourist dollar had multiplier effect of three. The later findings are 2.36.

International Tourism

India started promoting international tourism in a progressive manner, as early as 1950. Tourist offices of the Government of India were opened in London and New York in 1951, followed by several other offices abroad in subsequent years—now a total of eleven offices are operational worldwide.

The growth of international tourism in India has not been spectacular, mainly because the country did not have good hotels and its domestic airline—Indian Airlines—was perennially short of capacity when it had the monopoly in the sky. India had a poor image as a destination for holidays and it took the Government of India's tourist offices, a long time to change the country's image.

The growth pattern may be seen in the following table:

Year	*Arrivals*
1951	16,829
1960	1,23,095
1970	2,80,821
1980	8,00,150
1990	13,29,000
1995	21,23,683
1996	22,87,860
1997	23,40,940
1998	24,81,000
1999	24,82,000
2000	26,41,157

International tourism to India has some distinct features. For instance, the average stay of tourists is one of the longest in the world. The average stay has ranged from a minimum of twenty-seven days to thirty days annually. In the year 2000, the average was 30.2 days.

The average expenditure works out to Rs 291 per day for each visitor (1983)—the current estimate being Rs 1,000 per person per day.

Among international arrivals to India, the young predominate—fifty-two per cent in the age group of 25 - 44 years and another eighteen per cent in the age group of 45 - 59 years. The very young (3 - 14 years) are 7.5 per cent. The rest are of a senior age group, above 60 years. The average may vary slightly from year to year, but the general pattern has remained stable for some years.

The three months of October/November/December, attract the most foreign tourists (31.2 per cent), followed by January - March (twenty-seven per cent), July - September (23.5 per cent) and April - June (16.3 per cent). In other words, India's peak tourist season is October to March while the lean season is April to September. Arrivals, in the first and the fourth quarter of the year 1999, were 60.9 per cent and second and third quarter were 39.1 per cent.

While 98.5 per cent of foreign visitors to India travel by air, less than two per cent come by land or sea. The share of those coming by sea was insignificant—0.1 per cent.

Of the foreign visitors to India, seventy per cent declared that their purpose of visit was a holiday, followed by sixteen per cent who came for business; eight per cent came to visit friends and relatives, three per cent for study and the rest for conventions and conferences, etc.

About seventy per cent of foreign visitors to India are professionals, like company executives, scientists, doctors, entrepreneurs, government representatives. Only ten per cent are housewives. The rest fall in other categories. Males were sixty-five per cent among the visitors to India in 1999. The pattern is not very different each year. Japan had the highest number of male visitors—seventy per cent.

The Importance

Tourism, today, plays an important role in the economy of most countries of the world and India is no exception. India was a late starter in this field and the Indian Government did not realise its economic significance till the seventies, when the late Prime Minister, Indira Gandhi, set up a separate Ministry of Tourism and Civil Aviation, under a Cabinet Minister, Dr Karan Singh. Tourism now has been given the status of an 'export industry' by the Ministry of Tourism and the Planning Commission. This means that tourism-related activities can claim incentives and concessions given to other export industries, but the message does not seem to have percolated to all the wings of State and Central Governments. For instance, manufacturing industries pay a concessional rate of electricity, but hotels are charged a very high rate for the power consumed by them. There are other examples of double standards applied by the Government to the tourism industry—presumably because tourism has connotations of a 'luxury' which is frowned upon in the current political environment. Indians have to pay ten per cent 'expenditure tax' to the Central Government, if they stay and eat in hotels charging Rs 2000 or more for a room per night. It was Rs 400 per night till the Finance Minister raised it to Rs 1,200 in 1992 - 93 and later to Rs 2000.

In India, tourism has created direct or indirect employment for some seventeen million people. It generates earnings for hoteliers, travel agents, taxi drivers, craftsmen, souvenir-sellers, transporters, airlines, tourist guides and shoemakers.

Some Rs 1000 crore worth of handicrafts are sold every year to tourists, taking the benefit of tourism to the villages where our craftsmen live and work.

In certain parts of India, tourism is the only industry—Kashmir, for instance and now Himachal Pradesh and Goa. Or, consider Khajuraho. Tourism has transformed this once impoverished, obscure and backward village into a thriving tourist centre.

By the year 2010, India can earn Rs 30,000 crore from tourism. According to the Government of India's estimates—in the year 2000, it earned Rs 14,415 crore.

Tourism can yield enough revenue to purchase one Boeing 747 Jet for Air India every ten days. Or, one Airbus for Indian Airlines every five days. Or, one Jaguar deep penetration aircraft for the Indian Air Force every two days. From another point of view, tourism's earnings could pay for ninety medium-sized schools every day. Or, four hospitals of two hundred beds each for the country, everyday.

Tourism could pay for almost the entire Tenth Plan bill for the power projects. Most important, tourism can help pay for our imports.

As a Career

Travel and leisure tourism being a labour-intensive industry has numerous job opportunities for educated young Indians—and it is one industry which does not go into recession even in the recessionary time. People normally do not miss holidays and entertainment—even though they may reduce the expenditure a little, etc.

However, for seekers of careers in tourism industry, the author has a story to tell. After successfully running his travel agency for forty years, a travel agent died and reached the doors of heaven and hell. Saint Peter, as usual, stopped him at the gate and asked him his profession on earth. The travel agent was shivering as he was convinced that he will be thrown into the hell, as during his years on earth he was so busy that he did not find time to worship God. As he reluctantly told his profession to Saint Peter, he was in for a surprise. Saint Peter smiled and said, "My Man, I will let you go in heaven as you encountered enough of hell on earth at the hands of your customers." So, if you are seeking an entry in tourism field at any level—you must have an aptitude for meeting and liking the people. You must be patient, caring and attentive to the customers—even though some of them may be rude and obnoxious. You must keep your cool— you are being paid to be nice and caring, reflecting a pleasant personality. Although interesting, exciting and reasonably remunerative, tourism jobs make a lot of demand on your physical energy and time. If you have these qualities, you are a man for a tourism job.

How to Enter the Industry? How to enter in this industry? There are scores of training institutes in the public and private sector to teach you the skills for personnel needed in airlines, hotels, motels, resorts and transportation companies, or as tourist officers for State and Central Governments. The Central Government has some twenty tourist offices in key cities of India and eleven overseas offices, manned by India-based staff. Each State Government too runs its Department of Tourism and scores of tourist offices in and out of its state boundaries. They also need trained staff. Each State of India has at least one Government-run Hotel Management Institute run by the Centre, to train people, needed in accommodation and catering industry. Similarly, there are institutes to let you in on the skills for travel agency, airline ticketing, etc.

Tourism is a diverse and complex industry. It is entirely service-oriented where customers demand value for money. It is bought unseen on trust, assuming that the people involved in the service chain will be honest, dedicated, polite and nice. And, by and large, the industry has been functioning smoothly and efficiently. It is evident from the way it has been growing—five to six per cent average growth per year. The tourism tally for the year 2000 was—worldwide arrivals six hundred and ninety-eight million and revenue US$ 476 billion. It amounts to over 1.2 billion spending per day. It is expected to double in two decades, according to the estimates of the WTO. India's share in the international arrivals was 2.6 million—a meagre 0.4 per cent of the world arrivals. Despite this dismal performance, foreign exchange earnings in one year exceeded US$ 3055 million—next only to gems and jewellery, our top export. Add to it the revenue accruing from domestic tourism, which according to the 2000 statistical report of the Department of Tourism was over sixty crore travellers. Statistics can be mind-boggling. But compared to some of our neighbouring countries like Thailand and Singapore, the arrivals were near ten million in their case and foreign exchange earnings too left us far behind. Why?

Where are the Jobs? Now, let us explore the job opportunities. Tourism today is made up of many segments—the principal ones being transportation, accommodation, food service, shopping, travel arrangements, and activities for tourists such as history, culture, adventure, sports, recreation, entertainment and other similar activities. It is almost impossible to list all the jobs available in various sub-segments of travel industry, but for the convenience of our readers we can list the main segments.

The complexity of the industry can be explained with one product—say an all-inclusive package tour from Delhi to London for a group of fifteen, marketed by a Delhi-based travel agency, which collected Rs 1 lakh each for a fourteen-day holiday in Great Britain. The package included at least two airlines, providing transportation, handling at the London airport to the hotel, three meals daily, ground transportation for sightseeing, entry fees to monuments, guide services, shopping assistance and the return arrangement. At London end, all these functions were performed by Delhi-based agents' ground-handler in London for a fee. The Delhi agent had sent an experienced escort to go with the group to coordinate all arrangements. The package involved service at every step by the trained staff of the various service providers—we call them, in tourism terms, as 'suppliers'. The chain that serviced this group of fifteen Indian holiday-makers will be called tourism staff—it is here that we need right people with a sense of duty and purpose.

The World Travel and Tourism Council (WTTC) has estimated that the total number of tourism related jobs worldwide, in 1998, were two hundred and thirty million which will grow to three hundred and twenty-eight million by 2010.

Airlines : Airlines are the major travel industry employers, offering a host of jobs, at various levels—ranging from entry point to the top management. Illustrative jobs are reservation agents, flight attendants including air hostesses, pilots, flight engineers, aircraft mechanics, maintenance staff, baggage handlers, airline food service jobs, sales jobs, computer professionals, training staff, office assistants, clerical jobs and research jobs—the list can be quite long. Airlines services related jobs can be in the government as well as private sector—Civil Aviation Ministry, Airport Authority of India controlling some one hundred and thirty big and small airports all over the country. They further subcontract activities to the private sector.

Travel Agencies and Tour Operators : There may be a million small outfits which call themselves as travel agencies. Many of them are 'fly-by-night' outfits. Only sixty thousand of them in the world—one thousand five hundred in India are Government and International Air Transport Association (IATA)-approved travel agents. Rest of them are commission agents who sell airline tickets, splitting commissions with approved agents and the consumers. The new aspirants should seek entry only in IATA-recognised travel agencies which are under a financial bond and are, therefore, reliable. Agencies can be big and small—some like American Express and Thomas Cook have presence in most countries of the world. Others are very small, employing family members and a few others, if necessary. There is a good opportunity for self-employment in travel agency business. The types of jobs available are varied and include commercial account specialists, domestic travel counsellors, international travel counsellors, research people, advertising managers, computer specialists, sales people, operations, etc.

Tour operators are often dealing with in bound tour operations of visitors to a country as well as domestic tour operations. They normally do not undertake airline ticketing. For staff members, they need tour planners, tour escorts, publicity, reservation specialists, hotel coordinators, transport coordinators, office supervisors, managers, etc.

Hotels, Motels and Resorts : Next to airlines, hotels and motels offer the most jobs. Motel normally is a highway hotel with a lot of parking space for car parking. The following list may give an idea of job opportunities—general manager, resident manager, accountants, management trainees, director of personnel, director of research, director of sales, director of convention sales, mail clerks, room clerks, reception, and public relations staff, housekeepers, bellhops, lobby porters, chamber maids, chefs, cooks, kitchen assistants, storeroom employees, laundry staff, waiters, bartenders, air-conditioning maintenance staff, engineers electricians, plumbers, carpenters, painters, etc.

Resorts have more opportunities for trained staff—events management and recreation staff, sports such as tennis and golf, and ski instructors if the resort is in the mountains. If the resort is on the beach, there is need for many beach sports.

The American Hotel and Motel Association has estimated that lodging industry in the USA employs 1.64 million people and by 2005, there will be twenty-five per cent more jobs in this field.

Railways : Indian Railways is the largest public sector employer in the world as well as in India—employing some sixteen lakhs of people directly and another five lakhs indirectly. The range of jobs is well-known to our readers.

Transport Companies : Companies owning tourist transport fleet do a roaring business. Their services are hired to provide deluxe buses and cars to the visiting tourists, both foreign and domestic. Self-drive car rental companies though now functioning in India, are not too many, but their future is very bright. In the USA, by a phone call, one can rent a car and drive to wherever he wants and then return the car at the other end of the journey. Car rental companies have offices in each city including foreign countries. Some of the internationally known companies are Avis, Hertz, etc.

In India, cars with drivers are easily available and the tourists can afford them as the drivers do not cost the sky.

Food Services : Many job opportunities await young people in the growing food service industry such as captains, head waiters, waitresses, chefs, cooks, bartenders, restaurant managers, personnel directors, dieticians, menu planners, helpers and dish washers, etc.

Recreation and Leisure : An important area of new jobs in tourism sector is activity directors, aquatic specialists, ski instructors, river rafting instructors, golf instructors—all part of sports and health tourism. Major hotels in India now have Yoga, Meditation and Ayurvedic treatment centres. Drama and dance directors, camp planners too find jobs in recreational field and event management areas. Trained people are needed for amusement parks, and theme parks as these are important source of tourists. Several small Disneylands are coming up in all major cities of India.

Conventions and Conferences : Conventions and conferences are multi-billion dollar business all over the world. Every major tourist destination tries to attract conferences to its shores because the conference delegates spend more money than the average tourist. So, we have convention promotional centres run by governments, to promote conferences through seasoned marketers and conference planners. For India, it is a very promising business—every hotel is trying to get a conference whether international or domestic as it gives it assured business.

Other Areas : The other areas of jobs in tourism industry are tourism research, tourism education, travel communications. Hundreds of journalists are now working for travel magazines and newspapers. There are at least a dozen travel magazines or tabloids in India alone, in English and they have produced scores of travel writers who earn their bread through travel writing and reporting.

Gaming—casinos are another area for new jobs, but India does not allow casinos though most of our neighbouring countries like Nepal do. Recently, an off-shore casino has been allowed in Goa which may start a new trend and new job opportunities.

Welcome aboard on the tourism ship—if you are interested. In this field, there is seldom a dull moment. The author of this book has spent some forty-five years in this business and is still enjoying it.

Facts and Figures

- USA generates US$ 461 billion from domestic and international tourism. Tourism accounts for 4.5 million jobs for 3.5 per cent workforce of the country.
- Australia generates A$ 58.2 billion dollars from domestic and international tourism. Tourism accounts for 388,500 jobs for 5.4 per cent of the Australian workforce.
- France generates FF605 billion from domestic and international tourism and is credited for 624,400 jobs or 2.7 per cent of the French workforce.
- Canada earns Canadian $ 54 billion from tourism and tourism employs 546,400 for 3.5 per cent of the Canadian workforce, *(Source: WTO).*
- India employs some seventeen million people in tourism-related jobs—some five per cent of the Indian total workforce *(Source: WTTC).*

To summarise, tourism is one of the world's biggest businesses with a turnover as large as that of the oil industry. Although travel has a very, very long history, modern tourism really started in the fifties with the invention of jet aeroplanes. It is, therefore, a young industry. Yet, it is the fastest growing one in the world. It has not looked back since 1950.

Tourism is labour-intensive and creates many jobs. It generates economic activity in the host cities, states and countries.

Developing countries benefit from tourism or the money earned from foreign visitors can be used for imports of essential goods from other countries.

International tourism is one 'export' for which a country does not have to move goods from its shores. It is an invisible export as a country earns foreign exchange without exporting tangible goods. Tourism is called a 'smokeless' industry as no factories are needed to make goods for export. It earns about Rs 15,000 crore annually for India. By the year 2010, India hopes to earn Rs 30,000 crore every year.

Although money earned from international tourism looks impressive, India's share in international tourism is very small—0.37 per cent only. India has a lot more potential. Compared to some of our neighbouring countries like Thailand and Singapore, India's performance in tourism is rather unimpressive—2.6 million annual arrivals compared to seven million of Singapore.

An international tourist is defined as a visitor who spends not less than twenty-four hours in a country other than his own, spending his own currency. Visitors coming to a country for employment and education are not counted as tourists. Each country keeps a count of foreign visitors and also monitors the expenditure incurred by them. Expenditure is generally calculated by sample surveys.

Similarly, a domestic tourist is one who spends at least a night in commercial establishments like hotels, in a place other than his own—at least fifty kilometres away from home.

India's domestic tourism is growing, but it is still relatively small. Over a hundred million domestic holiday travellers move about in India every year—not counting the pilgrims. Worldwide estimate of domestic tourists is five billion in a year. Domestic tourism is as important for India as international tourism. The money spent by domestic tourists has the same impact on the local economy as the money spent by international tourists. Money has no nationality or colour. Tourism provides more jobs than many other industries.

5

The Components

Tourism represents one of world's largest industries with nearly 700 million estimated international visitor arrivals in the year 2000. This phenomenon today has become a very complex activity encompassing a wide range of relationships. As the global economy surges, resulting in improvements in standard of living and disposable income coupled with more leisure time, the overall number of tourists are expected to grow further. Factors like availability of cheaper and convenient transport, fewer or no restrictions on travel, availability of a mass of information on various destinations and newer marketing techniques, the contribution from tourism to world economy and overall number of tourists are expected to grow further.

World Tourism Organisation (WTO) statistics indicate that tourism industry will continue to expand over the years. According to WTO, international tourist arrivals worldwide will reach 1.5 billion by 2020. These tourists in their turn spend trillions of dollars in the host countries visited during their travel, resulting in great increase in economic activity. From the time a decision is taken to visit a particular destination for the purpose of tourism and travel, till the time a tourist returns home, a wide range of activities would have taken place involving many organisations and components.

Involvement of millions of tourists with a wide range of activities first in their own country prior to their departure and later on in the host country, has made tourism an increasingly important activity of great magnitude. Over the years, the multiplicity of activities have changed. From a simple holiday enjoying good weather and scenery at the destination, tourists have now greater interest in learning and understanding more about the host destination and the people with whom they interact. Tourists are also placing increasing emphasis and concern on green issues as also environmental quality of destinations, better services both in their own country and in a host country as also value for money.

The Fundamentals

The force behind this very complex activity encompassing a wide range of relationships in tourism is a phenomenon of modern times. Understanding the meaning and the nature of this phenomenon and its various components is very essential. In order to understand tourism systematically, it is necessary to know the various components which together make tourism happen. Three of these are considered to be basic:

(a) Transport;

(b) Attractions / Locale;

(c) Accommodation

Transport : There can be no travel if there were no transport. Travel involves movement of people and this is possible only if there is some mode of transport. Connectivity is very vital for tourism development. This could be possible only if adequate transportation infrastructure and access to destination is efficient, comfortable and inexpensive. A tourist, in order to get to his destination therefore, needs some mode of transport. This mode of transport may be a motor car, a coach, an aeroplane, a ship or a train which enables a traveller to reach his pre-determined destination.

Basic Components

Transport	Attractions	Accommodation
Air Transport	Ancient Monuments	Resort Complexes
Rail Transport	Historical Buildings	Hotels
Road Transport	Theme Parks	Motels
Ocean Transport	Wildlife Attractions	Youth Hostels
	Museums	Holiday Centres
	Art Galleries	Inns
	Archaeological sites	Farm Houses
	Cultural Centres	Sleeper Trains
	Amusement and Leisure Parks	Campsites
	Beaches	Caravans
	Mountains	Villas
	Open Countryside	Apartments
	Climatic Features	

Locale : The locale may include the holiday destination and what it offers to the tourist. The holiday destination may offer natural attractions like sunshine, scenic beauty or sporting facilities, etc. The locale, with its attractions and amentities, is the most important as these are very basic to tourism. Unless these are there, the tourists will not be motivated to go to a particular place. However, since interests and tastes of tourists vary widely, they might choose from a wide range of attractions available at various destinations all over the world. Tourist demands are also very much susceptible to changes in fashion. Fashion is an important factor in the demand for various tourist attractions and amenities. The tourists who visit a particular place for its natural beauty may decide to visit some other attractions due to a change in fashion. Peter has drawn up an inventory of the various attractions which are of significance in tourism. The five categories are given in the following table.

Peter's Inventory of Tourist Attractions

Cultural :	Sites and areas of archaeological interest; Historical buildings and monuments; Places of historical significance; Museums; Modern culture; Political and educational Institutions; Religious institutions.
Traditions :	National festivals; Arts and handicrafts; Music; Folklore; Native life and customs.
Scenic :	National parks; Wildlife; Flora and fauna; Beach resorts; Mountain resorts.
Entertainment :	Participation and viewing sports; Amusement and recreation parks; Zone and oceanariums; Cinemas and theatres; Night life; Cuisine.
Other attractions :	Climate; Health resorts or spas; Unique attractions not available elsewhere.

According to Robinson, the attractions of tourism are, to a very large extent, geographical in character. Location and accessibility (whether a place has a coastal or inland position, and the ease with which a given place can be reached) are important. Physical space may be thought of as a component for there are those who seek the wilderness and solitude. Scenery or landscape is a compound of landforms, water and the vegetation and has an aesthetic and recreative value. Climatic conditions, especially in relation to the amount of sunshine, temperature and precipitation (snow as well as rain), are of special significance. Animal life may be an important attraction, firstly, in relation, to bird watching or viewing game in their natural habitat and, secondly, for sporting purposes, e.g., fishing and hunting. Man's impact on the natural landscape in the form of his settlements, historical monuments and archaeological remains is also a major attraction. Finally, a variety of cultural features - ways of life, folklore, artistic expressions, etc. provide valuable attractions to many.

Accommodation : Accommodation plays a central role and is very basic to tourist destinations. World Tourism Organisation in its definition of a tourist has stated that the tourist must spend at least one night in the destination visited to be qualified as a tourist. This presupposes availability of some kind of accommodation. The demand for accommodation away from one's home is met by a variety of facilities. The range and type of accommodation is quite varied and has undergone considerable changes since last half a century. There has been a decline in the use of boarding houses and small private hotels. Larger hotels are increasing their share of holiday trade, especially in big metropolitan areas and popular tourist spots. In more traditional holiday and seaside resorts in Europe and elsewhere, big hotels are keeping their share of holiday resorts. In recent years some changes have been reflected in the type of accommodation. There has been a increasing demand for more non-traditional and informal type of accommodation. The latest trends in accommodation are holiday villages. In recent years there has been an increase in the popularity of such accommodation.

Accommodation may in itself be an important tourist attraction. In fact, a large number of tourists visit a particular destination or town simply because there is a first class luxury hotel or resort which provides excellent services and facilities. Some countries like Switzerland, Holland, France, Austria and Belgium have gained a reputation for providing excellent accommodation with good cuisine. Many hotel establishments elsewhere in various countries, especially the resort hotels, have gained a reputation for their excellent cuisine, services and facilities. The French Government for instance, paved the way for tourist development of Corsica by launching a big hotel development programme.

Main Features

In addition to the three basic components, there are certain elements or ingredients which are also crucial to tourism. These include:

(a) Pleasing weather

(b) Scenic attractions

(c) Historical and cultural factors

(d) Accessibility

(e) Amenities

Pleasing Weather : One of the most important and crucial attractions of any tourist place is fine weather with warm sunshine. For holidaying, good weather is a particularly important ingredient, since it plays an important role in making a holiday a pleasant or an unpleasant experience. Millions of tourists from countries with extreme climates visit beaches in search of fine weather and sunshine. Sunshine and clear sea breeze at the beaches have attracted many since a very long time. In fact, development of spas and resorts along the sea coasts in many countries, were a result of the travellers' urge to enjoy good weather and sunshine. In Europe, countries like France, Italy, Spain and Greece have developed beautiful beach resorts. North Europeans visit Mediterranean coasts searching for older resorts like Monte Carlo, Nice and Cannes on the Riviera and new resorts in Italy and Spain. Italy has built beautiful resorts in its southern parts of Calabria, Sicily and Sardinia along the Adriatic and Mediterranean coasts taking advantage of brilliant sunshine. Many of the Mexican resorts, of the Pacific and California, Florida, and Hawaiian Islands in the United States are yet other examples where weather has played a prominent part in attracting tourists. Beautiful beaches of India, Sri Lanka, Thailand, Indonesia, Australia and some other new destinations are yet more examples of what good weather can do. All these areas, in fact, capitalising on good weather, have become important tourist spots. Destinations with attractive winter climates, winter warmth and sunshine are also important centres of tourist attraction. Many areas have become important winter holiday resorts attracting a large number of tourists. Around these winter resorts, a variety of winter sport facilities have been installed to cater to the increasing needs of tourists. In countries with tropical climates, many upland cool areas have been developed as 'hill station resorts'. Climate then, is of particular significance to tourism and, there are many areas which, because of their beautiful, bracing climates, can be potential tourist areas.

Scenic Attractions : Scenic attractions, like good weather, are very important factors in tourism. Scenery or the landscape consisting of mountains, lakes, waterfalls, glaciers, forests, deserts, etc., are strong forces attracting people to visit them. Breath-taking mountain scenery and the coastal stretches exert a strong fascination for the tourist. The magnificent mountain ranges provide an atmosphere of peace and tranquillity. Tourists visiting the northern slopes of the Alps in Switzerland and Austria and the southern slopes in Italy and also the Himalayan mountain slopes of India and Nepal for the first time, cannot but be charmed by their physical magnificence. Great natural wonders such as the Grand Canyon in the United States, the Giants Causeway of Northern Ireland, the Niagara Falls, the Geysers of Iceland, the glaciers of the Alps, the forests of Africa, the mighty rivers, the lakes and the deserts are a source of great interest to many tourists and have become the basis of an expanding tourist industry.

Historical and Cultural interest characteristics exert a powerful attraction for many. Since many centuries these have had a profound influence on the traveller. A large number of tourists are attracted every year by the great drawing power of Stratford-on Avon in England because of its association with Shakespeare, or the city of Agra in India with its famous Taj Mahal or Pisa in Italy for its famous Leaning Tower. Thousands of Americans and Canadians visit Europe because of its long historical heritage; besides, many view Europe as their original homeland and have a sentimental attachement to it. Any foreign visitor to England must visit London not because it is the largest city in the country and the capital, but because of its historical associations and traditions and its many cultural attractions. In a similar way the visitor in France includes Paris in his itinerary as he does Rome and Moscow in a visit to Italy and the Russia respectively. Many countries which are developing tourist industries are using the legacy of their historical past as their major tourist attractions. In India, the world-famous caves of Ajanta and Ellora are an example. These caves are India's oldest and most beautiful testimony of religious architecture and painting, and are man-made caves hewn out of rocky mountains, conceived and executed some 2000 years ago.

Accessibility : Accessibility is a very crucial factor as it is a means by which a tourist can reach the area where attractions are located. Tourist attractions of whatever type would be of little importance if their locations are inaccessible by the normal means of transport. If the tourist attractions are located at places where no transport can reach or where there are inadequate transport facilities, these become of little value. The tourist attractions which are located near to the tourist generating markets and are linked by a network of efficient roads and can be easily reached by air receive the maximum number of tourists. The distance factor also plays an important role in determining a tourist's choice of a destination. Longer distances cost much in the way of expenses on travel as compared to short distances. An example can be that of India. About two million and a half tourist arrivals for a country of the size of India may look rather unimpressive. However, if one looks at certain factors like the country's distance from the affluent tourist market of the world such as the United States, Europe, Canada, Japan and Australia, one may conclude that the long distance is rather one of the factors responsible for low arrivals. It costs a visitor from these countries quite a substantial amount to visit India for a holiday. It has been stated earlier that Europe and North America continue to be the main generating and receiving areas for international tourism, accounting for as much as 70 per cent and 20 per cent, respectively, of international tourist arrivals. The intra-regional tourism (tourism between countries of the same region) has an appreciable influence on the distribution of world arrivals. Of the total international tourist movements within Europe and North America, at least 75 per cent are intra-regional. In the Americas the United States and Canada alone account for nearly 50 per cent of all international tourist traffic in the regions, where intra-regional international tourist movements are also predominant. In Europe, intra-regional tourism accounts for over 70 per cent of international tourist movements. Easy accessibility thus is a key factor for the growth and development of tourist movements.

Amenities : Facilities are a necessary aid to the tourist centre. For a seaside resort, facilities like swimming, boating, yachting, surf-riding and other facilities like dancing, recreation and amusements are important for every tourist centre. Amenities can be of two types: *natural,* e.g., beaches, sea-bathing, possibilities of fishing, opportunities for climbing, trekking, viewing, etc. and *man-made,* e.g., various types of entertainments and facilities which cater to the special needs of the tourists. Excellent sandy beaches, sheltered in sunshine with palm and coconut trees and offering good bathing conditions form very good tourist attractions. Certain other natural amenities such as spacious waters for the purpose of sailing, or the opportunities for fishing and shooting are also very important.

Geographical Components : Robinson has brought out a list of components of tourism which have been termed as geographical components of tourism. These are brought out in the following table :

Geographical Components

1. Accessibility and location
2. Space
3. Scenery:
   - (a) land forms, e.g., mountains, canyons, coral reefs, cliffs, etc.
   - (b) water, e.g., rivers, lakes, waterfalls, geysers, glaciers, the sea.
   - (c) Vegetation, e.g., forests, grasslands, moors, deserts, etc.
4. Climate Sunshine, clouds, temperature conditions, rain and snow.
5. Animal life :
   - (a) wildlife, e.g., birds, game reservations, zoos.
   - (b) hunting and fishing.
6. Settlement features
   - (a) Towns, cities, villages
   - (b) Historical remains and monuments
   - (c) Archaeological remains
7. Culture : ways of life, traditions, folklore, arts and crafts etc.

Geography of Tourism

Geography is a science that deals with the description, distribution and interaction of the diverse physical, biological and cultural features of the earth's surface. Travel geography is based on physical geography, which encompasses the seven continents, twenty one oceans and seas and over 200 countries in the world. Travel geography concentrates on those aspects of geography that facilitate travel and make it more interesting. Knowledge of the continents, countries and oceans of the world add dimension to life and is a requisite for travel and tourism professionals. Travel geography also encompasses cultural geography what all those more than six billion people are like, something of their ethnic and social codes, and what they expect from and dislike about foreign visitors.

There are two main aspects of travel geography:

1. The world's geographical resource base for tourism, and
2. The spatial patterns of world tourist activity. The distribution of tourism in the different regions of the world and geographical explanations of these patterns.

There are several factors that lead to changes in travel flows and patterns of tourist development. In order to understand these processes, it is necessary to know tourists' motivations and other social, political and economic circumstances that both generate tourism and control its spatial expression.

Main Regions : Geographically four main regions have been identified that function as tourist attractions, the way in which transport networks evolve to link tourist generating regions with potential destinations and their regional expression. These regions are :

Europe : The world's focus of international tourism generation and the world's primary destination region.

North America : An equally significant world tourist region in terms of volume of tourist movement, whose general patterns of tourist development show striking similarities with those of Europe.

The Pacific and Australasia : The world's most rapidly growing tourist region

South Asia, Subsaharan Africa, The Middle East and Central and South America : These regions are peripheral in terms of their economic relationships with the developed world and in terms of their tourist linkages with the major western tourist generating regions.

Travel geography is about the geographical distribution of tourism throughout the world. It seeks to describe and explain the spatial patterns of tourist activity and development on regional, national, international and world scales. It is about the location of tourist resources and the factors (e.g. economic and political etc.) that influence when, how and where they are used for tourism. It is about the people who are tourists, where and why they travel and the effect they have on the places they visit. The tourist travels away from home for a variety of reasons (other than work). The essence of tourism is therefore; that it involves travel to a location, that is not the tourist's home.

The simplest *spatial model* of the tourist system consists of three spatial elements :

(i) The tourist's home area (the tourist generating region)

(ii) The places people travel to (the destination regions)

(iii) The routes people follow between the generating and destination regions.

Travel geography is concerned with the study of all three elements of the system, at all spatial scales (from the study of domestic tourism with a city or region, through to the world of international travel).

Geographical Resources

There are certain geographical features of the world that attract travellers to them, i.e. which types of climate are most suitable for different type of tourist activity, what sort of coast and landscapes tourists find attractive. Which historical cultural and wildlife resources have the potential for tourism? It is also important to know where in the world these features are located i.e., what is the world distribution of climatic, landscape, coastal, wildlife, historical and cultural resources for tourism?

Following are the main geographical features which attract travellers to them.

Climatic Resources for Tourism

(i) Rainfall
(ii) Cloudcover
(iii) Sunshine
(iv) Hot climates
(v) Tropical climates
(vi) Mediterranean climates
(vii) Cool temperate climates
(viii) The cold climates
(ix) Mountain climates

Coastal Resources and the Sea

(i) The sea
(ii) The beach
(iii) The waves
(iv) The tides

Landscape and Wildlife Resources

(i) Natural landscapes
(ii) Tropical forests
(iii) National parks
(iv) Wildlife sanctuaries
(v) Hot deserts

Historic Resources for Tourism

(i) Early civilization
(ii) The classical world
(iii) The age of migrations
(iv) Medieval times
(v) 17th century to the present

Cultural, Entertainment and Man-made Resources for Tourism

(i) Theme parks
(ii) Entertainment
(iii) Leisure shopping

(iv) Sporting events

(v) Nightlife

Geographical Resources for Tourism : All the tourist resources discussed are to be developed in such a way that these develop into tourist destinations. It is necessary to know:

1. How do the world's physical, historical and cultural resources become developed for tourism? What part do the tourists themselves, the tourist industry and the host community play in this process of development?
2. How are the world's tourist resources used, who uses them and what impact does tourism have on the resources?
3. How does tourist development spread to new destinations throughout the world? Is this spatial spread of tourism inevitable?
4. How do host communities react to the development and spread of tourism? Do they encourage it or seek to control it through their economic and planning policies?

Geographical Resources for tourism:

Coastal Resources

(i) Beach Resorts

(ii) Resort land use patterns

(iii) Impact of beach resort development on the host region

(iv) policies for beach resorts

(v) ports and harbours

Landscape Resources

(i) Rural tourism

(ii) Impacts of rural tourism in regions

(iii) Landscape tourism

Wildlife and Wilderness Resources

(i) Ecotourism

(ii) Nature tourism

(iii) Ecological carrying capacity

(iv) National parks

(v) Wildlife tourism

(vi) Policies for national park development

Historic Resources

(i) Spatial distribution of historic resources

(ii) Historic towns and cities

(iii) Museums

(iv) Historic buildings

(v) Management of historic town and sites

Cultural Resources

(i) Cultural and ethnic tourism

(ii) Impacts of cultural and ethnic tourism

(iii) Policies for cultural and ethnic tourism

Urban Resources

(i) Urban resources and market for Urban tourism

(ii) Location of tourism within the city

(iii) Impacts of Urban tourist development

(iv) Policies for Urban tourism

Common Patterns

Where do international tourists come from; i.e. which countries and regions of the world generate international tourism, and is there any clear spatial pattern of tourist generation in the world ? Why do these countries and regions generate tourism, i.e. what combination of social, economic and political circumstances leads to the development of international (and also domestic) tourism in a country ? Has the level of world tourism generation changed over time, i.e. has the performance of world economy affected the generation of tourism on a world scale? The tourist generation is particularly closely related to economic circumstances, and that tourist generation on a world scale is heavily concentrated in Europe, North America and to some extent, in the Pacific region. There is a relationship between the performance of the world's economy and the generation of international tourist travel. This relationship also holds good at the level of the individual country.

A country's ability to generate tourism is related to its social, political and economic character. Each country goes through a clearly defined sequence of phases of tourist generation from phase 1 when only a tiny elite travel abroad, through phase 2 and 3 when first mass domestic and then mass outbound (international) tourism develops, and through to phase 4 when, finally, the proportion of the population travelling abroad is greater than that holidaying at home. These phases occur in parallel with economic and political change taking place in the country. Different countries of the world are at different stages of economic development and tourist generation. The countries of the affluent economic core (mainly the continents of Northern Hemisphere) currently generate the vast majority of the world's international and domestic tourists. Thus tourist generation on a world scale in heavily concentrated in Europe, North America and to a lesser extent, in the Pacific region. The countries on the economic periphery (essentially the countries of South and South East Asia, Africa and Central and South America) play a relatively small part in generating world international or domestic tourist traffic.

Systems of Transport

How do transport systems evolve, to link tourist generation regions with the attractions tourists wish to visit i.e. their destinations? In general, transport routes and systems evolve, (or are planned) to enable three main types of tourist movements to take place :

(i) A flow of tourists to the coast.

(ii) A flow of tourist to and between Urban areas.

(iii) Flow of tourists from the towns to the mountains and countryside.

However, on both the national and international scales the overriding influence of the climate imposes a clear directional influence on these : tourists in the Northern Hemisphere tend to travel South, while those in the Southern Hemisphere tend to travel north, towards the warmer climates.

World Geographical Units : The world can be divided into four functional tourist regions which can be clearly distinguishable in terms of tourist activity (both in overall volume and directional flow) These are :

1. Europe and the Mediterranean basin.
2. North America, plus Mexico and the Caribbean.
3. East Asia and the Pacific.
4. South Asia, Middle East, South America, Subsaharan Africa.

The above region are, however, very large and cut across the boundaries of the continents and overlap the division of the world into the economic core and periphery. The world, however, can be subdivided into the following manageable geographical units :

Europe

(a) The Iberian peninsula : Spain and Portugal
(b) The Balkan region : Albania, Greece and former Yugoslavia
(c) Turkey : Cyprus and Malta
(d) The Alps : Austria and Switzerland
(e) Central Europe : France, Italy, Benelux and Germany
(f) Eastern Europe and the CIS
(g) UK and Ireland
(h) Northwest Europe : Scandinavia

North Africa and Middle East, Subsaharan Africa

The Americas

(i) North America
(ii) Mexico and Carribean
(iii) Central and South America

Asia and the Pacific Region

(i) Australia and New Zealand
(ii) The Pacific Islands
(iii) East Asia
(iv) South East Asia
(v) South Asia : The Indian Subcontinent

Travel geography plays a crucial role in understanding clearly the distribution of tourism throughout the world and is a key element in planning and marketing a destination. While seeking to describe and explain the spatial patterns of the tourist activity, it gives direction to planners and developers of tourism to utilize scarce resources in the best possible manner.

Caring the Customer

A choice of a tourist destination, however, depends on a variety of other factors in addition to the ones discussed above Hospitality is one such factor. A friendly and appreciative attitude on the part of the nationals of the host country will make the visitor feel at home and help him enjoy his stay better. A satisfied tourist is an asset and helps promote a destination in a much more effective way than any tourist promotional campaign or publicity. The French government, for instance, regularly mounts a campaign to explain to their citizens the advantage to be gained from a flourishing tourist trade and the value of being courteous and helpful to the visiting tourist. At each of the innumerable tourist places, one encounters friendly guides who answer any questions a tourist might have. Clear directions at roads, metro stations, shopping areas theatres and a host of other places make a visit of a tourist very comfortable and memorable. Many other countries including India have also launched similar campaigns for their citizens.

Establishment of Information Bureaus is another important step in the direction of welcoming a visitor. It is very necessary to have information bureaus where the foreign visitor who, unfamiliar with the country or a resort in a country, and who perhaps is not familiar with the language of the country, can readily acquire information about places of interest and the various facilities available there. Trained and competent guides familiar with the tourist's language are also essential and are a great help to the tourist. The various formalities to be completed by the tourist should be reduced to the minimum. The United Nations Conference on Tourism held in Rome in the year 1963 had recommended the gradual elimination of all barriers, restrictions and formalities to facilitate international travel. In fact, some countries have already gone a long way towards abolishing certain formalities for visiting tourists resulting in increased facilitation. Many countries in Western Europe have abolished the system of visas between themselves and have done away with entry permits for nationals of all countries on a unilateral basis. Apart from certain essential formalities such as health, customs and currency restrictions, it is desirable that formalities should be reduced to the minimum.

Modern tourism has had spectacular growth especially since World War II. From 25.3 million international tourist arrivals in the year 1950 the figure went up to over 380 million in the year 1988. According to the most recent estimates produced by the Secretariat General, World Tourism Organisation, international tourist arrivals in 2000 are expected to total 715 million.

While economic and political conditions may continue to fluctuate throughout the world, there is every reason to believe that more and more people throughout the world will continue to travel. Tourism has become an irreversible fact in most parts of the world, and the expected upturn in overall economic growth, together with success in stabilising prices is likely to promote further increases in international tourism demand. With the expanding right to paid holidays and the irreversible increase in travel for cultural purposes, the number of persons taking to travel is bound to increase. As a result of labour legislation in various countries introducing paid holidays, over 750 millions workers and their families have acquired a right to travel. However, not all of them are able to exercise the right because of non-availability of sufficient facilities and increasing prices. However, a vast potential exists which needs to be exploited by those responsible for tourism development and growth.

Tourism for Social Purposes

The demand for tourism in any country is influenced by a number of factors including the very society and the socio-political system in which the potential tourists live. In many countries especially in East Europe and CIS, the state plays leading role in promoting tourism for their citizens. In these countries, the government provides relief to their citizens by way of giving them a holiday as a reward. In fact, in some countries of Eastern Europe there are government policies whereby the State provides a holiday to everyone. In Russia the worker knows in advance when and what type of holidays he is entitled to. In fact, social tourism can be said to be a form of tourism whereby the State renders facilities to its citizens to engage in tourism.

Definition : Although there is as yet no agreed definition of social tourism, there has been a considerable study on the subject. Dr. W. Hunziker at the second Congress of Social Tourism held at Vienna and Salzburg in Austria in May 1959, proposed the following definition. "Social tourism is a type of tourism practised by low income groups, and which is rendered possible and facilitated by entirely separate and therefore easily recognizable services". Another recent definition, propounded by M. Andre Poplimont, is as follows: "Social tourism is the type of tourism practised by those who would not be able to meet the cost without social intervention, i.e., without the assistance of an association to which the individual belongs." From these definitions of social tourism it is clear that it has certain elements. The first is the idea of limited means. Manual workers are thus included in the scope of social tourism. In addition to manual workers there are also others who cannot save enough to pay for travel and accommodation because their incomes are too low or their commitments too great. On the whole, however, the majority of such tourists are manual workers. Secondly, social tourism is subsidised. The subsidies may be provided by the states, local authorities, trade unions, employers, clubs or other associations to which the worker belongs. Thirdly, it involves travel outside the normal place of residence, preferably to a different environment.

Paid Holiday : The element of limited means is most important. Social tourism as we have seen, is concerned specifically with the participation in tourism of people with limited means and with the measures to encourage this participation and to make it possible. In fact, it may be correct to state that the establishment of annual paid holidays in the west heralded the birth of social tourism. Social tourism as we understand it today, in fact, owes its origin to annual paid holidays. The concept of annual paid holidays was established during the inter-war years as a reality for a considerable part of the working population. By the year

1939, in UK alone, some eleven million people were covered by the Holidays with Pay Act (1938). The paid holidays provided both the leisure time and the financial means to profit from it by travel and relaxation. Since paid holidays were introduced, thousands of millions have benefited from them. Paid holidays now have universal recognition and are established all over the world, and in most countries a minimum duration (one, two or three weeks) is specified either by law or by collective agreements. Today it is recognised that in Western Europe the fifth week, even from the standpoint of output may also be regarded as a productive investment. Sweden recently enacted legislation introducing this additional week of paid holidays.

State's Role

A number of countries in the world have special schemes whereby youth, workers and other groups, economically not affluent, are offered concessions and facilities for travel. In some countries, such as the Russian Federation, workers are enabled to travel as tourists with all the facilities provided by the State. Many private enterprises in some countries offer holiday coupons, holiday cheques, and leave of absence vouchers, to their staff. Many firms offer paid excursions, study trips and entertainment facilities to their staff. For a growing number of enterprises the cost of leisure activities has became an integral part of a wage structure based on the need to supply employees with certain minimum social benefits. Some governments have enacted special legislation on social tourism, directed mainly to:

(i) Holidays for certain groups of workers, especially the young;

(ii) Assistance in creating suitable accommodation facilities;

(iii) Holiday financing; and

(iv) Special incentives.

Most of these benefits, however, are available to the workers in the developed countries. Workers in the developing countries, do not enjoy benefits to such an extent. All such benefits depend on the state of the economy of a particular country.

Although many individuals and groups with whom social

tourism is concerned are often identified with manual workers, and social tourism is often identified with workers' travel, it is neither exclusive to them nor confined to them. Many manual workers do not have limited means and there are many non-manual employees on the other hand of limited means, particularly where families are concerned. The concept of social tourism, is therefore, largely based on subsidies, special facilities and other measures, sometimes of a cooperative nature, sometimes by state or another third party. Social tourism in the broadest sense, therefore, involves chiefly the extension of reasonably priced international travel to the widest possible circles. This can be achieved most effectively through cooperation with organisations which by their nature are already committed to the development of social tourism, such as trade unions, cooperatives, workers' educational associations and certain types of youth organisations.

The social scientists who forecast the nature of society in the future seem to indicate that all modern countries are progressing towards life-styles which favour the growth and development of tourism. Increasing number of young people all around the world are participating in tourism. Those in their teens and twenties tend to be more venturesome and willing to travel to places all over the world. They also use means of travel which, perhaps, the older persons would not favour, such as hitch hiking, staying and eating at youth hostels, or other low-priced accommodation. Several factors are responsible for the increased interest in tourism, namely the rising standards of living, technological improvements resulting in increased productivity per worker, increase in leisure time with decrease in work-week, and longer vacations. Changes in the age compositions in the population, the increasing levels of educational attainments, better communication, increased social consciousness of people relating to the welfare and activities of other people throughout the world, and the shrinking of the world by fast jets, have all combined to produce a greater interest in travel. Domestic travel within all countries has also been increasing and the above-mentioned sociological, economic and technological changes likewise favour this type of travel.

The role of travel to increase understanding and appreciation among peoples of the world is very significant. It has a great educational value. Realising the tremendous social benefits which accrue due to tourism, government policies in progressive and enlightened nations encourage travel, particularly domestic travel as a means of acquainting the citizens with other parts of their country and creating an appreciation for these. The importance of tourism was acknowledged formally when the XXI United Nations General Assembly designated 1967 as the International Tourist Year' with a unanimous resolution recognising that tourism is a basic and most desirable human activity deserving the praise and encouragement of all peoples and all governments.

Inland Tourism

While discussing the tourism phenomenon, the emphasis was only on international tourism, its meaning, components, elements and significance. However, one of the important elements of tourism is the subject of domestic tourism. A distinction is drawn between domestic or internal and foreign or international tourism. In domestic tourism, people travel outside their normal domicile to certain other areas within the country as contrasted with travelling outside the boundaries of the country as in international tourism. The basic difference between domestic and international tourism is that of jurisdiction of travel. The tourist activity of residents of a country within their own country, which does not cross the boundaries of the country, is thus described as internal or domestic tourism. Because the travel takes place within the limits of the boundaries of a country, the various travel formalities which are necessary in international tourism are not observed in domestic tourism. Travel thus is an easy affair. The barriers of currency exchange, language, passport, visa, health documents, etc., are not to be faced by a domestic tourist. A tourist's own language serves as a medium of communication. The currency which they use in their everyday transactions continues to be the medium of exchange.

Presently there exists no generally accepted definition of the term 'domestic tourist'. The domestic tourist is generally regarded as a person travelling for a purpose other than exercising a gainful activity or settling at the place visited. The XXIII General Assembly of IUOTO held in Caracas, Venezuela in October, 1973 recommended that a study should be carried out at the international level with a view to arriving at a standardised definition of domestic tourism. The following definition was put forward by IUOTO in 1974-75. This however was not adopted as an official definition, but merely as a basis for discussion.

For statistical purposes, the term 'domestic tourist' designates any person who travels within the country where he resides to a place other than his usual place of residence for at least twenty four hours or one night, for a purpose other than exercising a gainful activity and which may be classified under one of the following headings:

(i) Leisure (recreation, holiday, health, study, religion and sport).

(ii) Business, family, mission, meeting.

There is not yet any internationally accepted definition of domestic tourism. However, three elements are common to the definition normally in use. These elements are: (i) Place of residence; (ii) Geographical setting of travel; and (iii) Duration of travel. With regard to place of residence most countries regard domestic tourism as travel by a country's residents within that country. The geographical setting is the national territory. Duration of travel is an important element in a number of definitions. The unit most often mentioned is the night spent at an accommodation establishment. By analogy with the accepted definition of 'international tourist', the domestic tourist is one who spends not less than twenty four hours or makes an overnight stay away from his usual residence.

Two further elements are common to most definitions of domestic tourism. These are as follows: (i) Distance travelled; and (ii) Travel motivation. With regard to distance travelled, some countries specify a minimum distance in their definitions. The distance may vary between 25 and 100 miles (between 40 and 160 kilometres) approximately. The concept of the travel motivation is considered important by most countries. The domestic tourist is generally considered as a person travelling for a purpose other than exercising a gainful activity at the place visited. Sometimes, domestic tourism is considered as including holiday or leisure travel only.

6

The Promotion

These are so many variables of marketing mix. Promotion is the most important and visible of the variables. Promotion is the mix of various communication activities which tourist firms or national tourist organisations carry out with a view to motivate or influence those target customers on whom their product sale depends. It is however, not only the target customers who need to be influenced by the various promotional techniques, there is the need to influence intermediaries like retail agents and suppliers as well as opinion leaders like journalists, travel writers etc. However, the primary target for promotion is the target markets, group of current and potential customers.

As applied to service industry like tourism, the most important function of marketing is to bring about an awareness of the product and its benefits in the minds of both current as well as potential customers. The message about the product must, however, reach the customer through a variety of channels. All this activity form a part of overall marketing communication. Systematic communication both with the actual as well as potential customers as also with trade intermediaries and opinion leaders is very essential with a view to bridging the gap between the producer of services on the one hand and the customer on the other.

Communication is therefore necessary like in any other industry, successful marketing in tourism cannot rely on a product of the right kind or a market related pricing policy or reliable and effective distribution network alone.

The primary role of the promotion thus is to convince the potential customers of the various advantages of buying or using the products and services of a particular enterprise, organisation or a firm. Coulson-Thomas in the year 1986 has defined the concept as : "The role of promotion is to communicate with individuals, groups or organisations so as to directly or indirectly facilitate exchanges by informing and persuading one or more of the audience to accept an organisation's products." Basically, the term promotion is interpreted to refer to informing, persuading, encouraging or more specifically influencing the potential customers and trade intermediaries like travel agents, tour operators, reservation services, hotel and charter brokers, about the benefits of the product. In other words promotion is creating awareness among the potential customers about the product. The question now arises as to how this awareness is to be brought about in the minds of consumers and intermediaries. Tourist enterprises use different methods of communication to achieve their objectives. However, there are certain identifiable methods which are being used by almost all the marketing organisations. Broadly these are : (i) Advertising; (ii) Press or public relations; (iii) Sales promotions; (iv) Publicity.

Various Methods

Advertising : Advertising is a paid form of non-personal communication about an organisation's product or service communicated through a message. The sales message is delivered through a paid medium for the purpose of influencing the buying behaviour of the purchasers. The term may be defined as "any activity designed to spread information with a view to promoting the sales of marketable goods and services." As such, it operates in two ways: firstly, by spreading information among consumers, about the possibilities of consumption, and secondly, by seeking to influence their judgement in favour of the particular goods which are the subject of the advertisement. Use of certain paid media space is, however, a prerequisite. It can also be defined as a "paid public message designed to describe or praise a product." Unless a communication has as its purpose a sale of a product or service, it is not properly considered to be advertising. For example, the publication of a message in a newspaper by a philanthropic organisation soliciting funds is not an advertising activity. It is only a public announcement as there is no sale of a product involved.

The Backdrop : The original advertisements, perhaps, were announcements written on public walls several thousands of years before the birth of Christ, offering various commodities for sale. As economic forces expanded with the rapid growth of population and the discovery of new worlds; so did the advertising activity prosper. Since the effect of advertising is directly proportionate to the strength of the channel of communication or medium carrying the message to prospective purchasers, it was not until the late seventeenth century that the subject took on any great importance. Printing process from movable type had been in existence, for about 200 years, and primitive newspapers were beginning to flourish.

As the various media were being developed particularly newspapers and magazines, merchants were able to offer their products to larger group of consumers, and expenditures for advertising increased correspondingly. Thereafter, the advances made in the sphere of photography, photo-engraving, and printing served to bring advertising into focus as a major economic force. Finally, the spurt in mass media magazines and newspapers with circulation in several millions, radio broadcasting facilities capable of influencing millions of people simultaneously have raised the business of advertising to a major importance in the world's economy. Added to all this the introduction of television gave a real boost to advertising in recent times.

Aims and Objectives : An advertising objective is a clear and concise description of exactly what the advertising programme is intended to accomplish in a given period of time. Very often the management is not sure exactly why it is spending money and time on advertising without realising what it expects to achieve from this in return. Advertising is an investment and like all investment should produce measurable results. Measuring results vis-a-vis inputs put in terms of investment is, therefore, very important and a crucial aspect which each organisation needs to take care of. The first and the foremost reason for setting advertising objectives is, therefore, to measure the return on one's advertising investment. The second reason is that organisations must seek the most efficient way of marketing the goods and services if they are to remain competitive. There is another important reason for setting objectives. An advertising campaign is the product of the combined work of an entire team of specialists. The team consists not only of top management, marketing, advertising and product managers, but also of agency copyrights, media personnel, art directors, TV producers, etc. It is, therefore, important that all these people are concentrating on a single product and putting their concerted efforts in the same direction. Without written and concise objectives all this would be difficult to achieve. Objectives, therefore, serve the purpose of coordinating, and integrating marketing and advertising efforts.

Professor Robert Buzzell of the Harvard Business School, in a written submission to the Federal Trade Commission during hearings on modern advertising practices in July 1971, gives the following example of possible advertising objectives for a manufacturer's consumer product advertising.

To increase sales directly by:

(i) Encouraging potential purchasers to visit dealers or distributors;

(ii) Announcing special sales, contests or other promotions;

(iii) Securing new dealers or distributors;

(iv) Inducing professional person's e.g. (doctors, architects) to recommend a product;

(v) Distributing coupons to be redeemed on purchases.

To create awareness and interest in the company's product by:

(i) Informing potential buyers about product features;

(ii) Announcing the availability of new products;

(iii) Demonstrating the benefits of a product's use;

(iv) Comparing a product with a competing product;

(v) Showing how a product should be used;

(vi) Informing potential buyers about the company's technical skills, production facilities, technical services, etc;

(vii) Informing purchasers about where products can be obtained;

(viii) Announcing changes in prices, packages, labels, etc.;

(ix) Publicising a new brand name or symbol.

Although the examples given above refer to possible advertising objectives for manufacturers, consumer product advertising, these are also relevant for tourism product advertising. The broad objectives in tourism advertising include making of the tourist product as widely known as possible and to make it attractive for the prospective consumer.

The Advantages : Advertising has several inherent advantages. The most important advantages of this method are :

(i) Wider coverage

(ii) Frequent appeal

(iii) Accessibility

(vi) Lower cost

Wide Coverage : Advertising is especially appropriate for communication with a large number of perspective purchasers of a commodity or a service. A uniform sales message is directed towards all prospective purchasers. An advertisement can be placed before a large number of prospective customers as compared with the efforts of a salesman. *Frequency* is another advantage. It can make its appeal frequently, whereas the calls of salesmen are usually not so frequent. Another advantage is its *accessibility.* It may reach prospects whom salesmen would find difficult to interview, owing to lack of interest or inaccessibility to salesmen. Advertisement may reach such prospects through many types of media and under a variety of circumstances, and may thus attract their attention and arouse their interest. *Lower cost* is another major advantage. Large numbers can be reached economically, i.e., at a lower cost per contact than in any other technique available.

Advertising may be used to do a variety of selling tasks. A great deal of advertising attempts to win acceptance for the product. Such advertising may produce few specific demands for the advertised brands, yet when retailers display or show advertised goods they sell more readily than non-advertised ones. Therefore, retailers often hesitate to handle non-advertised goods unless they are obtainable at low prices. Advertising thus directly stimulates sales to retailers. Advertising may at times be used to make the complete sale. Some direct mail and periodical advertising attempts to make sales by requesting readers to forward orders accompanied by the necessary payment. When the number of potential buyers is small and when they are widely scattered it could be extremely costly to reach them through salesmen. Advertising then becomes the most economic means of doing the entire sales job.

The Planning : Careful consideration must be given to the actual make up of the advertisement while planning. The headline copy, illustrations, colour scheme, size, layout, and method of printing or reproducing the advertisement must be planned very carefully. This is necessary in order to gain attention of the customer, maintain his interest in the message, and secure the action desired by the seller. Closely related is the question of periodicity of advertisement. How frequently to advertise? For instance, is it better to use a full-page advertisement once a month or a quarter-page weekly? A frequently presented thought is likely to force itself into our consciousness. People are inclined to believe statements they hear or see repeatedly and hence the logic of frequent repetition of advertisements. In starting a special campaign the advertisements should not be spaced regularly. Early in the campaign they should be used close together, while later on they can be issued at much longer intervals. This is desirable because consumers forget rapidly at first and much more slowly later on. After the facts are retained by the prospects, the advertisements can be presented at much longer intervals.

Selection of Media : The advertiser should give careful attention in planning to the selection of the medium or media especially adapted to his needs. The selection will depend upon the factors like the area to be covered, the type of audience to be reached, the appeals to be made and upon the services and facilities of the particular medium in relation to costs. The important factors which influence the media selection are:

(i) Media habits of the target audience;

(ii) Product characteristics: for example, TV may be the appropriate media for those products which may require a demonstration of their operation for effective impact on the target audience; and

(iii) Cost of the media.

Message Selection : The massage selected for use in the advertisement should be such that it retains the interest in the minds of the customers about the product. The customer must maintain his interest in the message, and secure the action desired by the seller of the product. The objective is to present the advertiser's message in such a way that the illustration may lead the leader to favourable considerations of the advertisement. The important characteristics of an effective message are:

(i) *Information:* it should be adequate for a decision,

(ii) *Interest:* it should be able to catch the attention of the largest audience,

(iii) *Authenticity:* it should avoid exaggerated claims,

(iv) *Persuasion:* it should be capable of creating a favourable conviction in the target audience, and

(v) *Memory value:* it should have something in it which can help the target audience to remember it.

Cost Effectiveness : The advertiser must relate the estimated cost of the objectives planned and the contribution expected from advertising. Can the advertiser carry on a campaign large enough to make it effective? Are the funds available or will they become available through the sale of the product. How much does the advertiser spend for the advertising? The various methods commonly used are :

(i) *Affordable method:* here, the advertising budget is set on the basis of what the agency can afford;

(ii) *Percentage of sales method:* in this case, the agency sets the advertising budget on the basis of specific percentage of sales;

(iii) *Competitive parity method:* here the agency sets its budget to match those of its major competitors;

(iv) *Objective and task method:* in this the advertising budget represents the outlay required to perform the various tasks which are necessary to achieve the properly defined advertising- objectives of the company. This method is considered the most rational.

Determining Effectiveness : Today advertisement through any media has become -extremely expensive. In view of this it becomes very important for the agency to ensure that the money spent on it does bring returns by way of increased sales. This could be done by way of evaluating or testing the effectiveness of advertising. Testing methods may be used to evaluate the results of an advertising campaign. By evaluating and analysing the effectiveness of advertisements that have been used, future advertisements may be improved. In addition, tests may be applied before advertisement has been run. Pre-testing of an advertisement prevents expenditure that would not be profitable and leads to expenditures that give the best results. In determining advertising effectiveness the commonly used methods are given below:

(i) *Inquiries:* Answer-back coupons, with some inducement, are incorporated in many advertisements. The amount of response is an indication of the effectiveness of the concerned advertisement.

(ii) *Recall tests:* Here the respondents are shown the magazine cover or any other media vehicle in which the concerned advertisement had appeared. They are then asked to tell which advertisements in that publication they remember.

(iii) *Recognition tests:* Here the respondents are shown the advertisement and asked if they have read them.

(iv) *Sales tests:* Here, the actual sales results before and after the concerned advertising are examined. The sales results in the selected 'test markets' are also compared to those in some chosen 'control markets', i.e., the markets where the concerned advertising is not done. This is done to eliminate certain factors, other than advertising, which may also have influenced the sales.

In the field of tourism, advertising is mainly used to create initial awareness and interest in the tourist service or a tourist destination to be promoted and it motivates the potential tourist to make further enquiries about the facilities, cost, bookings etc. As advertising requires careful handling and expertise it is normally handled by an agency which undertakes the job on behalf of an advertiser. A large number of tourist enterprises as also national tourist organisations assign the job of advertising to different advertising agencies.

Advertising Agency

An advertising agency may be explained as an organisation consisting of one or more persons, the function of which is to provide advertising; merchandising, and other services and counsel relating to the promotion of a client's goods and services. The advertising agency is a service organisation which undertakes the planning and preparation of advertising. The agency service consists of interpreting to the public, or to that part of it which it is desired to reach, the advantages of a product or service. Originally agencies were media owners, service departments and not independent organisations as they are today, In the early days of advertising, agencies acted as representatives of newspapers and sold space in them to advertisers. At first, the agencies bought space in bulk, and made their profit by selling it in smaller units for as much as they could get. Later, agencies started to sell space on a commission basis, and a commission system is still the current basis for agency remuneration, agencies taking their profit from commissions granted by media owners rather than from advertisers.

The scope of the work of the agencies however expanded further. The agencies started a copy writing service and, soon after, design and art services were added to their functions. By this time agencies were really working more for the advertisers than for the newspaper proprietors and before long they became full-fledged service organisations giving their clients a complete range of advertising services.

The Selection : Selection of a suitable advertising agency is a major factor which determines the success or failure of a promotional work of an organisation. The choice of an advertising agency will depend on the size of a promotional budget, the range of services required and above all the objective assessment of the professional qualities of the agency. Most of the national tourist organisation and major tourist enterprises have appointed their own advertising agencies. The advertising campaigns of these organisations are run through the agencies. The national tourist offices usually hire the services of the specialised advertising agencies in various tourist generating markets to help them in market research, audience information gathering, designing messages and getting advertising schedules in well-selected media.

Scope of Work : Each major advertising agency has various departments whose area of work are well defined. The following are the major departments of an agency and their scope of work.

The Research Department: When the agency staff attempts to define their clients marketing problems they may decide that they lack sufficient information to reach a sound judgement and will take the assistance of the Research Department. A good amount of information is readily available in published form. Before any field research is undertaken there is always desk research which involves checking through existing sources of information. As soon as information collected has been checked, there are further meetings of the 'Plans Board' to consider the advertising and marketing campaign. Once this is done, the individual departments set to work to crystallize their ideas and to produce detailed proposals in accordance with the agreed broad plan.

The Media Department : Once the general strategy is agreed, it is now up to the media department to get down to detailed planning with the aim of spending the client funds in such a way that his advertising message reaches prospective buyers as effectively and economically as possible. The media-department then evaluates the media and selects the most suitable one in the light of clients' requirements.

The Creative Department: The Creative Department takes its work to a more advanced level. Copy is written for press advertisements or printed material and layouts prepared. For posters or display material, roughs and dummies are made and story boards drawn up for TV or cinema commercials.

Review of Proposals : As soon as detailed media and creative proposals are ready, the Plans Board meets again to review the progress of the work. The purpose is to check the proposals point by point to be submitted to the client to ensure that there are no discrepancies in the work of the individual departments.

Presentation of Proposals : Once the detailed proposals have been approved by the review board, they are made ready for presentation to the client. The media schedule is typed out in its final form as is the advertisement copy. The finished versions of designs are prepared by the creative staff. These are then presented to the client. Creative and media proposals are presented together. Where the presentation is on the major campaign, the agency may call on all those concerned to make a 'dry run' beforehand, amounting almost to a rehearsal. Some agencies even put the entire presentation on film or video-tape and screen this to the client rather than risk the possibility of error that is always present in the 'live' presentation.

Execution of the Proposal: Before giving an agency a go ahead' or a formal approval to proceed, the client checks the proposals to ensure that they are sound and that they dovetail with his company's marketing objectives. Once the agency has the client's agreement, the advertising proposals are put into effect.

Sources of Income : An agency's income is derived from media in the form of commissions and from clients in the form of service fees. The proportion of income derived from these two sources varies from agency to agency depending upon the pre-arranged agreement made with the client in any of the following ways:

(a) Receiving commission from media and billing the client for non-commissionable expenses plus a service fee;

(b) Charging the client a minimum fee and rebating all commissions to the client until the point is reached when commissions equal the fee, after which all commissions are retained and the fee is discontinued;

(c) Charging the client a set fee and rebating to him all commissions received, production expenses being billed to the client at cost;

(d) A cost-plus arrangement whereby the agency bills the client for a specified sum to represent the agency's profit, and invoices the client for all media and production expenses at cost.

However, in actual practice the most prevalent form of compensation is the first described above which is commission plus service fee.

Public Relations

In simpler terms, public relations involves measures designed to improve the image of a service, to create a more favourable climate for its advertising and sales support activities. It covers such a wide range of activities and is used for so many different aims that it becomes difficult to define it. Public Relations is the "art and science of planning and implementing honest, two-way communication and understanding between a company or an organisation and the many different groups with which it is concerned in the course of its operation." It is also defined as "continuous and consistent representation of an organisation's policies to the public at large and to sections of the public who have a special interest in the organisation's activities, e.g., to various strata of employees, shareholders, actual and potential customer as well as its local and national governments. Public Relations News, a weekly newsletter written for the PR profession in United States of America, defines PR as "a management function that evaluates public attitudes, identifies the policies and procedures of an individual or an organisation as they affect the public interest, and executes a programme of action, to earn public understanding and acceptance." The internationally accepted definition of PR however is that it is "the deliberate, planned and sustained effort to establish and maintain mutual understanding between an organisation and its public."

From the above definitions of Public Relations it is evident that its main function is to inform public about the activities of an organisation. In other words, it is a part of an organisation's total communication effort. Its purpose is to create best possible reputation for the organisation by way of presenting facts. Implicit in all the above definitions is the function of the professional public relations expert, which is threefold:

(i) To ascertain and evaluate public opinion;

(ii) To counsel management on ways of dealing with public opinion as it exists; and

(iii) To use communications to influence public opinion.

Public Relations is often confused with and used as a handy synonym for some of its functional parts, for instance, press agency, publicity, institutional advertising, propaganda, product promotion, and lobbying. The field with which PR is most closely identified is advertising. However, advertising pays for the print space, air time or electronic space in order to sell a specific product, while on the other hand public relations, which may include some forms of advertising as its tools, covers a much wider and broader range.

Generally, speaking, PR is the overall catchword for all of its functions.

Public Relations in Tourism : Public Relations in the field of tourism assumes special significance because of the peculiar nature of the product. Here the need for making complete information and facts available to both potential and actual tourists assumes special significance. It involves measures designed to create and improve the image for the tourist product, create a more favourable climate for its advertising and sales support activities, especially in regard to travel trade intermediaries and news media. Favourable acceptance of any tourist destination by the public is of utmost importance. In fact, no business is more concerned with human relations than the business of tourism. Public relations in tourism is used to create and maintain a positive image for a country, a tourist destination in the minds of people who are in a position to influence public opinion (journalists, editors, travel writers etc.), or in the minds of sales intermediaries (travel agents, tour operators, etc.). It is oriented towards creating and maintaining an atmosphere whereby travelling public at large is convinced of the advantages of visiting the country concerned.

Public relations is one of the important functions of the official tourist organisation. In fact, tourist organisations primarily are public relations organisations. The objectives of public relations in the field of tourism may be divided into two parts, firstly the dissemination of information, and secondly the creation of a favourable image for the tourist product.

The Techniques : Public Relations make use of several communication techniques. These include:

(i) News and feature stories

(ii) Press releases

(iii) Films and slides

(iv) Booklets and brochures

(v) Photographs, displays and exhibits

(iv) Advertising

(vii) House journals

(viii) Radio and TV scripts

(ix) Newsletters

(x) Stockholder reports

Public relations consist of a number of interrelated activities oriented towards creating and maintaining a favourable positive image for the tourist product. The main tools of public relations used by national tourist organisations in tourist promotion are as follows:

(i) Organising familiarisation tours for travel writers, editors, travel agents, photographers and other key personnel from different parts of the world as guests to visit the country and to get first-hand knowledge about it. These persons then write about the country visited in the well known travel and other general interest magazines.

(ii) Organising radio and television contests featuring the destination country.

(iii) Organising press releases and arranging press conferences with key personnel connected with the tourism field with a view to disseminate information about the destination.

(iv) Arranging seminars and workshops in the place where the tourist promotion office is located.

(v) Organising cultural programmes, musical and folk shows, TV interviews, exhibitions and national friendship weeks in the country where the national tourist office is located.

(vi) Organising various types of contests about the country.

(vii) Encouraging large departmental stores, organisers of fashion shows and manufacturing companies to project the country or a part of the country as a promotion show case in their premises.

A Professional Public relations approach of a tourism organisation can develop and maintain :

(a) Positive image for a country;

(b) Increased visitor numbers;

(c) Investment in tourist plant;

(d) Interest of intermediaries like tour operators and travel agents.

It can best be achieved through:

(a) Professionally prepared publicity material distributed judiciously to main population markets;

(b) Arranging for key influential media representatives to visit the country on familiarisation tours;

(c) Promoting package holidays and transport services;

(d) Creating major events which will draw attention to the country.

Planning and organisation of public relations should be an integral part of a management strategy and must be conducted on a continuing basis. A public relations function of an organisation cannot be considered as an end in itself or something which can be introduced at a short notice to cope with a crisis situation. An organisation should have a positive and planned public relations policy. It is no coincidence that most of the national tourist organisations devote considerable effort to their public relations programmes.

Handling the public relations function requires the same expertise as handling advertising. The public relations functions of an organisation may be handled independently either by its internal staff members or by outside agencies. A public relations department within a company or organisation may consist of a single person, or a group of persons, depending upon the scope of work as also the size of an organisation. The larger the staff, the more specialised would be the work of each of the staff members. A number of organisations appoint Public Relations agencies outside of their organisation to look after their PR work.

Public Relations Agency : Public Relations agencies generally are retained as either an additional arm of an existing PR department or, if there is no PR department, as the sole PR wing. The agencies are hired either on a early retainer basis or on special projects/assignments. In the field of tourism, a number of national tourist organisations have been taking the services of PR agencies to take advantage of the market. The tourist destinations have recently become increasingly competitive in the luring of tourists and visitors from various tourist-generating markets. It is a well known fact that all those countries which appear to be attracting the largest number of tourists are succeeding because they market their country's attractions, to the right potential audiences, professionally and systematically as well as positively. Much of their success can be attributed to a direct result of positive and competent PR efforts.

PR agencies play a significant role in assisting a country getting a larger share of tourist traffic provided they do their job properly. The selection of a proper PR agency, therefore, is very crucial. While advertising and other marketing tools increase the number of visitors to a country, the communications equipped to complement advertising, and thus fully realising a country's potential draw, can be accomplished through programmed media activity and with well-launched public relations support programmes. It is here that PR agencies come into the picture. Public relations, properly planned and executed through a public relations agency in a tourist generating market, can present a country in a favourable light and help in the country's efforts to attract more tourists. Public relations also go a long way in positioning a country as a nation whose people welcome tourists, whose hotels and resorts, transportation systems are accommodating and efficient and whose history and culture are fascinating.

Public relations agencies take up specific areas on behalf of their clients and apply public relations efforts to them. These are the basic areas of concentration on which a beginning is made in building an improved image of a country and its tourism environment. Given below in an outline format are specific areas to which public relations efforts are applied by PR agencies in the field of tourism.

Audience (Non-media)

1. Individual consumer travellers.
2. Special interest travellers.
3. The travel trade industry travel agents, in particular.
4. Business travellers.
5. Corporate travel managers.
6. Meeting planners as appropriate.

Media Audience

1. Consumer travel magazines and newsletters.
2. General interest publications (consumer).
3. Consumer newspapers (particularly those which contain travel sections) both metropolitan dailies and suburban weeklies and dailies.
4. Travel trade publications.
5. Broadcast both radio and television when appropriate and on a 'selected' basis.
6. Special interest publications which deal with recreational or sports activities, entertainment, architecture, and the like.

General Activities

1. In-depth discussion of the country's current and future plans, its marketing goals, its research findings, and its specific problems.
2. A review of the country's consumer and trade media placements over the past two years.
3. Coordinating public relations efforts with advertising, sales and marketing personnel.

4. Establishing methods of contact and information getting from all those entities which participate in the country's programmes of tourism.
5. Reporting actions and results on a periodic basis.
6. Writing with style, clarity and command of the country's many dimensions.
7. Determining media needs...apropos tourism to the country.
8. Providing media writers, reporters and editors current data and background information on the country.
9. Providing media with story ideas as well as with finished product news releases and feature stories.
10. Knowing consumer and trade media requirements so that information about the country is timely and presented in an understandable manner.
11. Arranging media interviews with key personnel.
12. Coordinating and advising on visits to the country by media personnel.
13. Assisting with travel agent familiarisation trips.
14. Participating in domestic and foreign trade and association shows, conventions, seminars and the like.
15. Updating and keeping current a country press/ information kit.

Media Activities

Trade Media : Ensure continued and complete exposure in all travel and tourism industry trade publications in the market. Among the many opportunities for editorial coverage:

1. Destination stories and reports (features)
2. Personnel announcements
3. Visiting tourism personnel
4. Inclusions in "business activity" stories and general industry round-ups
5. Reception photographs
6. Policy changes
7. Hotel renovations, redecorations and additions

8. Sales and marketing information
9 General news

Consumer Media Print works toward the placement of feature stories about the country in a variety of consumer publications with particular emphasis on travel and travel-oriented magazines and newspapers. The story ideas are limitless (destinations, resort areas, historical attractions and sites, architecture, beaches, skiing, wildlife preserves, hotels). Sometimes, such stories are agency-written, often, contributions and help can be given to writers and editors.

Radio and T.V.

More and more radio and television time is now devoted to travel subjects. With the penetration of cable-programming (television), there is now more opportunity to broadcast media placements concerning travel and tourism topics. Therefore, and as appropriate, monitor the broadcast situation and work on placements for the country's positioning.

Special Events

Travel Trade Events Participation : Advise on and assist with all the travel events meetings and conventions, both within and outside the country.

Tie-in Events and Promotions : From time to time, opportunities for charity events, fashion shows, athletic competitions and other events of a one-time nature arise. Sometimes such activities are worthwhile, depending on the publicity value and the business and/ or social importance of these varied possibilities.

Press/Information Kits : A well informative information package, in the traditional press kit form, is imperative for dealing with the media. Such press/ information kits are very often handy for supplying information about the country and its tourism resources to people and organisations outside the media.

Suggested Contents

(a) A good selection of black and white photographs, suitable for newspaper and trade magazine reproduction.

(b) Photographs of top executives.

(c) Two or three feature stories about the country (in press release format).

(d) Hotel and accommodation information (in brochure format or as lists).

(e) Airline information.

(f) Within country transportation information.

(g) Map of the country.

(h) Shopping, climate, currency and other pertinent information.

(i) Some typical giveaways

Promotion of Sales

Sales support activities are all those activities and measures which establish personal or indirect contact with customers or trade intermediaries. In the field of tourism, it is considered to be all those promotional activities designed to transmit to the public and to the travel trade specific and detailed information on aspects like transport, accommodation prices, attractions etc. concerning the tourist services to be promoted in the tourist markets. In addition, the sales support is also a process of training employees of an organisation to be sales-minded. In other words through the process of information dissemination regarding a product the sales team becomes motivated to participate in the product sale. Sales support has certain distinct closely related functions which neither advertising nor public relations can be expected to fulfil effectively. It is a channel of communications between the manufacturer or the 'producer' of a tourist service (accommodation unit, transport company etc.) and the 'distributor' or the 'seller' of that service. Secondly, it aids and assists the seller to do his job more effectively with the support of different techniques. The aim of the sales support activities is:

(a) To inform the customers (tourists-both actual and potential) or trade intermediaries, travel agents, tour operators, airlines, etc.) about the various services available, their price and quality, etc;

(b) To assist them in selling these services to the ultimate users;

(c) To motivate them to devote a sufficient level of sales activity to the service promoted.

Tourist service enterprises, tour operators, and national and regional tourist organisations, recognise fully well that their sales and profit depend to a very large extent on the support and assistance they provide to travel agents and also the way in which they motivate travel agents. This is done by way of sales support activities. In order to be able to sell a service (a room in a hotel, seat in an airline) or a destination to the prospective tourists, travel agents or other sales intermediaries need to be aware of certain factual information which includes:

(i) The country's tourist facilities such as, existing as well as new establishments, accommodation capacities, price schedules for various services.

(ii) Various travel regulations and formalities such as visa regulations including different certificates needed, custom rules, rates of exchange for currency.

(iii) The various transport and communication services available. The schedules of airlines, railways, road transport services, shipping services (where available), their rates.

(iv) Weather conditions at different times of the year, and types of clothing required during different seasons.

(v) The utilisation (occupancy rates) of existing tourist facilities at different times of the year.

(vi) Plans for opening of new destinations, hotels, transport routes (railways, airlines etc.) and also plans for expansion of existing tourist facilities.

Advertising creates a demand in the form of enquiries made by potential tourists, travel agents and other intermediaries. They now require, in addition to the type of information mentioned above, materials such as brochures, folders, booklets, guidebooks, directories, maps and illustrations in order to be able to transform demand into definite bookings. Most of the above material is meant for distribution to potential tourists by the travel agents and other sales intermediaries like tour operators, airlines, etc.; either directly or through mail. Almost all the tourist organisations and tourist service enterprises produce the material extensively and make use of it by way of distributing it to travel agents, tour operators, etc. Tourist sales intermediaries on their own also produce sales support material for distribution to potential tourists.

Sales Support Techniques : Sales support techniques can be grouped into the following two main areas:

(i) Printed material

(ii) Special offers.

Printed material includes brochure, folder, direct mail material, display material etc.

The Brochure

The tour operator's brochure is the most vital marketing tool. Since tourism is an intangible product, which cannot be seen or inspected by the customer prior to purchase, the brochure becomes the principal means of both informing them about the product and also persuading them to buy the product. Brochure is a document bound in the form of a booklet. It is a voluminous publication with special emphasis on the quality of paper, the reproduction of illustrations, graphic design of the cover and the layout of the pages. Special emphasis is laid on the quality of the paper and the printing. In view of the quality, the brochure represents a major proportion of a tour operator's marketing budget. Larger companies get their brochure designed and prepared either in their own advertisement departments or in conjunction with the design studio of their advertising agent who negotiates with printers to obtain the best quotations and ensures that print deadlines are met.

The brochure contains a comprehensive and detailed information about a destination including cruises, bus tours, safaris, charter vacations etc., with colour photographs regarding all the destinations which a company is promoting. Detailed information about hotels, weather conditions frontier formalities etc. is also given. The price of various tours is invariably mentioned along with the dates when tours take place. Many established tour operators take great care with production of their brochures. There are, however, no travel industry standards or guidelines for the production of brochures. The following are some important areas which need to be taken care of while getting the tour brochure printed: (i) Quality of paper; (ii) Layout; (iii) Quality of printing; (iv) Photography; (v) Detailed itineraries; (vi) Special features; (vii) Weather conditions; (viii) Maps of areas; (ix) Tour conditions; (x) Tips.

Folder : A folder is a single piece of illustrated paper which can be folded. As compared to the brochures the folder is less voluminous and its production is less time consuming. These are usually printed on a single sheet and then folded ranging from a simple centrefold to more complicated folds. It is, perhaps, the most widely used sales tool by official tourist organisations and by tourist service enterprises. It can be used alone or in conjunction with a 'sales letter'. It is less expensive and can be used in a variety of ways. While producing, special care needs to be taken about the quality of the paper and printing. The folder as compared to the brochure is short, tastefully illustrated and attractively designed and produced.

Shell Folder : Shell folders are blank folders interspersed with pre-printed photographs and are provided free or at a low cost by airlines or national tourist offices to encourage tour operators / travel agents to run programmes using their services or destinations. Tour operators travel agents can overprint a suitable text describing their programmes. Since only the text needs to be added, a one colour print run at low cost meets the requirements of tour operators etc. The use of a shell folder is a convenient way to reduce printing costs and is suitable for limited capacity tour programmes or ad hoc special tours.

Sales Letter : Sales letter is a direct mail material. It is a tool through which an attempt is made to gain agreement or favourable action towards a product. The sales letter offers many opportunities for selling travel services. These could be used alone or in combination with travel brochure or folders. "These are sent out to those people whose addresses have been selected according to the likelihood of their being potential users of the services offered. A proper mailing list is a prerequisite for effective use of this tool. Sales letters require very little time to prepare and to distribute. The effectiveness of a sales letter can be measured very rapidly from the response it draws. This is done by way of a reply card which is included with which the recipient can request further information and also travel literature.

Display Material

Display material includes posters, dispensers for sales literature, cardboard stands, articles of handicrafts, exhibits, etc. This material is used in the agency's office or in the travel agent's sales-rooms. The material is displayed in such a way that it attracts the attention of a visitor as soon as he enters the office. In many cases, cinema slides are also used, either fixed or on an automatic projector for display purposes.

Special Offers

Temporary price reductions, free gifts, premiums and various types of contests are being used extensively in competitive industries like cosmetics, packaged foodstuffs, etc. The tourist industry has also started to adopt these techniques as an additional sales support tool. Reduced airfares for students, 'affinity group' special off-season rates at hotels and tourist resorts are the examples of some of the special offers in the tourist industry.

Newsletters

Newsletter is yet another important promotional medium utilised extensively by tourism organisations. Its main purpose is to get the organisation's message across. A newsletter can be considered to be a major advertising medium. It is a personal reminder to regular clients that a company is still in business. Newsletters are also the best possible instruments for image building. The strength of the newsletters is in the continuity they create. Published monthly, a newsletter maintains a running dialogue with customers. It is also an inexpensive form of media to inform about staff etc. Similar information through newspapers and radio commercials may cost a lot of money.

A newsletter, however, has certain hazards. First, it requires a lot of time. It can also be quite expensive. With constant increases in postal tariffs and production costs, even a simple newsletter with minimal artwork and illustrations costs quite a lot. Besides, a newsletter must compete with a lot of other mail for attention. Because information changes so rapidly in travel today, a newsletter can be outdated even before its mailing is complete. In order to make full use of newsletters an organisation has to take into consideration certain essential ingredients for production. These are as follows :

Mailing Frequency: Mailing should go out often enough to maintain the agency's identity with readers. In fact, it should be so frequent and regular that customers look forward to it and, in fact, even miss it when they don't get it. At least four mailings a year are required to maintain identity and continuity.

Attractiveness: Newsletters should have short and crisp paragraphs with clear photographs to illustrate or document a story. Layout must have a good look so that the message is readable and pleasing to look at.

Relevance: In general, newsletters should address readers in their own frame of reference. Each idea or expression should be spelled out.

Simple Text: A professional journalist is not required to write a newsletter. However, a copy should be clear, crisp and colourful. The message should be clear and simple. Any grammatical errors or misspellings should be avoided as this can damage the image one is trying hard to develop.

Mailing Lists : Even the best newsletters will lose much of their impact if mailing lists are not kept up-to-date. There should be a proper system through which these could be regularly updated. A responsibility should be fixed on someone in the organisation for this. Feedback It is necessary to get a regular feedback from the clients regarding the newsletter. This would ensure whether the newsletter is being received or not as also the interest clients are having in it.

The Publicity

Publicity refers to the dissemination of information without charge or its news value in order to inform the prospect about a particular product. A publicity programme should include regular publicity, stories and photographs to newspapers, travel editors, contact with magazines on stories, ideas, and the preparations of story outlines and pictures in order to induce magazines to do feature stories on a particular destination. News releases to travel trade magazines on items of interest to the travel industry, such as opening up of a new area, total expansion, increased transportation facilities, development of a new resort, are measures which are adopted, together with other publicity through the media of radio, television, lectures, seminars, travel films, etc. Tourist publicity initially developed in an empirical way under the pressure of the growth of international travel, and to the extent that information had to be supplied to an ever-increasing number of tourists. Thus at its outset, it was simply informational publicity. With the growth in volume of commercial tourist publicity, particularly in the sphere of transport, and great increase in the number of tourists, various countries realised the importance of tourism in the national life. They recognised it, especially in economic terms and in the earning of foreign exchange This necessitated that countries organise their institutional tourist publicity with a new approach and employ experienced commercial publicity technicians to draw up a long-term publicity strategy.

Tourist Publicity Media : The publicity itself is carried out through media whose scope is that there are constantly new possibilities which suggest themselves to the resourceful publicity expert. This is of particular relevance in respect of tourist publicity whose new forms and scientifically based planning in publicity are not so frequently discernible. At any rate, tourist publicity media seem to be construed as a result of the fact that in general their publicity effect is limited to the visual and auditive sense. Illustration, copy and the spoken word are, therefore, the primary publicity media for tourism. They are multiplied through the media compounded out of them.

The greatest importance appertains to illustration, for it can achieve emotional effects in the reproduction of a landscape and its atmosphere and is also universally understood. Even if one is inclined to accept the psychological argument that every human being only projects his own personality in every consideration, the illustration retains from this standpoint also considerable publicity effectiveness, because it is viewed and perceived differently by different persons. Given the differences of individual tastes, the illustration naturally plays a decisive role. Consequently, the best illustration is just good enough for tourist publicity. It depends on the planning and shaping of the publicity medias to decide whether the illustration is to be employed in the form of a drawing, a printing or a photograph. Generally, the photograph is adjudged as possessing a greater objectivity in the statements. On the other hand, an artistic representation can be the expression of cultural activity and hence equally effective as publicity. Illustration can be developed through stylisation into a brand and thus create a concept which is derived from the meaning.

With copy as a publicity factor, there also arises the necessity for originality with the object of giving expression to the publicity idea. The purpose of every publicity media is to arouse and sustain attention. Illustration and copy must therefore create desires. In tourist publicity the tendency towards schematisation is extremely strong and counteracts necessity for publicity orginality. The similarity in the printed publicity material of hotels, travel agencies, tourist resorts, areas and even countries furnishes proof of this.

The spoken word is of importance in the case of personal publicity. The proper use of the spoken word is difficult but effective. "Words are not only conveyors of thoughts and ideas, but also of emotional contents and consequently they reach not only the intellect but also the psyche of the recipient and are expressed to this end." (Walter Hegeman on the Myth of the Mass). Thus the spoken word helps us to approach the imaginative world of the person addressed and this accounts for the importance of the information or sales talk as well as of publicity lectures, radio broadcasts, television speeches and publicity receptions. The spoken word is here supported by the appearance and presence of the speaker, as well as by his psychological capacity to adjust himself to the individual as also of listeners. The three primary publicity media mentioned - illustration, copy and the spoken word - form the basis of the composite publicity media which can suitably be arranged in the following groups:

(i) Printed publicity, (ii) Advertising publicity, (iii) Projected publicity, (iv) Structural forms of publicity, (v) Personal publicity.

Printed Publicity Material : Printed publicity in the field of tourist publicity is mainly composed of the publicity leaflet, folder, brochure and poster. The publicity leaflet is used among others as inserts and enclosure in the case of conveying an information or communicating the knowledge to the largest possible number of persons. *The folder* is the most commonly used and the most important publicity medium for tourist publicity. We encounter it in numerous forms and multiple variations which leaves unsolved the question of the optimum effective folder. The question culminates in the investigation as to what the recipient expects from a folder, what he looks for in it, what he hopes to find in it and whether the folder corresponds to the imaginative conception of the country or region which it should advertise. The logical conclusion would be that account should be taken of the mental outlook of the recipient at the time of producing the folder. In the main, what actually takes place is that different versions of the folder are printed for different countries. This practice is further confirmed by the production of special folders like the cultural folder and those for motor tourists, mountain climbers, fishing and hunting enthusiasts, etc. These folders should deal with the special interests of the recipient and above all must be composed in "the idiom of the client".

The production of a general folder which has to be advertised for a whole country with its variety of attractions, specialities and circumstances requires much expertise. Here, there exists the danger of "too much" as well as "too little' besides the pitfalls of a dry description, superlative forms, over estimation and misappreciation of the points of attraction. A folder is not a travel guide nor a manual of geography. But it must not also be forgotten that the present day travellers are very often "illiterates in the field of tourism" who consequently require directions and help as well as information. This renders the page setting and composition of the text of an effective general folder, a task which has not yet been 100 per cent satisfactorily solved. "A folder has not incorrectly been compared with a representative. It is the silent representative of a firm, a resort or a country through which most often the first link is established with the future guest, the recipient"

The folder must also possess all the necessary qualities like proper appearance, faultless exterior, an unobtrusive and engaging presence, exact information about everything which is offered, truthfulness in assertions and no fanciful exaggerations. The text should never be long winded. A concrete and concise description containing exact comprehensive information corresponds to the quick rhythm of our time. To be adequately effective, however, the publicity medium of the folder needs to be not only well set up, but also to be produced in sufficient quantity and have a planned distribution.

The poster is the most important publicity medium of tourism. Difficulties touched upon in respect of the production of the general folder occur, especially in the case of the poster. The tourist poster should combine its effectiveness based on psychological factors with the task of depicting a country as tourist destination working on the limited means at its disposal. The tourist poster further suffers from the fact that there is no well considered distinction in the production of the poster for application as an interior or outdoor poster. In the majority of cases, there is an interior poster for the premises and show windows of travel agencies and information centres, whose use as an outdoor poster in the streets of large cities is consequently hardly discernible. Nevertheless, it should simultaneously satisfy the imperatives of a good outdoor poster and be designed as an eye catcher. The problem of publicity is further complicated by the discussion on the pros and cons of graphic and photographic posters. *The publicity* journal which is utilised at present by almost every national tourist publicity organisation is more representative than all other forms of printed material. As such it is expensive and therefore limited in its circulation. For the sake of comprehensive coverage, mention may also be made of the printed publicity material which really belongs already to the sphere of customer service, like maps, guidebooks, directories, inserts, etc.

Projected Publicity : Projected publicity media comprise film and slide publicity. Of particular importance is the film which is an outstanding medium, not only on account of its representational potentialities, but also because of its suggestive power. The colour film is assuming increasing significance within the framework of tourist publicity. The central idea of the film should be expressible in terms of motion and this accounts for the cardinal rule of all publicity films, short text but plenty of action which should captivate the attention of the spectators and also aim at influencing memory through emotional factors. Publicity effectiveness is a characteristic not only of the purely publicity film, but also the feature film as well as the instructional impact of the didactic film. In the United States of America and Western Europe the travel film with a commentary known as the "travelogue" has won extensive popularity. Television is a suitable medium to spread the interest in foreign countries and thus serves tourist publicity.

Structural Forms : Structural forms of publicity comprise publicity measures which manifest themselves in constructions and structures, as for example, in the establishment and equipment of a tourist publicity office abroad, in participation in fairs and exhibitions, in the preparation of show cases and window displays, etc. Here no restrictions are set on the inventive resources of the architects. There is also the possibility of publicity combinations whereby tourist publicity can be undertaken in conjunction with business publicity. For example, shops selling sports goods, fashion articles, travel accessories, etc. are willing to have such combinations in their show windows.

Similarly, at fairs the joint stands of a country procure publicity advantages for tourism because the exhibition as a whole shows tourism in relation to the country and succeeds in creating lasting impressions.

Personal Publicity : Personal publicity in tourism has various forms of application ranging from the informational and sales talk to publicity travel, which serves the need of maintaining contact with the travel industry and to support it in its sales efforts, and includes the publicity lecture. In all these spheres the personal effort holds sway. Also to this category belong interviews, radio broadcasts, receptions, etc.

The role of promotion in tourism is of paramount importance. The various promotional techniques like advertising, public relations and sales support are used together by tourism hospitality and leisure providers. All the three techniques are however, complementary to each other. The proper and judicious mix of these is very essential for the successful promotion of a product or a programme.

7

Tourism Product

Often, managers use the term marketing to describe their companies as modern, dynamic and forward looking. But, marketing in its real sense is seldom applied in most businesses and even to a lesser extent, in tourism-related businesses.

There is far greater awareness about the need for marketing in industrialised countries of the West than in a developing country like India. Marketing concept and philosophy were invented in the USA, moved slowly in the sixties to Western Europe and Japan. Japan perfected the marketing concept by totally catering to consumers' needs in most of its products. Japan's success story in exports apart from the team-work of its people has been ascribed to their ability to apply marketing techniques to production, sales and distribution in their country.

Historically, marketing in its present form was not needed when production of goods was only enough to meet the current demands. Even after the Industrial Revolution, goods were produced only to meet local demands. In the absence of fast means of communication and transport, there was no national market in any country. In the nineteenth century, when countries like England and France acquired excess production capacity, they dumped it on their colonies. There was, therefore, no need for marketing to create a new demand. Production was oriented to sales. So long as you could sell what you produced, marketing could be dispensed with.

It was only in the sixties of the twentieth century that techniques of production improved to a point that more goods were available for the market than there was potential demand. In recent decades, production capability has progressed so far that continuous production of many products has become a condition of producing them. Examples: motor vehicles, TVs, refrigerators, etc. If you slow down their production, cost goes up.

"The basic pattern has been from a seller's market and production orientations through a buyer's market and sales orientation to a buyer's market and marketing orientation. During this period, growth in output has gone hand in hand with growth in market."

In India, applications of marketing principles was not necessary till production was controlled. Any expansion of a plant was disallowed without prior approval of the government. Open competition was not permitted in any sector of production. Production of cars like Ambassador and Premier was so controlled that it took a decade for a customer to buy one. The companies, therefore, did not need marketing. It was a seller's market. It continued till the second half of the eighties when competition was allowed in some sectors.

A similar condition prevailed in the tourism sector. Government owned all airlines and no private airlines were allowed. Passengers had to wait for days to get a booking on Indian Airlines. It was also true of Air India. Thousands of potential tourists were wait-listed on Indian Airlines for months till they gave up their desire to visit India. Entry of private airlines was not allowed. For construction of new hotels, the central and state government financing was also controlled by the government. Till the early nineties, hotels were not allowed to fix their own tariff based on demand and supply. The Department of Tourism fixed at what price they should sell their rooms. Government-owned public sector hotels were openly preferred and patronised by the government departments. Despite these restrictions, the travel industry has not only survived but also grown. Government did not allow the travel agency industry to function freely — a few government owned travel agencies competed with private sector travel agencies. They prospered under government patronage. Indian Airlines did not allow all IATA approved travel agents to sell their tickets. Indian Airlines chose its own agents — it became a matter of political patronage. The only free area was inbound tourism in the hands of the private sector, again with a couple of exceptions. But, the inbound tour-operators were controlled indirectly by the government. The government alone had power to release foreign exchange to travel agents and tour-operators who wished to travel overseas to solicit business for their companies from foreign tour-operators. At times, the government told them where to go for business and where not to go. It was also used as a form of patronage. New entrants in inbound tourism business had to face a lot of difficulties. There was no easy way for them to travel overseas.

For inbound tourism, private tour operators assisted by Indian Tourist Office had to compete in an environment of global competition. They, therefore, acquired some expertise in marketing. They had to offer to foreign buyers a tourist product which they needed and not what India wanted to sell. Other destinations were there in the markets to offer alternate products. Although Indian tour-operators were fast learners, the Tourist Officers posted abroad were reluctant learners. They could not get away from the fact that the bureaucrats were always right and went back to their old ways after serving overseas for 3-year tenures. For both Department of Tourism officials and Indian Tour-Operators, modern marketing techniques are essential for broadening the base of Indian tourism. Indian tourism, too, is, therefore, gradually becoming customer oriented.

It is only after the gradual elimination of controls on economy by the Government of Prime Minister Narasimha Rao in 1991, that industry and business are readjusting to the needs of free competition. And one can see from the results that for the first time tourists arrivals exceeded two million in 1995.

The travel industry-which was already exposed to international competition in the past is expected to do better.

Concept and Perception

As in industrial production, tourism entered the new era of mass production in the early seventies. The introduction of Boeing 747 and the large-scale construction of hotels at popular tourist destinations led to the belief that overproduction of both Airlines seats and hotel rooms is a distinct possibility. The rapid growth of package tours in Europe convinced us that during the coming years, most people will be able to experience holiday travel. Travel will not be limited to a few. The people are already learning the skills to take advantage of the new opportunities offered by mass tourism. The following case study of packaged holiday in United Kingdom shows how it was done in the past and how it can be done even on a large scale in future. It also marked the beginning of a mass tourism.

Marketing of Package Tours in Great Britain (A Case Study) Holloway and Plant relate the story of the spectacular growth of package holidays in Britain as a good example of marketing.

In the sixties, some entrepreneurs in Great Britain saw a new opportunity to create holidays utilising spare airline capacity that resulted from the introduction of new technology aircrafts and the low cost accommodation available at new Spanish holiday resorts. The tour-operators in Great Britain were able to offer exciting holiday packages to the British public at far less cost in Spain than dreary and cold vacations in their own homeland. These holiday packages soon became very popular. There was tremendous demand from the public to increase the volume available. But, hotel accommodation in Spain could not be expanded to meet the demand. The visitors from Britain had complaints against the greasy Spanish food which they called the 'Foreign Rubbish'. There was also apprehension about the safety of old second-hand aircrafts used by tour-operators.

The marketing experts pondered over the matter and came to the conclusion that consumers faced the following problems:

1. Fear of flying
2. Fear of foreign food. The British travellers of the sixties were not yet exposed to foreign foods.

3. Fear of foreigners. They did not understand Spanish customs, manners, and habits.

After some research, it was realised that profitability could be improved if the tour-operator gave up the use of cheaper, redundant aircrafts. They purchased new and modern aircrafts. The new planes gave them operational economy through better utilisation of planes which were fuel efficient increasing profits. Besides, customer's confidence was restored. The new planes were safe and efficient.

The fear of foreign foods was overcome by adopting a novel way. The British tour companies sent their food experts to Spain who advised Spanish hoteliers to modify and adjust their cooking and services to suit the British tastes. They suggested that they could economise on the use of ingredients and reduce the grease content in the food cooked for the British customers. It worked. The British started enjoying the new Spanish cooking.

The fear of foreigners was based on the unreliability of the Spanish accommodations, their way of dealing and service. This lent to no easy solutions. So, the British travel companies invested a lot of money in Spain to build new hotels according to their own specifications. The new properties were managed by the British or by their own nominees. The British expertise and their inputs improved standards in Spanish hotels.

On a personal level the British representatives changed their style and became dedicated to the hotel's customer services.

"Now, the quality of the product of major travel companies is no longer in question, any more than a sweater from Marks and Spencer or TV from Dixons," noted Holloway and Plant.

Package tours now are so popular that over 50 per cent of leisure travel out of Britain is on such tours.

Tourism product has, therefore, to be consumer oriented. That implies we can no longer sell what we produce, we have to produce what customers consider as their needs. In the words of Professor Theodore Levitt, "Selling focuses on the needs of seller, marketing focuses on the needs of buyer."

Among several definitions of marketing, the one formulated

by the British Institute of Marketing explains the marketing process better.

Marketing is the Management function which organises and directs all those business activities involved in assessing and converting customer's purchasing power into effective demand for a specific product or service and in moving the product or service to the final customer or user so as to achieve the profit target or other objectives set by the company.

The American Marketing Institute defines marketing in the following words:

> Marketing is defined as those activities which direct the flow of goods and services from production to consumption. As in the two definition above, marketing is seen as coordinating all aspects of business. It is not the responsibility of one department only.

Tourist Product

It can be defined as a composite product which consists of attractions of a destination, air transportation provided by airlines, hotel accommodation offered by hotel companies and the local transportation, sightseeing and other activities provided by local tour-operators at the destination.

The most convenient and conventional method of buying the tourist product from a producer is the packaged tour.

But, a customer has other options. He can design his product—buy his ticket from an airline and reserve a hotel room by requesting the airlines to do it for him at the destination. He is free to ask a travel agency to put together for him the type of holiday he needs. He has a choice of a hundred destinations to select from. He can choose any one of them, any airline that flies to that destination and pick up a hotel of his choice at the destination.

The real tourist product is usually composite—whether the customer buys it in packaged form or assembles it himself.

Its three principal attributes are: attraction, facilities and accessibility.

The Peculiarities : The following are some other peculiarities of the tourist product which we must understand.

(a) A wide range of services which the tourist requires and which constitute the tourism product in his mind cannot be provided by a single enterprise. Each of its component needs a high degree of specialisation and every enterprise produces only a part of the final product. Naturally, the need for cooperation and coordination in marketing efforts is paramount.

(b) Marketing of tourism is further complicated by singular dichotomy between supply and demand. Supply is inelastic as considerable fixed investment is required to expand it and highly trained manpower is needed to operate it. It cannot be adopted quickly to demand variations. The existing facilities and establishments cannot be easily modified to qualitative change.

(c) Tourism demand is highly unstable. Seasonal factors can affect it. Political unrest and economic instability caused by inflation and currency fluctuations can damage it.

(d) Trade intermediaries in tourism—travel agents, tour-operators, charter brokers—are powerful factors in the marketing of the tourist product. They have bargaining power in relation to the suppliers of tourist service. They can also influence the choice of a holiday destination.

(e) Tourism product cannot be transported to the consumer. It is the consumer who comes to the product to experience it.

(f) The travel agent, tour-operator or producer of the product cannot stock it or hold it in abeyance. It is a highly perishable product. An airline seat or hotel room not used today is total loss.

(g) Entitlement to the use of service facility in tourism product does not mean that ownership passes to the user. Hotel rooms, transport seats are hired only for a specified period while the ownership remains with the proprietors.

Marketing of tourism product, therefore, is more urgent and more complicated than other products.

Process of Planning

Every business organisation dealing with tourism product needs a Marketing Action Plan. It can be short-term or long-term. The short-term plan will deal with immediate issues relating to cash flow required and what products will be marketed during a given period and at what price to meet the running costs and to make some profit. The long-term plan will establish goals and strategy for growth, diversification and profitability.

Process of Marketing

The first step in the marketing process is to carry out a Corporate Environment Analysis.

The Corporate Environment Analysis will list the company's corporate objectives, its strengths and weaknesses. It will also look into the financial environments under which the company will have to work during a given period.

The second step will be to identify the customers who will buy their products, where they live and what they want. This is called Market Research. Research may reveal that there is no point in advertising the beaches of India to Americans. They have enough of their own or in their neighbourhood—the Caribbean Islands. Northern Europe is India's best market for beach holidays because they do not have warm water beaches. And they are also geographically closer to India.

The third step is to look for the type of customers who will buy the product. Are your customers in the age group of 40-50 or do they come from the younger crowd? Are they professionals? Are they people who seek adventure or they are people looking for a cultural experience? Also who are the people who can afford your product? This is called Market Segmentation. We will, therefore, focus our promotion on the market we identify through this process.

The fourth step is Formulation of the Product. We formulate the product to suit each segment of our customers. The product must meet the needs of the customer.

The next step is Pricing. The company must price the product attractively to interest the customers. It should be affordable to customers we seek.

Distribution come next. Where do we sell our product, in which areas and through what kind of sales network? The product should be easily accessible to enable potential customers to buy it.

The next and most important part of the marketing process is to make sure that potential customers know about the product. It is called Promotion. It includes every aspect—mass-media, advertising, public relations, press releases, direct mail, etc., to draw the attention of customers to the product.

In diagrammatic terms, it looks like the following:

Marketing Process

Financial and Economic Planning

Corporate Analysis

Analysis of Current Environment under which Business Operates

Establishment of Goals

Market Research

Market Segmentation

Product Formulation

Pricing

Place (Distribution)

Promotion

A combination of four Ps—Product, Price, Place (Distribution) and Promotion—is popularly called the Marketing Mix. The right mix for marketing purposes produces profits.

Each of these elements mentioned above may be thought of as tourism marketing, but not in isolation. Together they make up marketing. It is a cyclic process, with periodic review of product — market mix and the promotional strategy to measure their success. The strategies can be modified or changed if it is discovered that they are not effective.

A marketing plan should include the following elements represented by acronym SWOT:

1. *Strength:* How does the product compare with other similar product?
2. *Weaknesses:* Its deficiencies in relation to competing products.
3. *Opportunities:* What new markets and market segments are available for the product?
4. *Threats:* Who are the principal competitors to the product in the marketplace and what are they doing?

Corporate Analysis

The Corporate Analysis implies that a company decide on its goals and objectives. The goals are determined after an objective study of the current economic and market environment. The company examines its strength and weaknesses in relation to the existing competition. It must examine threats to business as well as opportunities.

The goals would include achievable targets — how many tourists to attract in a given period and from which markets or market segments, etc.

Research and Survey

A tourist product cannot be used by everyone. Many people cannot afford it. The first step for a marketeer, therefore, is to know his product well—its advantages, disadvantages, attractions and position vis-a-vis the competitive products. He finds out all this information through research on potential users of the product.

The research must provide answers to the following questions:

- What is the total size of the tourist market?
- Who are the existing customers?
- Where do they live?

- What are the present customers seeking in our product?
- What level of pricing will the customer accept?
- What are the trends in the market — past and present?
- What are the factors influencing the trend?
- Who are our potential future buyers?
- What are the strength and weakness of our product compared to the competition?

Market research depends on the types of data needed. It could be primary or secondary data.

Primary data is available in house or through field surveys. In-house data provides information on the performance of business, number of visitors, occupancy ratios, visitors, spending, source for business, profits, costs, etc.

This information can be collected for individual businesses, groups of businesses or on regional or national level depending on the requirements.

Field Surveys : Field surveys can be done in several ways. The most frequently used method for collecting primary data through field survey is through the use of questionnaires. Questionnaires can be completed by the respondent directly or with the help of trained interviewers. Self-completed questionnaires are often used by airlines and hotels. But, they suffer from one major disadvantage — they allow no control over the sample of people filling the questionnaires and responding. Therefore, this method cannot be very useful for market research. Such questionnaires are often filled by dissatisfied customers.

The other method in field survey is to determine the sample in advance and use the services of trained interviewers to get the response.

The questionnaires generally provide two types of data. The first, demographic and socio-economic profile of the people interviewed including family composition, occupation, place of residence, their spending pattern, etc. The second type of data relates to motivation, perception, etc. The questionnaires can be designed according to the needs of an organisation.

In India, the questionnaire method has been more frequently used by Indian Tourism Authorities to know the visitors' profile—the places they come from, their expenditure pattern, motivations to come to India and their perceptions, etc. It is done every four to five years.

Secondary data can be obtained from what is called Desk Research. This kind of research uses census reports, annual company reports, surveys done by the regional and national tourist organisations and at international levels reports of IATA, ICAO, WTO, PATA, OECD, EEC, World Bank, UNESCO and other international bodies. These organisations compile information on aspects of travel industry in which they are interested.

Travel industry magazines are a useful sources of information. In Asia, important travel industry magazines are Asia Travel Trade and TTG-Asia published from Singapore, Travel News Asia, Hong Kong, Travel Trade Report, Bangkok, Travel Trends and Trav Talk, New Delhi.

Another reliable source of tourism information is an annual publication, Travel Industry World Year Book — The Big Picture published from New York. It has been published annually for 30 years. It analyses comprehensively trends in travel industry every year in all parts of the world.

In USA, the US Travel Data Centre, based in Washington, produces excellent reports on US tourism. The Economic Intelligence Unit, London, provides some of the best reports on how tourism is shaping in different parts of the world. Of course, WTO has all kinds of reports and information on world tourism. Their publications are available for sale to non-members.

For carrying out market research, it is important that the organisation chosen to carry out survey is selected carefully. It should be professional, reliable and credible. The client's ability to understand the purpose and limitations of marketing research is also important.

Market Segmentation

The strategy of market segmentation accepts the fact that few travel destinations are universally acceptable and popular. The marketeer, therefore, need not dissipate his promotional resources trying to please all the population of a country. He is, therefore, advised to concentrate on selected target groups to whom the product may appeal.

Segmentation is the process through which a marketeer is able to identify the group/groups from within the population of a country to whom his tourist product will appeal. Identification of these segments too is done through market research.

There are a number of ways to segment the market. For the purpose of leisure travel, we can broadly segment it in four categories:

1. Youth Market
2. Senior Citizens
3. Family Market
4. Special Interests Market

The category four will obviously include Visiting Friends and Relatives (VFR), pilgrimages, adventure travel, wildlife, convention/conference, incentive travel market, etc. The other three segments do not need an explanation.

The most important travel segment is Business Travel — one which airlines love to pamper. It constitutes one-third of the total travel business. Business travellers pay full fares and their demand is not subject to seasonally. The choice of destination is determined by the nature of business and not by its attractions.

Under the broad heading of business travel, we can include the staff of the companies rewarded for doing a good job — achieving or exceeding sales targets or owners of stores who sell the most for their principals. This reward is often given in the shape of an all-paid holiday and is called Incentive Travel. Another form of business travel is the Convention Conference Travel, the people who travel on behalf of their companies for conventions, professional meetings, seminars, and conferences including large international gatherings of travel agents like the Americans Society of Travel Agents (ASTA), conferences of heart surgeons or a gathering of oil industry specialists. Thousands of such meetings take place every year in different parts of the world. The expenses are paid by the companies in most cases. For professionals like heart surgeon and others travel expenses on professional gatherings are tax deductible in most countries.

The leisure travel markets can also be further divided into geographical groups. It makes sense that the needs of Japanese tourists will be generally similar. For example, the work ethics of Japanese visitors does not permit them to enjoy a long holiday abroad — they prefer 8 to 10 days holiday. The marketeer will have to design his product accordingly. The British, on the other hand, have no difficulty in spending 15 to 21 days in a country like India because of their long association and common bond of English language. The Indian marketeer will not go wrong in offering the visiting Britons a holiday of 15 to 21 days.

While segmenting on geographical basis, the market can be grouped as Primary, Secondary and Emerging markets.

Primary markets are those which generally send most tourists. For India, it is USA, UK, Germany, France, Japan, Italy and Canada. For USA, the primary markets are Canada, Mexico, Japan, UK, Germany and France. Most promotional resources are spent in the primary markets. Secondary markets are those which do not generate very large number of tourists but the numbers are adequate to convince the marketeer that some promotional resources should be allocated to these areas. For India, secondary markets include Singapore, Malaysia, Thailand, Korea and Taiwan. These markets have not been traditionally generating large volumes for India but their rapidly growing economies lead us to the conclusion that these markets may become India's primary markets in the near future.

And finally, there are the emerging markets. Presently, their people may be more interested in existing popular tourist destinations but soon they could be persuaded to look at other destinations. For India, South Africa, Israel, Korea and Mauritius may be considered the emerging markets which should be attended to.

Segmentation is a comprehensive philosophy and can be worked out to the minutest details by studying consumer behaviour and consumer psychology. For readers interested in going into greater depth of the segmentation process, the following books are recommended:

1. Mastering Marketing, Douglas Foster, Macmillan, London, 1984.
2. Marketing of Tourism, Holloway and Plant, Pitman, London, 1988.

Some important travel market segments have been discussed at the end of this chapter.

Formulation of Product

Based on market research and market information, the marketeer can plan to formulate the tourist product. The process of product formulation is frequently referred to as the "Five Rights": the right product, at the right place, at the right time, at the right price and in right quantities.

A product is much more than a combination of raw materials. It is really a bundle of satisfactions and benefits for the consumers. When we design and develop a tourist product, we must see it from the consumers' point of view.

Creating a right product or right service is no easy matter. Consumers' needs, wants, desires and interests are constantly changing. Competition also brings in similar products, a result of which a product once successful starts a declining trend.

At national level, a National Tourism Administration has great responsibility to work out a unique identity of its tourists product. In the case of India, Taj Mahal is uniquely Indian. The mere mention of Taj Mahal conjures up the vision of India. So are the Himalayas. Another good example of successful product development in India is the development of Goa as a beach holiday resort. Now, Goa is in the world map a desirable beach destination. Twenty years ago, it was virtually unknown.

The Lifecycle : Each product has a lifecycle. It shows the phases that a new product goes through from its inception till its decline or decay. The phases are introduction, growth, maturity, saturation and decline.

However, the life of the product can be extended in the following two ways:

1. By finding new or alternative markets for the products.
2. By redeveloping the product to meet the changing tastes and fashions.

The product lifecycle is measured in years or decades. The product lifecycle is explained in the following diagram:

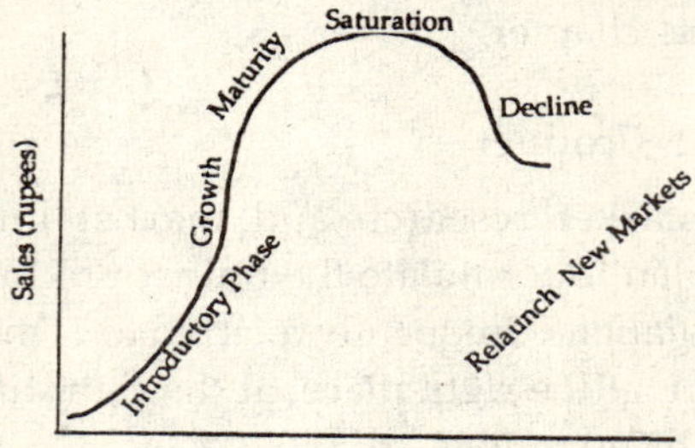

Policies for Pricing

A crucial element in marketing strategy is pricing. In order to arrive at the right price at which the product will sell, the following information is required:

1. The cost of product.
2. The planned volume of sales.
3. Price charged by competitors of similar or the same products.
4. External factors such as interest rates, taxes, etc.
5. Consumers perception of price—what the market will accept as the right price.
6. Level of investments to achieve the target sale plus profit margin.

Price is fixed depending on the nature of the product and its estimated lifecycle. If an enterprise is entering a new market, a lower price with lower profit margin may be introduced assuming that price could be increased later when the product has been well accepted. This is called Penetration Pricing.

At times, travel companies introduce promotional prices to attract new customers for a new product or for an old product where sales are sagging — the price in this case has to be lower than normal.

If you have introduced a new and unique quality product, a higher pricing may be desirable. It may help recover the huge initial investment. Subsequently, when the sales increase the price could be rationalised to make the product more saleable.

Pricing policies are also used as a planning tool. For instance, if a country, region or a resort wishes to sell its product only to the up-market and rich consumers, it can price it high. Bhutan, for instance, controls its tourism by charging over US $ 200 per day from visitors, thus eliminating the fear of mass-tourism.

'Palace on Wheels" train in India is also priced at the rate of $ 200 per night and above. It offers only 140 seats every week and its occupancy is 90 per cent by foreigners who can afford this price.

Distribution (Place) : To make the tourist product easily accessible to consumers, a marketeer has to decide what distribution channel or channels will be used to sell the product. The decision will also affect other elements of the marketing mix and has, therefore, to be taken very carefully by:

(a) Analysing the product.

(b) Determining the extent of the market.

(c) Costs/profits of using a distribution channel/channels.

(d) Expected cooperation from the channel used.

(e) The extent of assistances demanded and expected by the channel used.

(f) The number of sales outlets to be used.

If a marketeer wants large sales, he will have to use a large number of travel agents, retailers to sell the product. Alternatively, he can give exclusive distribution rights to a few selected travel agencies to sell the product.

Tourist product can reach the consumers through retail agencies or through speciality channellers like incentive firms, convention and conference planners. Each has power to influence the sales.

The modern Computerised Reservation System (CRSs) of airlines and hotels have a role in distribution. Many airlines sell their own packaged tours produced by their subsidiaries or by some favoured private wholesalers who agree to use the services of their airline.

Promotion of Sales

This includes advertising, production of brochures, public relations, sales promotion, etc. It is the most recognisable of the four Ps and is often taken to be synonymous with marketing. But, it is only part of the marketing process, as important as the other three Ps. Each of the four Ps' have a role in evolving a total marketing strategy.

The basic function of tourist promotion is to communicate with the consumer through media advertising, brochures, posters, leaflets. These are all designed to inform, persuade and motivate people to create a state of mind well disposed towards the sale of the tourist product. Consumer attitudes and behaviour change rapidly.

Communications is a continuous process. Messages have to be repeated to change attitudes. To get a positive response from the consumer, the communication process passes through the following phases:

(1) Creates an awareness that the product exists, that it is easily available, useful and reliable.

(2) Comprehension of what the service or product can do for him.

(3) Conviction that the service or product will give him value for money.

Promotion includes marketing communications to convey information about the business to all participants in the chain of distribution, as well as to the end user — the consumer. This necessarily includes all facets of public relations, publicity, media advertising, sales and sales promotion to direct response, collate materials, merchandising, signage and training—anything to do with the total image of the product.

Under the broad head of promotion, Communications Mix is the term used to include advertising, sales promotion, public and press relations, personal selling, merchandising, packaging, etc.

The right combination of these techniques is the 'Mix' that helps sale. Their combined action provides sufficient information to everybody in the distribution chain to take a positive action by seeking more information, placing orders or purchasing the product.

The above, broadly, is the way a marketing plan is developed and marketing strategies determined. How much promotion and promotional mix is required to make the plan successful is decided by people who are entrusted with the task of making the plan successful.

In recent years, marketing philosophies have undergone several changes. To make marketing effort a success, it must seep into the subconscious of every staff member. Intensive training of staff is necessary to make them respond to the needs of the customers. The action of each staff member of the company reflects the company's marketing philosophy. The British Airways, soon after its privatisation, started the Customer First Training Courses with their own staff. It made the British Airways a successful airline that it is today. But, to make the staff responsive, the management had to look after their needs too which the British Airways did. Marketing is total effort of Management and staff to make the customer satisfied and happy.

In India, managements are becoming aware of staff training based on the tenets of Bhagavad Gita and other Hindu scriptures. Realising that Indian cultural traditions are rich in leadership value, business corporations have begun to analyse and absorb the wisdom of scriptures "Corporate playing fields are like the Kurukshetra," said Management Consultant H.B. Atherye. The

Hindu philosophy is helping resolve conflict in the management of business more effectively than the Western or Japanese ways, he believes.

To summarise, after having examined travel and tourism industry in its different facets, this chapter proceeds to tell the reader how tourism product is marketed both at home and abroad.

Till the mid-eighties, the Government of India had total control over all industries. It decided what industries would be allowed and expansion was also subject to government permission. Whatever was produced in the country was sold immediately. In fact, in some industries like motor-vehicles, steel and cement, demand far outstripped the supply. The producers, therefore, did not need marketing efforts as they had no surplus production.

Marketing viewed from the customer's end is relatively a new phenomenon in India. The liberalisation of economy during the last five years has led to a new resurgence of spirit of enterprise fuelled by competition. Tourism is no exception to the spirit that prevails. Both the Department of Tourism which is India's National Tourism Administration (NTA), and the travel industry are trying to adjust to the new environments. The Government of India has taken new initiatives to encourage travel industry to develop new products and go out and sell them in the potential markets of the world.

In the changing environment, it is essential that the travel industry of India understand the principles of marketing and apply them rather than do lip service. The lesson to be learnt is that the producers should begin looking at their tourism products from customers' angle and not their own. Before developing a product, it is necessary to find out through credible research what the customers want in the product and at what price. Since not all the people in a country can afford to travel or are interested in a tourist product marketed by an NTA, the marketeer will have to find out which segments of population will be interested in the product. He must be aware of the age-group of his potential clients, their lifestyle, income, education, etc., to formulate the product according to their needs and requirements. Once the product is formulated and the marketeer knows what segments of population may be inclined to buy the product, the next step is to use an adequate dose of communication mix to reach those segments of population who can afford it. For this purpose, the promotional mix required include advertising, public relations, sales promotion, merchandising, etc. The product is then put into the market through different distribution channels. It is the management's responsibility to make sure that the sales graph moves up fast and if there are difficulties, let the marketing plan be re-examined and modified accordingly to the feedback from the market.

Every product has a lifecycle of its own. If the lifecycle appears to be declining, new products have to be put into the market. The lifecycle can also be extended by introducing the same product in other markets or by redesigning the product according to the changing pattern of demand.

Case Studies

Youth Tourism : Youth tourism may be described as that segment of domestic and international tourism market, which for statistical purpose would apply to 15 to 29 age group.

WTO prescribed the above definition of youth tourism in their New Delhi Declaration on Youth Tourism after a prolonged international conference held in the Indian capital in November, 1991.

The youth market was estimated to be over 84 million trips in 1990, and was 19 per cent in all international travel. And, it is growing annually at an average rate of 8.8 per cent — higher than the normal growth of international tourism at 6.5 per cent.

European railways have done pioneering work in encouraging youth to travel extensively by permitting people below the age of 26 to purchase tickets at grossly reduced rates. International travel is also included in such discounts in some of the railway systems. Young people from abroad are issued special European Rail Passes, with high discounts. National Bus Companies have followed the lead of the European Railways and introduced special fares on their national and international bus routes.

Unfortunately, airlines have not extended special concessions to young people under 26. Zvi H. Raven, Director of International Product and Marketing, Council of International Educational Exchange (CIEE) proposed at the WTO Conference on Youth Tourism in New Delhi, "If an airline can improve its load factor from 65 to 85 per cent through internationally accepted youth or student cards, youth tourism will blossom."

Youth tourism is no longer all budget. Gentiki Travel Organisation, one of the world's largest tour-operators catering to young people between the ages of 15 and 35, sold US $ 1700,14-day European profile itinerary to thousands of young Europeans.

Citing the case histories of many European countries, Professor Lee H. Kreul of Pardu University of USA told the WTO Conference that the young people today travelled out of their countries to foreign destinations more frequently than the rest of the population.

WTO Security General Atonio Enriques Savignac predicted that more European young people will in future travel long distance — especially to countries of Asia-Pacific.

For the first-time in history young people in developed countries have become a very important consumer group. This reflects their growing financial independence, especially in relation to the rest of the society. Young people now are a big market of consumers with their own rules, products and distribution channels, including a specialised travel market segment.

Professor Raven has, therefore, urged National Tourism Administrations to cater to young tourists by providing specialised information regarding sports activities, accommodations, youth hostels, sights, transport, language courses, etc. "Specialised information for young people is still a rare phenomenon," he opined.

Senior Citizens Tourism . Senior citizens in each country, especially in developed societies, form an important and fast expanding segment of travel business.

The following facts tell us the potential of this segment:

1. In Europe alone, there are 185 million persons aged 60 and above.
2. In the USA, the median assets of senior citizens are nearly twice that of other population segments.
3. Unlike other established groups, senior citizens in the main generating markets are less likely to be affected by the economic hard times than other segments of population because many of them have fixed incomes.

Given the current health benefits and facilities, senior citizens are more likely to be travelling during off-season than other people. They also enjoy flexibility—they can choose their time for travel.

Most people in that age group who are likely to travel, live in North America, Europe, Australia and Japan.

They seek high quality tourism and tend to travel to regions with milder climates and good facilities. For individual travel, they prefer package tours rather than travelling independently. Senior citizens usually dislike being confined to their own age groups when travelling and prefer to mix with younger crowds.

Most older people prefer to travel within their own regions, using buses and trains rather than private automobiles.

Thanks to better health facilities, there is a sizeable market of affluent senior citizens who can afford to travel. Need is for a good organisation which can take advantage of this opportunity. In USA, there is a powerful organisation, American Association of Retired Persons (AARP). The AARP has a membership of 30 million and admits anyone above fifty years of age as its member on a payment of $ 5 only. The association has negotiated discounts 10 to 50 per cent on travel services for older people. The association is able to provide travel to senior citizens on a very large scale at affordable prices:

Conference and Conventions Incentive Travel : There are 33,000 international conferences and conventions held worldwide every year and generating revenue of US $ 105 billion.

The tourism industry has coined a special acronym MICE for this business. MICE stands for meetings, incentives, conferences and exhibitions.

Incentive travel is the reward given by business organisations to their best workers or top sales people for their achievements. In developed countries, people have little value or attraction for rewards and incentives like a TV or a refrigerator because they already have one. A nicely packaged all-paid holiday with spouse is considered a more attractive proposition. Several million people are recipients of such rewards every year. About 4 million people travel internationally on incentive trips every year. Besides, there are many more millions who get to travel on similar incentives domestically.

Specialised travel organisations have been set up to professionally deal with this segment of travel. They provide complete service to business houses — from developing an incentive product to its materialisation. Most organisations try to make these trips exciting and unique by organising theme parties and other interesting activities. Indian travel agents have organised special rural 'Melas' as well as entertainment at exotic sites like forts and palaces for incentive groups. The guests are welcomed by caparisoned elephants on arrival. Similarly, the business of conferences and conventions is handled by experts at both ends. Nothing is left to chance.

Incentive travel was started by Americans but it has since spread to Europe, Japan and Australia. Indian enterprises are also in it now offering incentive holidays to their good salesmen. Holidays are offered within India as well as overseas destinations like Nepal, Singapore..

A Gallup survey conducted in 1988 for Society of American Travel Executives (SITE) revealed that 6 per cent of all US air travellers (3.5 million people) took an incentive trip in 1988. The average length of stay was 5 nights and the group size 131. Not all the 3.5 million people went to far away fantasy lands — 67 per cent went to domestic destinations for holiday.

The Women : Women are the fastest growing segment of travel in the world, especially business women.

With women rising on the corporate ladder and having independent jobs and professions, their travels are touching new heights. In some developed countries, they are already catching up with their male counterparts. In the travel industry of USA, women seem to have left their male counterparts far behind. An ASTA survey of 1992 reveals that 84 per cent of US travel agents and 81 per cent of the agency managers are women. In the Far East, women account for 23 per cent of the region's senior posts in business, professions, government and education. In countries like Thailand and the Philippines their share is around 30 per cent.

Overall, 40 per cent of American business travellers travelling domestically are women, according to a survey done by New York based research firm, Erdos and Morgan. A Marriot Corporation study reveals that 32 per cent of the extended stay-hotel guests in the United States are women.

Of an estimated nine million most affluent and frequent business travellers, women accounted for 2 million. The United States Travel and Tourism Administrations (USTAA) has compiled statistics on American women travelling abroad. For instance, women constituted 27 per cent of the Americans travelling to Far East, 37 per cent to Oceania and, 35 per cent to Europe. Among the Americans visiting India, the percentage of females was 34 per cent in 1992. India could certainly try to attract more American women travellers as it is a safe country.

Thailand was the first country to identify the importance of women in their tourism profile. It successfully celebrated 1992 as Visit Women Thailand Year. Thailand had the image that it was more suited to men where women were easily available. But, the Tourism Authority of Thailand tried to change that image and sex tourism is now frowned upon.

Hotels too, have identified the importance of women travellers. Bangkok's leading hotel, Dusit Thani, has gone out of its way to offer a special all women floor with separate elevator, specially appointed rooms for women business executives staffed with female butlers.

According to a survey done by a travel magazine, Asia Travel Trade, women executives expect good room service and good food from the hotels where they stay. Other things listed by women travellers important to their needs were walk-in closets, extra hangers, skirt hangers, hair-dryers, a good international newspaper with breakfast, choice of television stations, a swimming pool, facial and massage services and overnight pressing services.

8

Information Series

The faster rate of expansion of both international and domestic tourism is a manifestation of increasing higher standards of living, more leisure time, technological advances in transport and communication systems and better marketing and promotional techniques. Emergence of newer patterns in world tourist flows — as a result of psychological, sociological and economic factors related to purchasing power and some other factors — are responsible for rapid expansion in tourist activity. The rapid pace at which tourism has expanded over the past decades specially the decades following world war II, clearly indicates the importance of this sector of activity not only from the economic standpoint but above all as an essential need of people everywhere.

Today there can be little doubt that tourism has assumed considerable economic and social significance globally. For the year 2000 the world tourism organisation (WTO) estimated the number of international arrivals at about 710 million expecting this figure to reach 1.5 billion by 2020. Domestic tourist movements are generally several times more than international tourists in many developed countries especially the western countries.

The various benefits especially the economic benefits which the large number of tourists bring to the host countries have made these countries spend huge sums of money to develop infrastructure and other facilities. It is a recognised fact that the developed countries in West Europe, North America and Canada are the ones which are major receiving areas for international tourism and are, therefore, the principal receivers of economic advantage. However, as a result of constant growth of tourism to developed countries, especially Asia, and Pacific, these countries are also getting considerable economic benefits from international tourism. The major economic benefits of these countries are in terms of foreign exchange earnings.

The measurement of this phenomenon assumes a great importance in view of the fact that the countries benefiting from this activity need to know how this is affecting their economy. The measurement of this phenomenon also helps countries in their efforts in planning for the infrastructure as well as marketing of the product. Tourism can only be grasped in all its complexity and its multiple relations with other economic and social sectors and properly understood, if there is a statistical tool able to measure its development according to the determinant factors and at the same time permit a country comparison of such a development. This is possible only by the use of the statistics.

Statistics can be defined as that branch of science which deals with the frequency of occurrence of different kinds of things or different attributes. It is a method specially adopted to the elucidation of quantitative data affected by a multiplicity of causes. It can also be defined as that branch of applied mathematics, by which data of various observations are collected, summarised and presented. The objective of statistics is not merely the description of an existing situation, but also the study of procedures of scientific inference and proof.

Basic Information

Travel Statistics : Travel statistics constitute the basic and essential information series through which the development and performance of the tourist sector can be evaluated in a particular region or a country or worldwide. The collection, study and analysis of the statistics enables new decisions to be made, and the past to be monitored. In addition, the statistics also help in planning and forecasting travel requirements. Broadly, tourism statistics can be grouped into two. Those which relate to Demand, are "Flow Statistics" and generally relate to tourist movements, stay and payments in national, or international markets. Those which relate to Supply refer to a stock or capacity of tourist facilities, mainly accommodation establishments. Changes in the mangnitude of the stock of accommodation, when related to changes in tourist demand, have significance in deciding, for instance, what policy should be pursued to encourage hotel construction so as to accommodate increased demand.

The Measurement : The systematic measurement of tourism began not very long ago. The need was felt as the volume of tourist traffic began to reach significant proportions in the early years of the twentieth century. As the tourist movements grew tremendously, particularly in the last six decades following the First World War, their measurement became very significant for various purposes. The frequency of occurrence of tourist movements in various countries engaged the attention of the statisticians and the social scientists in Switzerland, Italy, Austria and France which emerged clearly as tourist countries early in the century. Before the commencement of World War I, Switzerland was a very popular destination for the rich and leisured class and was known to have received half a million foreign visitors annually. In the year 1929 foreign visitors to Austria were estimated at about two million, to Switzerland about one and a half and to Italy about a million and a quarter. In Europe such statistics of tourism, as did exist up to the First World War, were mainly derived from government controls and enumeration records for health, safety and taxation and, in particular, for police and migration purposes. No distinction was made between tourists and other travellers. These statistics provided only some indication of the volume and value of tourist traffic.

The records of individual passenger transport and accommodation operators were the other principal sources of quantitative data about tourism, the former giving numbers of travellers staying in hotels and similar accommodation establishments. These sources continue to be utilised for quantitative data about tourism by many countries. In the absence of a clear-cut definition of the term 'tourist', these sources rarely distinguished in any way between the actual tourists and other travellers and also between different groups of tourists. These were thus of limited value in the assessment of the volume and the value of tourism. Tourism had not yet received recognition as an economic phenomenon and, therefore, not much efforts were made to systematically and scientifically measure it.

Post-World War I period witnessed a large scale movement of tourists and, in the following decade, tourism received recognition as a great economic phenomenon. In the 1920s and early 1930s tourism came to be examined against the background of economic problems of most European countries. World War II, however temporarily stopped the tourist movements. Most of the European countries suffered tremendous economic losses as a result of war. In the years immediately following the war, European economies were dominated by reconstruction and recovery, by balance of payment problems, and, in particular by the dollar gap. Tourism in these countries was seen as an important factor in the solution of various economic problems, particularly the problems of the balance of payments.

Planning Statistics

The United Nations Development Decade in the 1960s focused much attention on the developing countries—their problems and solutions. Various development plans were prepared by the experts in which tourism played a significant and a dominant role. The need arose for primary data on tourism to measure the tourist flows to particular destinations and of the tourist expenditure to provide a basis for planning the future development. Statistics thus became an essential tool of measurement of the tourist phenomenon. The emphasis, however, was on international tourism. Most of the statistics which were collected and analysed concerned the international tourist. During this period domestic tourism also gathered momentum. The governments, realising the importance of tourism, gave a thought to its development. It was felt that both international and domestic tourism can contribute towards regional development within a country. Hence in recent years many countries have felt the need for the collection of tourist statistics of domestic tourist movements and expenditure and for the statistics related to a particular destination within a country.

Market research in the recent years has brought about the need for quantified data in addition to the basic statistics about the movement and expenditure. A prospective tourist's choice of a particular destination or destinations is from a certain priority and related to his wants which could be physiological, psychological and/or sociological. These wants could be related to factors like recognition, a new learning experience, response from others, relaxation, etc. Marketing, decision-making and formulation of promotion strategies involve specialised knowledge and information of the buyer's likes and dislikes, preferences, etc. Therefore, it becomes necessary for the purposes of marketing of the tourist product. Hence the need for quantified data.

The measurement of the tourism phenomenon thus is very vital. The importance of statistical measurement in tourism may be summarised as follows :

(a) For evaluating the magnitude and significance of tourism to a particular destination. The destination could be a country, a region or a district within a region. The data collected can be utilised to quantify the role and contribution of tourism to the country's economy.

(b) For planning and development of physical facilities and for infrastructural requirements. It is not merely that statistics are useful to know the numbers of tourist arrivals for a series of consequent years to show whether tourist trade in any particular country is growing, stagnant or declining; it is important to know the other attributes like the mode of arrival, the kind of accommodation used, the amenities desired by the traveller, the length of stay, the amount that he spends, the purchases he makes, etc. All this information is essential for tourism planning.

(c) For marketing and promotion, it is very essential to know the profile of tourists, both actual and potential. It is only after ascertaining the physiological, psychological, sociological wants of visitors that an effective marketing campaign can be launched.

(d) For understanding the changes in tourist fashion. Regular returns of statistics help the countries to find out about the flow of the tourist traffic to various destinations. The flow will indicate whether a tourist patronises a beach holiday, winter resort, archaeological site or any other area.

(e) For legislative and administrative purposes since legislation may apply to certain activities alone and not to others.

The statistics have become an essential factor in obtaining an overall view of the issues that determine or affect tourism development globally or in particular of a country or a region. The statistics are the key element in decision-making at the most diverse levels, given the increasing complexity of tourism and the swift changes affecting it. The collection, processing and dissemination of statistical data in each country is, therefore, a fundamental element in the overall tourism development process. Understanding the concept of tourism in general and a tourist in particular is very important in order to grasp the tourism phenomenon. When we talk about the measurement of tourism, we must know as to what is that which is to be measured? How is it to be measured? Are there any particular problems of measurement? When is it to be measured? These are all very crucial questions. One of the earliest definition of tourism was given by an Austrian economist, Herman V. Schullard in the year 1910 who defined it as : "The sum total of operators, mainly of an economic nature, which directly related to the entry, stay and movement of foreigners inside and outside a certain country, city or region." The concept of tourism found expression however, in a more technical definition of Swiss professors Hunziker and Krapf in the year 1942. The professors stated: "Tourism is the totality of the relationship and phenomenon arising from the travel and stay of strangers, provided the stay does not imply the establishment of a permanent residence and is not connected with a remunerated activity".

The definition was subsequently adopted by the International Association of Scientific Experts in Tourism (AIEST). The increasing importance of the quantitative aspect of tourism for planning and marketing decisions has led to various attempts by individuals and organisations in the field to arrive at an internationally accepted definition of the term "tourist" as the basic unit of measurement for tourism statistics. It is the tourist which is the principal character in the tourism phenomenon and when we talk about measurement, we refer to measuring a "tourist". The tourist becomes the unit of measurement.

Concept and Perception

The 19th Century Dictionary defines 'tourist' as a "person who travels for travelling, out of curiosity, and because he has nothing better to do". The term 'tourist', the Oxford Dictionary tells us, was used as early as the year 1800. According to the Dictionnaire Universal, the 'tourist' is a person who makes a journey for the sake of curiosity, for the fun of travelling, or just to tell others that he has travelled.

The term 'tourist' in the sense of pleasure tour is, however, of recent origin. In the words of Jose Ignacio De Arrilliga, "tourism in its first period was considered as a sport or rather as a synthesis of automobiles, touring, cycling, camping, excursions and yachting. In the early nineteenth century, the term 'tourist' assumed a meaning of 'one who makes a tour or tours', especially one who does this for recreation or who travels for pleasure, object of interest, scenery or the like."

League of Nations : All the above definitions of the term ' tourist' are of a general nature and, therefore, could not serve the purpose of measurement. It was, however, the League of Nations which did a pioneering work in defining the term for the purposes of statistical measurements. Realising the importance of collecting tourist statistics and of securing international compatibility, the Committee of Statistical Experts of the League of Nations in the year 1937 established the definition of the term 'tourist'. The League of Nations with the concurrence of member countries defined the term 'foreign tourist' as : "Any person visiting a country, other than that in which he usually resides, for a period of at least 24 hours".

The following persons were to be considered tourists within this definition :

(i) Persons travelling for pleasure, for domestic reasons, for health, etc.

(ii) Persons travelling to meetings, or in a representative capacity of any kind (scientific, administrative diplomatic, religious, athletic, etc.)

(iii) Persons travelling for business purposes.

(iv) Persons arriving in the course of a sea cruise, even when they stay for less than 24 hours. (The latter should be reckoned as a separate group, disregarding if necessary their usual place of residence.)

The following categories were not to be regarded as tourists:

(i) Persons arriving, with or without a contract of work, to take up an occupation or engage in any business activity in the country.

(ii) Persons coming to establish a residence in the country.

(iii) Students and young persons in boarding establishments or schools.

(iv) Residents in a frontier zone and persons domiciled in one country and working in an adjoining country.

(v) Travellers Passing through a country without stopping, even if the journey takes more than 24 hours.

The above definition was confirmed by the United Nations in the year 1945 and it was stated that the 'tourist' was a person who stayed in a foreign country for more than 24 hours and less than 6 months for any non-immigrant purpose. The definition was adopted by many countries for the compilation of travel statistics.

European Travel Commission : European Travel Commission (ETC), the organisation for European Economic Cooperation (OEEC), and the International Union of Official Travel Organisation (IUOTO) were the agencies through which the first regular reporting was developed on the basis of the definition established by the Committee of Statistical Experts of the League of Nations, in the year 1937 and subsequently confirmed by the United Nations in the year 1945. The European Travel Commission was a non-governmental body chiefly concerned with the promotion of American travel to Europe. The members of this Commission were the national tourist organisations of some countries of Western Europe.

The IUOTO representing national tourist organisations on international basis, established the Study Commission on International Travel Statistics and in the year 1947 began the publication of its Digest of Tourist Statistics. The document was a collection of national statistics of tourist arrivals and travel payments of some countries. In the year 1950 a permanent IUOTO Research Commission was established to study and recommend improvements in statistical methods. In December 1960, the Organisation for Economic Cooperation and Development (OECD) was set up under a convention signed in Paris. It took over the work in tourism of its predecessor, the Organisation for European Economic Cooperation (OEEC). Up to the year 1963, the Tourism Committee of OECD recommended to its member countries the adoption of the definition of the term 'foreign tourist' established by the Committee of Statistical Experts of the League of Nations in 1937. Both the OECD and the IUOTO brought out many publications in the subsequent years concerning tourist statistics.

United Nations - Rome Conference : The United Nations Conference on International Travel and Tourism held in Rome in 1963 considered a definition and recommended that it be studied by the United Nations Statistical Commission. A revised definition was prepared and adopted. The conference considered an overall definition of the term 'Visitor', which for statistical purposes describes: any person visiting a country other than that in which he has his usual place of residence, for any reasons other than following an occupation remunerated from within the country visited.

This definition covered:

(i) Tourists, i.e., temporary visitors staying at least twenty-four hours in the country visited and the purpose of whose journey can be classified under one of the following headings:

(a) leisure (recreation, holiday, health, study, religion, and sport);

(b) business, family, mission, meeting.

(ii) Excursionists, i.e., temporary visitors staying less than twenty four hours in the country visited (including travellers on cruises).

The above definition excludes travellers who, in the legal sense, do not enter the country (e.g., air travellers who do not leave an airport transit area).

The Expert Statistical Group on International Travel Statistics convened by the United Nations Statistical Commission recommended in 1967 that countries use the definition of visitor proposed by the United Nations Conference on International Travel and Tourism in Rome in 1963. The Group considered that it would be desirable to distinguish within the definition of visitor a separate class of visitors, who might be described as day visitors or excursionists defined as consisting of visitors on day excursions and other border-crossers for purposes other than employment, cruise passengers, and visitors in transit who do not stay overnight in accommodation provided within the country. The special characteristic of this category of visitor, distinguishing it from the main class of visitor, is that there is no overnight stay. In 1968 the Commission approved the Rome definition.

The various definitions discussed above have gradually received general acceptance. According to studies published by the World Tourism Organisation, nearly 75 per cent of the countries the world over use these definitions in the collection of international travel statistics.

Various Categories

The tourist statistics are basically concerned with the estimates of arrivals and departures, more particularly the former. In addition to statistics of arrivals and departures, the statistics of tourist spendings during their stay at a destination have important implications for the country's economy and on its balance of payments accounts. Yet another type of tourist statistics is concerned with the information on the tourist himself. This information is very crucial as it deals with various aspects of tourist behaviour and his characteristics. This information is necessary for the purposes of tourism marketing and development. The main categories of the tourist statistics therefore are: (a) Volume; (b) Expenditure; (c) Characteristic

Notes:

(1) Visitors who spend at least one night in the country visited.

(2) Foreign air or ship crews docked or in lay over and who use the accommodation establishments of the country visited.

(3) Visitors who do not spend at least one night in the country visited although they may visit the country during one day more and return to their ship or train to sleep.

(4) Normally included in excursionists. Separate classification of these visitors is nevertheless recommended.

(5) Visitors who come and leave the same day.

(6) Crews who are not residents of the country visited and who stay in the country for the day.

(7) When they travel from their country of origin to the duty station and vice-versa (including household servants and dependants accompanying or joining them).

World Tourism Organisation Classification of Travellers

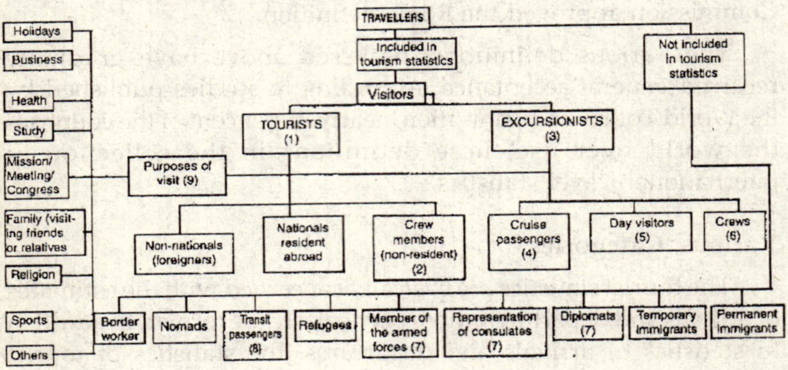

(8) Who do not leave the transit area of the airport or the port. In certain countries, transit may involve a stay of one day or more. In this case, they should be included in the visitor statistics.

(9) Main purposes of visit as defined by the Rome Conference (1963).

Volume Statistics : The basic Volume Statistics consist of the number of tourists to a particular destination over a given period of time. The unit of period could be a month, six months or a year. Most of the countries, however, consider a year as the unit of period. While counting, it is normally the number of arrivals or visits and not the number of tourists. This is because it is impracticable to allow for those who visit the same destination more than once in the same period. It is the events rather than individuals with which the basic statistics of volume are concerned. A half a dozen visits by the same person is counted therefore as separate six events or six tourist arrivals. Thus 700 million tourist arrivals in the world in the year 2000 denote 700 million visits made by a somewhat smaller number of individual visitors.

Duration of stay' is another main volume statistics. Duration of stay is measured in terms of days or nights spent by a tourist at the destination and is normally expressed as the average length of stay.

Statistics of numbers provide a general indication of the volume of tourist traffic to a particular destination. The statistics of length of stay on the other hand provide a general indication of the nature of the traffic, in particular of the extent of transit and terminal visitors and of their demand for overnight accommodation.

Expenditure Statistics : Expenditure statistics on the other hand are concerned with measurements of spendings by the tourists at the destination and also on the journey. These statistics are very important as these measure the value of tourism to a particular economy. Expenditure statistics make it possible to determine the monetary value of tourist movements. Tourist spending at a destination determines how much of the total volume of foreign exchange enters a particular country. Tourist spending for international tourism commonly covers all tourist expenditure in a country including foreign tourists' expenditure on transportation in the country and expenditure on shopping. It, however, excludes payments to international carriers in respect of journeys to and from the country visited. Similarly, for other destinations, expenditure covers what is incurred at the destination, but not expenditure on the journey to and from the destination.

Payments made in respect of journeys to and from the destination do not necessarily accrue to the destination and they are, therefore, normally excluded from statistics of expenditure at the destination. However, for purposes of total estimates of tourist expenditure, they may be included or separately evaluated. For the balance of payments purposes, fare payments by foreign visitors to a country's carriers represent income to the country visited. Although this item is usually included in the transport item of the balance of payments in conformity with the international recommendations, it is a part of tourist spending and a part of the country's earnings from tourism.

When the total visitor expenditure at the destination is divided by the number of arrivals or by the number of tourist days or nights, the result is the average expenditure per visit or per day or night. While the global estimates of tourist expenditure give a general indication of the value of tourism to an economy, visit and daily - averages provide, respectively, general indications of the type and quality of the traffic for a destination.

Characteristics Statistics : Characteristics statistics are yet another type of tourist statistics which are very essential for those concerned with marketing and development of tourism. Any information regarding the markets, the mode of transport used and the socio-economic characteristics of the visitors are all essential for tourism planning and development. The total volume of arrivals and tourist nights have to be divided into various market segments according to the purpose of visit, mode of transport used, place of origin, tourist profile characteristics and tourist behaviour patterns in order to provide meaningful information for marketing and development purposes. The main profile characteristics of tourists include age, sex, occupation and income. The behaviour characteristics include such elements as time of visit, mode of transport used, type of accommodation used, whether travelling alone or in groups and his activities at the destination. For the purposes of promotion, the profile and behaviour characteristics also include such information as the readership of newspapers and magazines, attitude of tourists and impressions about the visit. Information about the population which does not engage in tourism or the population which does engage in tourism but does not visit a particular destination is also very important. All this information provides a basis for evolving a realistic marketing strategy and for the physical planning of the amenities at the tourist destination.

Measurement Methods

The principal methods as far as basic volume statistics are concerned may be divided into three areas:

(i) Enumeration at the arrival and departure points.

(ii) Registration at hotels and other accommodation units.

(iii) Sample Surveys.

Enumeration at the arrival and departure points is an administrative procedure which assists measurements. For example, frontier arrivals may be counted by way of checking passports, visas, disembarkation cards and the like. The counting in this case is done at the point of entry or exit from the destination. The entry or exit point may be single or multiple depending upon the size and also the location of a country. In the case of a large country, the entry and exit points are many and the tourists have a choice of embarkation or disembarkation from any of these, depending upon their convenience and choice. On the other hand in smaller countries and, in particular, the islands, there is a limited number of entry and exit points. This method of enumeration at the point of arrival and departure is an accurate method of obtaining numbers and can also provide information on the length of stay of tourists. By way of linking arrival and departure dates of individual visitors, the information on the length of stay of tourists is arrived at.

The Registration : Registration of tourists at the place of their stay is another method of measurement. Use is made of registration at hotels and other such establishments, or even the cashing of traveller's cheques. The registration forms of hotels and other such accommodation units are the sources of eliciting information from the tourists who fill these forms at the time of registration. From these registration forms data are reported periodically to a central bureau which in turn supplies this to concerned authorities. This method of measurement, however, requires legal authority and enforcement. Unless it is binding on such establishments to collect such information, accurate and timely data collection may not be possible.

The data collected by way of registration at hotels and other such establishments provides a variety of valuable information which includes information on numbers, duration of stay and tourist nights, etc. It may also provide some profile characteristics of tourists such as their places of origin and may be classified by the type of accommodation and area visited: Statistics collected by this method are not necessarily entirely accurate. This method normally covers to a varying degree different forms of accommodation provided on payments. It is difficult to extend it to all types of accommodation including private homes where tourists often stay. Special care has also to be taken to avoid double counting of arrivals when tourists change their accommodation at the same destination. Many a times it happens that a tourist, after having registered at a particular hotel, decides to change it for another for reasons of convenience and/or economy.

The above two methods measure the volume of tourism to a particular country or destination, when and where it occurs, for instance, at an airport or at an hotel. In contrast to the above two methods of measurement, another important method is sample surveys. Sample surveys of a population are made by means of interviews and use of questionnaires. The question arises, of course, as to how one contacts and identifies visitors. The contact may be made at the time of arrival of the visitor, or subsequently when the traveller returns home after the event. In either case he is asked to complete a detailed questionnaire which elicits the information or details of his participation in tourism during the past period. When the surveys are detailed enough and cover places visited, duration of stay, and similar information, they may at the same time also provide basic statistics of volume of tourism to particular destinations, such as regions, in addition to profile and behaviour characteristics of the population in general.

Sample Surveys : Sample surveys of foreign tourism can be divided into several types, according to scope and purpose and also according to where and when interviews take place. The more comprehensive survey endeavours to include all or most visitors to a country and obtain volume and expenditure data as well as qualitative data about the tourists themselves and about various aspects of their trip. This survey is carried out at points of arrival and departure or en route. In order to be representative of the total traffic, interviews must be carried out at all major points of arrival and departure of foreign tourists and also on all or most routes continuously and also throughout the year. When, on the other hand, it is desired to obtain more detailed information about one part of the traffic, sample surveys may be used to cover that particular part only, for example, industrialists or motorists, in which case interviews are carried out only with the visitors on business or those arriving and departing by car, which may be restricted to certain times of the year.

Sample surveys may cover separately visitors of particular nationality or countries of origin. In this case interviews may be conducted at points of arrival and departure but there are sometimes advantages in the survey being undertaken in the country of origin rather than the country visited. The biggest advantage in this is that interviews can be conducted in the visitors own language.

Since only a small proportion of the total population in a particular country have visited the country studied as a destination, it is necessary to locate them in the first instance. This can be done, for example, by including questions in an omnibus survey in the country of origin, from which names and addresses of past visitors provide the contacts for interviews. The sample survey method is independent of the administrative process and has the advantage of making contact with the tourists from whom all kinds of information relevant to the industry may be elicited.

Statistics have become the essential basis of any policy for the promotion of international tourism. It is also acknowledged today that the lack of statistical data and effective methods for their collection, processing and presentation are factors which hamper decisions on tourism development in the countries of various regions. Statistical information is likewise recognised as a vital factor in the rational planning of tourism development and in evaluating progress made towards achieving both national and regional objectives set for tourism development and promotion.

Several countries have developed statistics of international tourism to meet their need for measurement of the volume and value of tourism. These countries use methods which have been earlier derived from immigration and exchange control systems. In recent years, however, increasing efforts have been made to produce, on the one hand more specific statistics and, on the other, to achieve a greater measure of comparability between statistics produced by individual countries. It is not possible to obtain adequate information by way of indirect methods derived from administrative systems as the volume of international travel has grown tremendously. Direct methods based on sample surveys of tourists are increasingly used, in addition to and in place of indirect methods with a view to obtaining adequate information.

General Problems of Measurement : Almost all international tourists have three actions in common according to McEven. These are:

(i) They cross international frontiers;

(ii) They exchange their own currency for foreign currency; and

(iii) They spend time outside their own country, and this implies using some form of accommodation.

It is possible to use these actions as methods for measuring international tourism, i.e., by enumerating arrivals at frontiers, by recording currency transactions and by recording the number of nights in various types of accommodation units by the foreign visitors. None of these methods is, however, foolproof. Each method has its limitations in respect of recording and enumerating foreign visitors. Counting foreign visitor arrivals is the most usual and most widely adopted method.

The tourist statistics is basically concerned with arrivals and departures and more particularly with the former. In arriving at these figures, it is, as indicated above, concerned with events rather than individuals and as far as these are concerned, half a dozen visits by the same person is counted as six separate events of six tourist arrivals. There are certain difficulties in the matter of counting. The main difficulty is, perhaps, the risk of double counting. Absolute figures of tourists visiting almost every country tend to be inflated because of double counting. For example, an Italian tourist on his way to holiday in Spain may travel by car for two days through France and on his return journey to Italy will also travel two days through France, hence his journey, i.e., his arrival in France is recorded twice.

Another problem of statistical measurement in tourism arises from the difficulty of differentiating between tourists and other travellers and between them and the resident and working populations. In their movements and in their stay at various places at destinations it becomes difficult at times to distinguish between them and the residents and the working populations. Also regarding the use of transport to destinations, tourists may use public transport or use their own private transport. They normally enter various destinations without stopping and often without registering their arrival. They do so increasingly even when crossing many national frontiers. At the destination the tourists use a variety of accommodation ranging from hotels, pension apartments, guest houses and friends' and relatives' homes. They eat in the same eating establishments and buy items for use and other services from the same sources from which these are bought by those who are not tourists.

It may, however, be stated that the various general problems of statistical measurements in tourism discussed above are to be encountered in countries having common borders. It is in these countries that distinction becomes difficult. A number of countries in Europe, Middle East, South America, South-East Asia encounter such problems of measurements.

WTO's Role

The World Tourism Organisation brings out a valuable document entitled The Yearbook of Tourism Statistics. This annual document gives a summary of the most important tourism statistics for 180 countries. The statistics included in the yearbook are official data obtained primarily by means of questionnaires sent to the competent government offices of the world. The main purpose of this annual publication is to present a comprehensive compendium, of the most important internationally comparable data, for the analysis of tourism development of the world at regional and national levels. These are obtained from official national publications and by correspondence with the national statistical services. The yearbook contains comprehensive statistical data on volume, expenditure and characteristics of tourists. It also contains data on individual countries giving information on areas like accommodation sector, length of stay, mode of transport used, international tourism receipts and expenditures, purpose of visit and data on domestic tourism.

9

Indian Market

India is one of the few countries in the world blessed with a tremendous variety of tourist resources. But, the country attracts only 0.4 per cent of the world's international tourism. A country which always attracted foreign visitors throughout its history, India has lagged behind in developing adequate infrastructure and creating the right image for international travellers.

India recognised the economic significance of tourism soon after independence and established a full-fledged Department of Tourism as early as 1958. In fact, India was one of the first countries among the newly independent Asian nations to undertake the promotion of international tourism in a professional way. It was the first country of Asia to open overseas tourist offices in USA and the United Kingdom as early as 1952.

Long Journey

In 1951, there were about 17,000 tourists who visited India, in 1982 the number went up to 12,88,162, in 1994 to 17,64,830 and in 1996 it was about 23,00,000, including visitors from Pakistan and Bangladesh. Earlier, India did not include visitors from Pakistan and Bangladesh in visitors' tally because these figures fluctuated drastically with political ups and downs. Now, the

Government of India has decided to include these arrivals. However, it is a matter of regret that as the size of international tourism grows, India's share in worldwide arrivals declines. While India's share in world tourism was about 1 per cent in the sixties, it has come down to 0.35 per cent in the nineties.

India's official targets for tourist arrivals laid down by the Ministry of Tourism in the late seventies were 3.5 million for the nineties. But, the country barely touched 1.5 million by the 1990. The tourism authorities have been giving unrealistic targets against the expert advice. Now, again the Ministry of Tourism has given a tall order of 5 million arrivals by 1997 — the last year of the 8th Five Year Plan. In the current scenario, India should be lucky to achieve 2.5 million arrivals by 1997.

Tourist traffic essentially moves from one developed country to another both for pleasure as well as for business. The developing countries do not receive major benefit from tourism due to various reasons, including their poor image as a holiday destination and inadequate tourist infrastructure. India is no exception.

However, the number of tourists visiting a country need not always be the norm by which a country's performance in tourism field may be assessed. It is also the quality of tourists a destination attracts and their capacity to spend money. From this angle, India is not doing badly. The average stay of visitors to India during the past two decades has been varying from 27 to 30 days — next only to Australian average. Similarly, India attracts tourists primarily from the affluent countries of the West whose capacity to spend is higher. Averages are made by the size and diversity of a country. In Europe, an American tourist may visit ten countries in 14 days, or at least 4 to 6. But, in India even the American average is 17days and the European average is over 20. A European tourist travelling from his home country to the next may not be spending much money in the host country. Often they pick up their trailers and camping equipment from their homes and drive 300 kms and pitch their tent in the host country, bringing with them their own food. They fill the gas in the car tank from their side of the border. After a couple of days stay in the neighbouring country, they return home again filling up the gas tank from their side of the border. This story was told by the head of the German National

Tourist Organisation to the author of this book about the Dutch tourists visiting Germany. Tourism in Europe is like domestic tourism in India — people of West Bengal going to Kashmir or people of Punjab visiting Darjeeling. Not even that. Often inter-European tourism is like the people of Punjab visiting Haryana or Uttar Pradesh and people from Madras going to Kerala !

The numbers can be misleading. Malaysia with 6 million arrivals may include two million Singaporeans who live only 30 kms across the border. If average stay is 6 days for 5 million visitors to Thailand, 2 million visitors to India with an average stay of 28 days can surely be more advantageous to India.

Reasonable Growth

International tourism to India had a reasonably good growth since independence. Comparison with some of its more popular neighbouring countries like Hong Kong, Singapore and Thailand can be misleading because the Government of India in its own wisdom accorded low priority to tourism till the early eighties. Despite the government's apathy, tourism registered an impressive growth till it tapered off in 1980. The Indo-Pak War of 1971 brought traffic to a virtual halt, but it revived soon after.

An analysis of the 1995 international tourist arrivals by the country of residence reveals that visitors from Western Europe accounted for 7,54,182 or 33 per cent; North America 2,67,188 or 11.7 per cent; West Asia 1,14,748 or 5 per cent; South Asia 5,40,209 or 23 per cent; South East Asia 1,29,449 or 5.6 per cent; Africa 87,238 or 3.9 per cent; Eastern Europe 53,275 or 2.3 per cent; and Central and South America 16,672 or 0.6 per cent.

Countrywise analysis shows the following countries are the top ten markets of India:

Top Ten Markets

Country	*Arrivals*	*Percentage of the total*
1. United Kingdom	3,00,696	19.2
2. USA	1,76,482	11.3
3. Sri Lanka	89,009	5.7

Contd..

Country	*Arrivals of the total*	*Percentage*
4. Germany	85,382	5.7
5. France	73,088	4.7
6. Japan	63,398	4.1
7. Canada	56,441	3.6
8. C.I.S.	56,387	3.6
9. Singapore	44,187	2.8
10. Italy	43,500	2.8

Note: Pattern of traffic has remained more or less the same — occasionally Germany and France exchanging places. Among other primary markets of India are Malaysia, Switzerland, Belgium and Holland. South Africa and Israel are also emerging as important markets.

Seasonality : There is a high degree of seasonality in foreign tourist traffic to India. While the peak is during the last quarter of the year, October to December, the arrivals at the lowest ebb are during the second quarter — April to June. That causes some problems as hotel rooms go begging during the off-season. Fortunately, due to the recent liberalisation of the Indian economy, a large number of foreign businessmen are visiting India during the off-season. The 1995 percentage for the first quarter was 26.5, second quarter 19.2, third quarter 24 and the fourth quarter 30.3 — an improvement on the past. It was little over 20 per cent in 1995.

Foreign Exchange Earnings : Because of longer duration of stay, India earns more per tourist than most other countries. Over half the visitors to India have an annual income of over one million rupees or US $ 50,000 or more.

The foreign exchange earnings were estimated by the Reserve Bank of India for the year 1995 at US $ 2.5 billion or Rs. 9000 crores. The average spending for visitors exceeded Rs. 35,000 — the average has gone up recently as the Rupee has been devalued by about 40 per cent during the past five years.

Tourism stands third in foreign exchange earnings after textiles and gems and jewellery.

The percentage share of India in world tourism receipts was about 0.40 in 1995-96.

Foreign exchange earnings from tourism as percentage of GNP were 0.65 only.

The percentage contribution of tourism to Net National Product was 0.70 (1991-92).

The estimated direct employment provided by tourism in 1991-92 was 6.39 million, including employment generated by domestic tourism. The size of domestic tourism was estimated to be 66 million in 1992 according to a report of the Department of Tourism. The 1997 estimate is 100 millions tourist movements.

Modes of Travel

Air travel continues to be the preferred mode of travel for tourists to India. During the years 1996 and 1994, 98.4% per cent arrived by air and less than 2 per cent came by land. Only a few thousand visitors came by sea.

Delhi was the major port of entry with 39.5 per cent, followed closely by Bombay — 36.3 per cent. Both these ports together accounted for 75.8 per cent of the arriving foreign tourist traffic. The pattern continues.

The arrivals at Madras and Calcutta were 11.9 and 3.1 per cent respectively. For road traffic Sonauli checkpost continued to be the most popular entry point (1.1 per cent).

Goa airport was opened to international traffic in 1992 and it is at present receiving about 70,000 visitors annually, mostly those coming by chartered planes from Europe.

Length of Stay : The estimated average length of stay in 1996 was 28.7 days against 30.2 days in 1991. The total tourist days spent by foreign visitors in 1996 were estimated to be 41,500,000.

Age Group : More young people visit India. In 1996, about 61 per cent of visitors to India were below 44 years of age and the remainder 40 per cent fell in the age group higher than 44. The percentage of women among the visitors to India has always been low. It was 39 per cent in 1996 compared to 28 per cent in 1987. The highest was 54 per cent among Hong Kong citizens followed by Sri Lanka 42 percent.

The Tourists

From time to time, the Department of Tourism has sponsored studies to know the profile of visitors to India. One survey was undertaken by a Delhi-based Research Organisation, J.K. and Associates, during the period February 1988 to September 1989. The method of survey was through personal interviews. As many as 19,000 foreign tourists and 2,000 transit visitors were interviewed—14,000 at exit points and the remaining 5,000 in their accommodations. The results were interesting. A majority of visitors to India were well educated professionals. The following is the break-up:

1. Scientists/Doctors - (20%).
2. Executives/Managers (12.5%).
3. Production, Sales, Service Workers (11.6%).
4. Students (9.4%)
5. Housewives (6.2%)
6. Entrepreneurs (6.1%)
7. Government Administrators (4.5%)
8. Retired persons (2.7%)
9. Others (27%)

Purpose of Visit

Of the visitors to India 57.9 per cent of them declared 'Pleasure' as their purpose of visit, while 22.4 per cent were on business. People visiting friends and relatives were 7.3 per cent followed by students 4.3 per cent and pilgrimage 3 per cent. The rest came for purposes other than the above.

Another interesting revelation was that 8 per cent of the foreign visitors were of Indian ethnic origin — down 0.8 per cent from an earlier survey conducted in 1982-83 by the Indian Statistical Institute, Calcutta.

Influencing Factors

Travel agents appear to be the major influencing factor to bring visitors to India — 14.6 per cent, followed by India's Tourist Offices overseas 12 per cent; foreign international carriers 7.4 per cent, Indian national carriers (Air India, Indian Airlines) 7.1 per cent. Among other organisations and people influencing them to come to India were Indian missions abroad 7.1 per cent and Indian hotel chains about 4.7 per cent. The remaining 47.1 per cent came to India influenced by their own curiosity or through the advice of friends who had already been to India, etc. India is, apparently, a destination loved by visitors. There are many who come to India again and again. The survey revealed that 52.2 per cent of the visitors were coming to India for the first time — the second timers were 16.5 per cent and the third timers 13.8 per cent. The remaining 17.5 per cent had been to India more than three times.

Among the visitors 40.9 per cent came alone; 23.2 per cent came with friends; 27.9 per cent with family.

Ratings : In the overall rating of their stay in India, 37.25 per cent rated it as excellent, 51.92 per cent rated it good and the balance from 'fair' to 'satisfactory'. Tourists also recorded favourable and unfavourable factors as perceived by them, of their visit to India. On an overall basis, the first five favourable factors were:

(1) Friendly people

(2) Beautiful scenery and sights

(3) Comfortable accommodation

(4) Good shopping

(5) Good climate.

The unfavourable factors listed were:

(1) Unpleasant climate

(2) Complicated travel formalities

(3) Uncomfortable travel

(4) Lack of good accommodation

(5) Lack of night life.

Satisfaction Index : Of the total visitors, 71.95 per cent liked the friendliness of the Indian people and 81.5 per cent of visitors were satisfied with their India tour.

Among the visitors who experienced difficulties following were some of the reasons:

(a)	Poor sanitation	-	31.60
(b)	Tiresome entry formalities	-	30.21
(c)	Unhelpful people/unethical traders	-	17.83
(d)	Non-availability of right type of food	-	15.45
(e)	Poor quality of accommodation	-	12.88
(f)	Difficult air-bookings	-	12.38
(g)	Difficult rail-bookings	-	12.22

Image among Americans : The following are the highlights of India's tourist image among the American visitors according to a survey conducted by the Indian Statistical Institute:

1. India has a moderate level of familiarity amongst potential US travellers.
2. India does not have an image advantage over other Asia-Pacific destinations.
3. Ratings for India with regard to reasonable costs for travellers' stay in the country having sunny comfortable weather and good shopping are moderate. India has not been effective in communicating these benefits to potential travellers.
4. Her image of having good shopping is below average rating.
5. Her ratings on hotels that meet American standards and a good place to relax are low.
6. India is not perceived as a place with activities for children, good recreation, sporting facilities or for familiar types of

food, not a relaxing place to visit with interesting night life or beautiful beaches.

7. India is also perceived as not a safe place to travel.
8. It is seen as having interesting customs, an exotic place, one with scenic beauty and unique natural attractions and a place that offers lots to see and do.
9. It is able to provide with a feeling of adventure and challenge and having many out-of-the-way places which are worth seeing even if it means roughing it up.

The Spendings : The average per capita expenditure of (Rs. 22,000 in 1982) by visitors to India is distributed as per the following chart:

Percentage Spent on	*Package Tourist*	*Non-Package Tourist*
Accommodation	33.5	11.0
Food and Drinks	20.5	13.5
Entertainment	2.6	1.8
Shopping	24.8	64.8
Internal Travel	13.6	5.3
Miscellaneous	5.0	3.0

Source: A Survey of Foreign Tourists to India —1982-83, Indian Statistical Institute, Calcutta.

Tourist Places

India is fortunate that its visitors are not concentrated in one or two cities of the country — they travel to far off places. In the 1975-76 survey, the number of places where a sizable number of foreigners travelled was only 40; the number increased to 58 in 1982-83 and the present number of places included in the itinerary of foreign visitors exceeds 75. This diversification brings about more evenly spread benefits to the Indian nation.

There is a trend to discover new tourist places in the country and the Government of India is also opening new travel circuits for foreign tourists.

Negative Aspects

The following are the reasons why tourists in millions do not come to India:

1. *Distance:* India is located far from the affluent tourist markets of the world. High airfares are major constraint.
2. *Image:* India is not yet well known abroad as a holiday destination. Its image is essentially that of an exotic country with an ancient history and civilisation as the two main resources.
3. *Facilities:* Tourist facilities in India are not adequate and well developed. There is inadequate hotel capacity, unsatisfactory domestic air and ground transportation, etc.
4. *Non-affluent neighbours:* India's neighbours are not rich. Their citizens cannot, therefore, afford to travel. European tourism is basically travelling to neighbouring countries. Even in ASEAN countries the international tourism is over 50 per cent from the neighbouring countries. In India, it is less than 10 per cent.
5. India's political problems with its neighbours, especially Pakistan, are a major constraint.

A country may be host to a large number of thrifty visitors, or a small number of high-spending visitors, but no country (except totalitarian regimes) can determine the kind of tourists it would prefer to welcome. While the number may be a test of the success, or otherwise, of promotional and marketing efforts of a country, in economic terms, what matters is the volume of tourism and foreign exchange receipts derived from this source. The volume depends on the average length of stay.

Analysis of Marketing

Having understood the current profile of Indian tourism, it is possible to analyse the marketing efforts put in by the Department of Tourism, Government of India. While starting tourism promotion in a modest way in the early fifties, the Government of India had no clear-cut objectives and goals about how to go about it. Tourism promotion was considered an information service like information on any other aspect of a country i.e. trade, economy, etc. Nothing more.

To most government officials involved in tourism promotion in the early fifties, international tourism meant that some affluent people from rich countries with a lot of money and some curiosity (especially from the US) were willing to travel to foreign lands. It was recognised that the first preference of such people in North America would be Europe which they considered the cradle of Western civilisation. However, the retired and more affluent among them could be persuaded to take round-the-world trips either by ship or by air which sometimes included India. That was the India's target group in the fifties and sixties.

In North America, or for that matter in the entire Western world, India, if known at all, at that time had the image primarily of an exotic country — hot and humid, poor and backward, a land of snake charmers and rope walkers — an image which the British authors like Kipling had built up over the decades. The British rulers projected this image as they had to stand the heat of long summers in India to administer the country. Their families retired to the hills with cooks, bearers, nannies and gardeners and there was little attempt at meeting the people of India and understanding their rich culture.

In the early fifties, the government decided that India should have overseas offices to project a new image of the country as a tourist destination. The markets chosen were the USA, the UK followed by West Germany, France and Australia. These offices were essentially information offices whose job was to distribute and disseminate tourist information through brochures printed in India. In an effort to do everything in India, they forgot that their publicity material exported out of India was not attractive enough and of the best quality.

Although these offices were useful in projecting the new image of an independent India, some of the offices were perhaps opened a little too soon. For instance, an India tourist office was opened in Germany in 1957 at a time when the Germans had just undertaken travelling outside their country. They were not ready for India. It took them a decade before they began taking long distance holiday trips to countries like India and that too only when holidays to India became relatively inexpensive due to the introduction of charters and the cheaper inclusive group fares on scheduled carriers. Similarly, India opened a tourist office in Japan in 1964, when Japan first liberalised its foreign exchange restrictions and allowed the Japanese to take only three hundred dollars for travel overseas. But traffic from Japan to India remained static for five years as the Japanese did not think beyond the USA and Europe as their preferred holiday or business destinations. In Australia also, the story was more or less repeated as Australians started taking India holidays or stopovers on the way to Europe only in the early seventies. However, these tourist offices were useful in paving the way for tourism from these markets in later decades.

Modest advertising campaigns were launched by the tourist offices overseas within their limited resources. It was generally a well thought out activity undertaken on the advice of the professional advertising agencies hired by each tourist office locally to improve the image of India as a land of Ajanta-Ellora, the Taj Mahal, the Himalayas and Mahabalipuram. Cultural tourism relating to monuments and an ancient civilisation was the initial thrust of promotion as people in the Western world could more readily identify India with such an image. The frequency and the size of advertisements was inadequate. Advertisements were released mostly in black and white as colour advertising was considered too expensive. At the same time, tourist offices, however, established contacts with the tour-operators and travel agents to persuade them to send their clients to India.

Organised Marketing

Market planning in the fifties and the sixties was not really feasible because the base of Indian tourism was narrow. The resources for promotion were even more limited and, tourism being a new industry, personnel were not well-trained.

For preparing any successful marketing plan, we deal with four variables, popularly known in the marketing jargon as the four Ps.

Product: It means attractions or tourist resources that a country can offer — beautiful monuments, scenic beauty, beach and mountain resorts, transportation services, good hotel accommodation, polite and friendly people, etc.

Price: It implies the optimal rates at which the tourism product (holiday) can be sold.

Place: Most suitable distribution channels. In other words, the markets where the product should be sold and the network through which it is sold.

Promotion: It implies the communication process, public relations, advertising, promotion, etc.

To begin with, the Indian tourist 'product' had several drawbacks. The major shortcoming was the image. India did not enjoy the image of a holiday destination.

Indians were often shocked to see the results of surveys conducted by organisations like PATA showing India in a terribly bad light. Despite the shock the fact remained that India had an image problem about its tourist product everywhere, especially in the USA. The picture in Western Europe was not very different. In 1961, the London Observer questioned its readers where they were planning to spend their holidays in 1962. India

was not even mentioned among the first twelve popular destinations. A member of the Indian Parliament on return from England in 1966 quoted a placard shown in London which read:

Positive news came from Germany. In a survey carried out in the Federal Republic of Germany, the respondents were asked in the early sixties: 'If you could do as you liked, where would you go and what would you like to see and do most of all'? They were given the choice of twenty two places and activities; for example:

The Egyptian Pyramids

The ruins of ancient Greece

The skyscrapers of New York

The Kremlin in Moscow

The Hollywood film studios

A journey across the ocean in a sailing ship

To watch a nuclear explosion

The Isle of Capri

Paris

St. Peter's in Rome

Tour to India

Surprisingly, India was the most popular country outside the European continent.

The image problem was further complicated by the inadequacy of transport and hotel accommodation, both in quality and quantity. In 1967, the Director of the Government of India tourist office in San Francisco called on a major travel agency and the following conversation took place with the President of the company, with the President doing the most of the talking.

"Sir you have beautiful, colourful literature on India. I must compliment you on its production."

"Thank you very much. How is the business?"

"You have a great country with varied tourist attractions."

"Thank you again for saying that."

"You have a very nicely located office in a central place in San Francisco. Your staff is polite and efficient."

"Well you are making my day...."

"But, Sir, why don't you close down your office?"

"Now, tell me, why do you say that after paying me all these compliments this morning?"

"Better buy some planes for Indian Airlines for tourists. I cannot get confirmation on Indian Airlines for my clients for months. How can I sell India?" he asked. "Presently, what you need is capacity on Indian Airlines and not promotion. Close your shop and go back home," he advised.

This was duly reported to the Government of India, but the government had its own priorities. It was a time when Indian

Airlines had not bought its Boeings and Airbuses, and the capacity on most routes was limited.

No amount of marketing and promotion could help India with these constraints.

The Indian Airlines' capacity was increased in December 1970 when Boeing 737s were bought; later their fleet was augmented by the addition of more such planes and in 1988 and after by the purchase of 19 Airbuses. Despite these purchases, Indian Airlines' capacity did not catch up with the increasing demand. The situation is a little better today though popular tourist routes are still overcrowded during the season. By 1997, the Indian Airlines had more planes than pilots, and Indian Airlines fleet was underutilised— the other extreme.

The introduction of a Hotel Loan Development Fund in 1968 eased the accommodation situation somewhat. While marketing India's tourist product, price too was an important factor to be taken into consideration. Although India's tourist facilities were relatively inexpensive, the high airfares were a negative factor in the major tourist markets of the world. The majority of tourists to India come by air from long distances — an expensive way of travelling compared to road or rail travel as in Europe.

It would be seen that India's share in world tourism cannot be very large till there is a significant inter-regional movement. If the experience of other countries provides a clue, large-scale tourism cannot originate from long-distance markets. European countries and Canada, Mexico and the Carribbean receive a majority of their tourists from the neighbouring areas. East Asia — Thailand, Singapore, Hong Kong, the Philippines and Malaysia — receives a sizeable number of visitors from neighbouring countries. Till such time as India develops large-scale inter-regional traffic, it cannot have "mass tourism" or even tourism on a large-scale. Tense political relations and economic weaknesses of India's neighbours preclude any such possibility in the coming years.

Keeping in mind these factors, Indian advertising strategy in the sixties was essentially to tell American travellers they could break their journey in India on round-the-world tours, and to the Europeans that India was a home of a great civilisation, culture and architectural wonders. A market study conducted in the United States through the Stanford Research Institute in the early sixties revealed that Americans having an annual income of US $ 10,000 to 15,000 per year alone could afford to travel to India and in addition, only those who had a lot of intellectual curiosity. Indian advertising was, therefore, targeted to the people in this income bracket and among them also to those who had already travelled to Europe. (Now, the target group is with annual income of US$ 50,000) The headline of an advertisement released by the Government of India Tourist Office in New York in the mid-sixties read:

A Message

The text of one advertisement told the readers about the great attractions of Europe but advised them to see India if they had already seen Europe and wanted to see something more interesting and different. Till the end of the sixties, India's tourism promotional campaign was in response to the existing market conditions — a low profile approach to the rich and educated segment of the population.

Integrated Planning

It was only in 1967 that a separate Ministry of Tourism and Civil Aviation was created under a cabinet minister. Tourism, Civil Aviation and the various corporations relating to these activities came under the charge of this ministry. The results were amazing, and for the first time an integrated marketing plan was developed. Air India joined hands with the Department of Tourism in active promotion of India as a tourist destination. A new scheme called "Operation Europe" was launched in 1968 in Europe to, market Indian tourism. Air India not only made financial contributions to the promotional budget of the tourist offices, but also allotted targets to their field offices in Europe to sell Indian tourism. More tourist offices were opened in Europe as a result of this scheme. The tourist officers became "market oriented" and they started travelling extensively to meet tour-operators selling India in major markets. The scheme was considered successful and was later extended to all parts of the world. Indian Airlines, which had not actively advertised overseas, also joined by allocating a modest budget for overseas promotion through travel trade press.

The new advertising strategy had an element of aggressive selling. Price became an important element in the advertising text to draw customers to India. The idea was to dispel the misgiving that the prices of Indian tours must be high and not within the reach of most people. An attempt was made to project India as a destination by itself and affordable too. Given below are some of the headlines of the advertisements released in 1967 and after:

The Taj Mahal is in India it is not India : The objective was to inform people about many attractions of India other than the Taj in the great subcontinent of India. A similar approach was directed towards trade advertising. An advertisement in 1968 said:

Ten Wonders of India Check the ones your Clients have Missed : The text described the ten wonders of India as Ajanta-Ellora, the Shaking Minarets of Ahmedabad, Khajuraho, Gir Lion Sanctuary, Tiger Shikar (it was not banned at that time), Sun Temple of Konarak, Kashmir, Cochin, Darjeeling and Goa.

Price, as mentioned earlier, became an important factor in Indian advertising from 1969 onwards. Special excursion and group fares had been introduced from USA and Europe which made Indian tourist packages attractive and competitive. For instance, India could offer package tours from Japan to India cheaper than the European and US tour packages. In Europe, India started marketing inexpensive tours at almost the price of charter tours. In 1969, an advertisement in the USA proclaimed:

India Give-Away 17 Days $ 799 The Text Ran : "If you thought a holiday in India was an expensive affair, we would like to give you a surprise."

A year later, India was publicising tours ranging from $ 654 for seventeen days to $ 1,757 for twenty-five days including Nepal and Sikkim. The above theme was adopted to meet the changing requirements of the new class of visitors—the budget conscious travellers. Tourist offices kept a list of tours marketed by various tour-operators abroad with departure dates. These lists were mailed to people who wrote to tourist offices for information. The idea was to support the marketing efforts of tour operators and to enable the potential tourist to make a quick decision in the choice of his holiday. A favourable climate for India was developing as far as tourism was concerned.

However, the old theme was not forgotten Expo'70 was held in Tokyo in 1970. To take advantage of the flow of traffic to Japan because of this trade fair, the India tourist office ran the following advertisement in the USA:

After Expo'70 and before Europe see India : The Government of India tourist office in Tokyo followed up this theme by opening a tourist information booth in the Indian pavilion at Expo'70 and distributed millions of pieces of tourism literature in Japanese and other languages.

India carried out a market survey in 1961-62, 1964-65 followed by 1972-73 on the behavioural pattern of foreign tourist traffic. The survey revealed that destination traffic to India had risen from 43.2 per cent in 1961 to 73.6 per cent in 1972-73 and the indications were that more people would come to India for a destinational holiday if right conditions were created. The market planners in India re-oriented their thinking on promotion towards developing the Indian tourist product with a new focus on beach and mountain resorts, supported by cultural tourism which is in abundance all over India. Air India helped by establishing promotional air fares through IATA from several tourist generating markets taking multi-stopover requirements into account.

Europe/India GIT had relatively a low discount of thirty four per cent, but this was because high proration was involved on domestic sectors. For instance, the GIT fare for routing Paris-Mumbai-Delhi-Srinagar-Varanasi-Kathmandu-Patna-Calcutta-Madras-Trivandrum-Cochin-Bangalore-Hyderabad-Mumbai-Paris cost F.Fr. 4,670 in 1976 of which the international carrier was eventually left with F.Fr. 2,447 for the Paris-Bombay-Paris sector. Simultaneously, separate promotional fares were established allowing higher discount of fifty seven per cent on point-to-point journey for Europe-India GIT, since the proration was nil.

In 1983, there was a free for all battle of airfares in European countries. In order to corner a larger share of the market, most airlines offered discounted fares. So the tourist traffic to India did not decline from Europe in spite of the overall recession. Europeans preferred India at that time over destinations like Hong Kong, Thailand and Singapore.

Taking advantage of stopover facilities under long distance IATA fares, the Government of India tourist office in Tokyo ran an advertisement all over East Asia with those headlines.

India's Nine Cities are Included Free in your Ticket to Europe/ USA : The text told the travellers that they could easily break journey in India as no extra fare was involved and that land arrangements could be made for ten to twenty five dollars a day depending upon one's requirements. The advertisement was so effective that a number of foreign carriers complained to the India tourist office that their workload had increased as making tickets with too many stopovers was not only a complicated job but also a risky one for them, as they could lose their clients to a competing airline.

With a little more confidence in selling India, the tourist offices settled down to diversify their product by spreading more extensive knowledge of India's tourist attractions. The theme changed to the variety that was India. A concerted drive was made to move traffic from the traditional golden triangle of Delhi-Agra-Jaipur to Kashmir in the North, and Southern and Eastern India. A study conducted in the USA in 1974 through the Opinion Research Corporation of USA regarding the new profile of the visitor to India summed up the profile of the potential American travellers to India in the following words:

Historically, travellers to India have come mainly from an elite group — people of wealth, with time for extensive travel, and often from the older age brackets or retired. A further distinguishing characteristic of this traditional, "quality" source of visitors has been relatively high frequency of foreign travel. Quite logically, frequent travellers are good prospects for India because they have been to a number of countries and are ready to see another one. This research confirmed the importance of the frequent traveller as good potential for India. There is every reason to continue to woo him/her through travel agents, advertising and other appropriate means.

Indian research identified another important group, perhaps not too well recognised hitherto — young travellers (18-29 years age group). While continuing to market Indian travel aggressively to the older market of frequent travellers, Indian tourism may well wish to direct additional marketing effort to the young potential group.

The newer potential group — young travellers — are a large group of prospects, relatively affluent, interested in India, and compatible in their thinking with the things India offers and requires of its visitors.

To broad base the market on the basis of identification of potential American travellers, the Indian tourist office in the USA, ran the diary of a traveller to India who tells his experience in the form of a series of advertisements. A new slogan was coined:

Another World

India was now being offered as a complete tourist product and experience, and not as a stopover point or part of a total tourist product. The Diary of a Traveller to India describes Kerala, Mysore, Madras, Kashmir, Khajuraho, Konark, Bhubaneshwar, Calcutta, etc. The readers of leading magazines were told in an Indian advertisements in 1974:

When you Visit Our Land, do not Rush about it take it Slowly. Let India happen to you : In 1975, advertisements were released to project a composite image of modern and ancient India. An advertisement proclaimed:

India is not for you if you want our past but not our Future : Similarly, travel agents were advised in trade magazines.

When you are Selling our Past Centuries do not Forget the Twentieth : Here, the 'copy' tells readers about facilities in India for golfing, skiing, modern hotels, bird watching, adventure, etc.

Promotional approach has to vary from market to market. UK citizens have a little better knowledge of India than the Americans. The Government of India tourist office in London conducted a survey to know what constituted potential market for tourism to India in that country. The Economist Intelligence Unit Ltd. (E.I.U.), London, which carried out the study, gave the following conclusion in 1974:

> The Indian tourist product, though heavy in parts, is not unsaleable, but is not being actively and effectively sold by the travel trade.

Marketing and promotional activities can counter any image problems by creating the picture of India as a fashionable place to spend a holiday, thereby stimulating IT (Inclusive Tour) holiday demand to India.

The most appropriate form of promotion likely to influence the short-term potential traveller is direct, face-to-face contact. For the long-term potential traveller an information and advertising programme through the mass media is likely to have more impact.

It's currently available to India to fulfil market requirements, but there exist opportunities for tourists to be sold on:

A. A theme basis like special interests.

B. On itineraries taking in Kashmir, the South and the beach resorts of Goa and Kovalam.

To follow up on the study, the tourist office in USA ran educational advertisements with headlines like:

Wherever you go in India you will find our People are all the Same : This colour advertisement carried a dozen photographs of the people of India from different regions in different costumes providing an interesting contrast. Another one had the headline:

Any Traveller to India always Comes Back Richer : The text tells the people about India's spiritual heritage. Other advertisements focused on beach resorts, mountain holidays, trekking and outdoor activities.

Arab countries—especially the Gulf States—had become potential tourist markets for India. At that time, the Arabs were mainly interested in Mumbai for shopping or for an interesting city life. India's market planners wanted to send them to areas beyond Mumbai. Advertisements were designed to bring forth new themes in the eighties. Some of these were North of Bombay.

Taj Mahal is only one of India's Thousand Wonders South of Bombay Fresh New Excitement awaits you : This advertisement referred to the tourist attractions of South India. A third one sold Kashmir in winter.

India projected "Unbelievable India" theme in North America, focusing also on Gandhi's India taking advantage of the better awareness of this country created through the film Gandhi.

For Business Travellers : In the nineties, the Department of Tourism in India realised the importance of business travel, especially from areas from where new investments were coming. An interesting advertising campaign was launched by the Government of India Tourist Office, Singapore, to attract business travellers and to tempt them with other opportunities for holiday / vacation during their business trips. Some of the headlines.

Favourable Tourism Climate at Home : The plan of integrated promotion included creation of a climate favourable to tourism at home. Since 1967, the Department of Tourism ran educational advertisements in the national press, both in English and in Indian languages, with slogans like: Tourism is the world's biggest industry. What are we doing about it?

Tourism is Everybody's Business : Both advertisements conveyed the message to the Indian readers that tourism was a major economic activity and that people should be courteous and nice to tourists and send them back happy and satisfied. A slogan was coined which went with all advertisements in the series: This was also part of a message given by the late Prime Minister Jawaharlal Nehru.

Welcome a Visitor - Send Back a Friend : The Department of Tourism advertising also laid emphasis on courtesy, cleanliness, helpfulness, etc., as tourist attractions. Example:

Joint Promotions with Industry : All these promotional efforts had the support of the travel industry. Hoteliers and travel agents joined hands in carrying the message of the government advertisements to Indian readers. To support India's marketing effort, the PATA (India) chapter was set up in 1969 as an Indian branch of the Pacific Asia Travel Association. It consists of PATA members from India who are active in the travel industry. The

Department of Tourism, India Tourism Development Corporation, Air India, Indian Airlines and other international carriers, major hotel chains and leading hotels are members of this organisation and make financial contributions for promotional work. During the last 30 years, the chapter has sponsored the visit of several travel industry teams overseas for holding promotional seminars. The chapter has a Publicity and Promotion Committee which determines the promotional themes to be projected in a different market before such travel industry teams take off.

Another helpful factor in India's tourist marketing was the emergence of major chains of Indian hotels like Oberoi's, the Taj Group, Welcomgroup and the Ashok Group, etc. Most of them have competent promotional managers who have been marketing their products with outstanding audio-visual presentations. Leading travel agencies like TCI, SITA, Mercury, Trade Wings, etc., have also produced films and audio-visual presentations. India has benefited from such worldwide promotions undertaken by these organisations. They have worked closely with the Government of India tourist offices and Air India offices overseas. The climate has improved further by training programmes conducted by the Department of Tourism for guides, tourism personnel, etc. PATA (India) chapter also started Tourism Research and Awareness Programme to create a favourable climate for tourism within the country stressing its significance and economic importance to influence the opinion makers in the country — members of Parliament, ministers, politicians and administrators.

Unfortunately, the programme has since been forgotten—at least for the time being.

A hopeful sign about Indian tourism is that those involved in it have a pride in their 'product' and have a sense of involvement with their profession. This has been, perhaps, the one reason for the success of India's tourism marketing efforts —' in spite of heavy odds. '

Indian tourism has grown reasonably well during the last four decades in line with the normal growth in world tourism. No extraordinary spurt has taken place in Indian tourism because of various factors.

The 1996 arrivals at 2.3 million — an average stay of 28 nights and an average expenditure of Rs. 35,000 per visitor—earned India US $ 2.5 billion.

Indian tourism, like other countries, suffers from seasonality factor — more visitors coming during cooler months of October to March and a lot less coming during summer months. During busy months, hotel rooms are in short supply while in the off-season, hotels are half empty. The gap has been reduced to some extent by the influx of business travellers coming due to a favourable business climate as a result of the liberalisation of the Indian economy in the nineties.

India cannot be a mass tourist destination due to its distance from principal tourist markets of Europe, USA, Japan and Australia. Airfares, therefore, are high. The influx of tourists from the neighbouring SAARC region is negligible as the economy of these countries is not doing well.

It is not fair to compare Indian tourism to countries like Hong Kong and Singapore in terms of numbers with that of India. The average stay of visitors to these countries is very small compared to India's — 28 days. However, it is not to suggest that India cannot improve its tourism profile. The government is trying to attract more visitors by upgrading the infrastructure and improving facilities to international levels. A target of 5 million arrivals was set for the year 1997, the last year of the Eighth Five Year Plan and earnings of US $ 5 billion in a year. The targets were too high and unachievable as has been proved.

India was the first country of Asia to set up Government Tourist Offices in London and New York as early as 1952, but the Government did not have a clear concept of matching promotion with the availability of good hotel accommodation and domestic and international air capacity. Since the opening of promotional tourist offices overseas, the domestic and international air transportation as well as hotel accommodation has not kept pace with the arrivals. Indian tourism has therefore, suffered from chronic shortages.

However, the overseas tourist offices of India took tourism promotion seriously and tried to take advantage of opportunities that the market offered. First, it was to woo the round-the-world travellers who were persuaded to stop briefly in India on their round-the-world trips followed by appeal to those Americans who had been to Europe several times to discover India. In the seventies, the market planners focused on holiday tourism as facilities were available for a beach holiday at Goa, Kovalam,

Mahabalipuram and a mountain holiday in the Himalayas. Integrated marketing commenced with the establishment of a separate Ministry of Tourism and Civil Aviation in 1968. Air India and the Department of Tourism were persuaded to join hands in promoting tourism all over the world. The travel industry, through PATA (India) chapter, has been regularly sponsoring travel industry missions to several parts of the world to spread the good word about India. Now, in the nineties, the focus is on the business traveller, telling him that India is good for business as well as all other forms of holiday. The new approach is yielding results.

10

Element of Distribution

Travel agency sector is the distributor element in the travel and tourism marketing system. It can be considered to be a link between the producers of various travel services like tour operators, airline companies, transport operators and hoteliers on the one hand and their customers on the other. In other words, travel agents bring buyers and sellers together with a view to creating markets in places where these did not exist or to make existing markets more user friendly and efficient in order to expand the overall size of the travel market.

Today, the travel agent has become an important, integral, part of the travel and tourism industry world wide. Majority of people are using the services of travel agents for organising their travel both international as well as domestic. It is estimated that worldwide almost 70% of all international travel and 45% of all domestic travel are arranged by the travel agents. The figure however, may vary from country to country. The important role of the travel agent in the modern world is summarised in the principles of professional conduct and ethics of the American Society of Travel Agents. The role of travel agents in summarised as follows :

> "We live in a world in which travel has become increasingly important and complex in its variety of modes and choices. Travellers are faced with a myriad alternatives as to transportation, accommodation and other travel services. They must depend on travel agencies and others in the industry to guide them honestly and competently."

Sale of Product

The main function of a travel agency is the product sale. Product sale is very complex subject specially when the product happens to be a tourist product. Because of the special nature of the tourist product and the multiplicity of manufacturers of the product, selling assumes greater importance. In addition, the distribution channels through which the tourist product finds its way to the consumers are multiple and varied. The tourist product, consists mainly of attractions, transport and accommodation. The producers of elements of the above products include air, sea, road transport companies and carriers, hotels and other forms of accommodation units, and the organisations which are responsible for putting together attractions both natural and man-made.

In most of the countries product sale is conducted through a distribution system controlled mostly by a network of retail travel agents, tour operators and wholesalers. The individual elements of a tourist product like international air tickets, domestic air or train tickets are also mostly sold through agents or representatives of airlines and railway companies, and purchased directly by consumers. The consumers have, therefore, a choice between direct booking and using the services of an agent. In addition, there are alternative channels available to the consumers through which they may buy their tourism products. These channels include clubs and societies, mail order, travel shops in supermarkets and departmental stores, tourist fairs and exhibitions and, more recently, electronic booking methods like computers.

Historical Backdrop

Any discussion on sale and organisation of travel must begin with the pioneer named Thomas Cook. The history of the business of the present Thomas Cook Group Limited can be traced back to over 150 years to its founder Thomas Cook, who not only was the first organised Travel Agent in the world, but who, it could be said, invented the travel business. A book salesman, a baptist preacher of Derbyshire was on his way to a temperance meeting in Leicester when he was inspired with "the idea of engaging a special train to carry the friends of temperance from Leicester to Loughborough in England and back to attend a quarterly delegate meeting." He thought that it was a sounder proposition to persuade a railway company, then in its infancy, to carry a train load of passengers at a very cheap fare than to run the train at 'standard' fares, but possibly only a quarter full. The man was Thomas Cook and his idea was put into operation with characteristic speed and efficiency. A few weeks later 570 travellers made the journey by the Midland Counties Railway at a specially reduced fare. This venture was soon followed by excursions to various other places, and in 1843, 3,000 school children were taken on a trip from Leicester to Derby in England.

Thomas Cook's real beginning as 'mass excursionist' was, however, the Liverpool-Caernaryon trip of 1845. The tourists travelled by rail to Liverpool, from where they took a steamer to Caernaryon. The advertisements for the trip caused a sensation and the response was so overwhelming that a second trip had to be arranged. Cook thought of every detail. He made a preliminary survey of accommodation and facilities and produced a handbook of the trip to Liverpool. The excursionist invasion of Scotland soon followed in 1846 and 1847. From 1848 to 1863 Cook conducted circular tours of Scotland, with 5,000 tourists a season. With the citadels of the landed aristocracy falling before him, he saw more enticing prospects opening before him: "I had become so thoroughly imbued with the tourist spirit that I began to contemplate Foreign Trips, including the continent of Europe, the United States and the Eastern land of the Bible."

Circular Tour

By the mid-nineteenth century 'Holidays away from home' had become customary for a larger social group than ever before. Cook's initiative and organising genius provided the final impetus.

In the winter of 1850-51, Cook was already negotiating for a tour of America, but his attention was diverted when he was offered the opportunity of conducting excursion trains to the Great Exhibition of 1851. Altogether, Cook conducted 1,65,000 people to and from the Crystal Palace. In 1856, Cook succeeded in organising his First grand circular tour of the continent. The tour was so successful that it had to be repeated six weeks later.

Thomas Cook's conquest of Europe began in 1862 when he made arrangements with Brighton and South Coast Railway for passenger traffic to the continent. Cook's Paris excursions are the first true 'package tours'; all the details of transport and accommodation were pre-arranged. In 1863 Cook visited Switzerland where his ideas were greeted with enthusiasm by hoteliers and railway proprietors. His next stop was Italy. Cook first made a personal survey of Turin, Milan, Florence and Genoa, to familiarise himself with their touristic attractions and facilities. In 1864 the first guided tour of Italy left England with applications far in excess of the available tickets. The 1860s also saw the introduction of Cook's 'railway and hotel coupons'. Cook personally examined the system by travelling through Italy to Vienna, down the Danube into Hungary and from there into Switzerland. By the 1890s, 1,200 hotels throughout the world accepted his coupons. Starting in 1868 Cook arranged regular circular tours of Switzerland and Northern Italy.

The first official London Office of Thomas Cook and Sons was established in 1865. John Mason Cook now joined his father as a permanent partner and took charge of the London office. From that year on, the history of Thomas Cook and Sons was one of continuous expansion. In the year 1880 John Mason Cook left for India and established offices in Bombay and Calcutta and formed the 'Eastern Princes' Department. In 1887 this department arranged the visits of Indian princes to Queen Victoria's Jubilee Celebrations.

By taking advantage of nineteenth century advances in transport technology, Thomas Cook and Sons had effected a revolution in tourism by the end of the century. No longer the preserve of the rich and the aristocrats, tourism was now an industry. Armed with Cook's hotel and rail coupons, the tourist could demand uniform prices and standards of service and accommodation. This new standardisation had distinct advantages. It meant comfort and convenience and less need for decision making on the part of the individual tourist. The tourist was less likely to experience discomfort or embarrassment.

The management of the Company passed on to John Mason Cook's three sons in the year 1898. At the time of John Mason Cook's death, the business included three main aspects of travel -selling tours, banking and shipping. Soon after the Second World War, the British government acquired the principal interest in the Company. In the year 1972, the British Government sold the company to Midland Bank Consortium.

Today, Thomas Cook Group is the parent company of a worldwide group of companies which are partially or wholly owned. The company also has a close trading relationship with Companie International des Wagon-Lits et Tourism, and the combined worldwide network of these companies, together with their authorised agents. The company also introduced traveller's cheques which were originally called 'circular notes'. Members of the Thomas Cook Group of companies now issue cheques as principals in different currencies and are associated with partner banks in various countries. It is also a large trader in the buying and selling of foreign currency bank notes. Thomas Cook Group Limited today provides a wide range of services to its customers in over 150 countries worldwide through their network of over 1,200 outlets. The company is considered to be one of the largest travel companies selling a wide range of travel services.

Much has changed since the year 1841, when Thomas Cook chartered a train to carry 570 travellers at a specially reduced fare from Leicester to Loughborough in England. Cook, who bought the railway tickets in bulk and resold them to members of his group, can be credited with being the first bona fide travel agent to work as a full-time professional. However, neither Thomas Cook & Sons, nor American Express Company or Cox and Kings were then a retail agent as the modern complex distribution chain had not yet evolved in any trade including travel.

Scope and Sphere

The scope and the role of the travel agency was limited in the beginning since mass tourism as we know it today had not yet begun. It was, however, the introduction of the air travel which gave a boost to the travel agency business. The introduction of an economy class by various airline companies crossing the North Atlantic heralded the era of travel agency and was responsible for their growth. The introduction of an 'economy class' in effect was nothing more than a projection of Thomas Cook's original idea of adjusting prices to encourage full capacity use of every means of transport.

Rapid development of transport system, especially the jet travel, improved living standards combined with reduction in working hours is the root cause of today's upward surge in travel. Side by side with the rapid improvements in industry and technology, practically all aspects of life have become more and more complex particularly during the past half a century. This is certainly the case in the travel industry in which, only a century ago, the job consisted almost entirely of arranging a simple reservation for the travellers in some means of transport. Today the functions and duties of a person at the travel agency counter are vastly different and more varied. He is now called upon to perform a variety of duties rather than just issue tickets and reserve seats in a train, aeroplane or accommodation in the hotel. Travel today is no longer the privilege of the few, but is sought by millions. No longer does the travel agency exist for the sole purpose of selling tickets from one point to another. The travel industry developed along certain well-defined lines as the worldwide demand on its services increased. The urge to travel became very intense over the years resulting in wide-spread growth of travel agencies in the world. Most of the travellers wished to have their travel arrangements made in advance and to be relieved of the difficulties of coping with various pre-travel arrangements of which they had only a very limited knowledge.

Modern Concept

Over the years the range and activities of a retail travel agent have increased manifold. In the modern context, the role of a travel agent is rather different to that of most of other retailers selling merchandise. The travel agent does not purchase travel with a view to reselling the same to its customers. It is only when a customer has finally decided on the purchase of travel that the agent approaches the principal on behalf of his customer. The retail travel agent, unlike most other retailers, does not carry an inventory or stock of travel products in his premises.

The main role of retail travel agents is to provide to their customers a convenient location for the "purchase" of various elements of travel like transport, accommodation and several other ancillary services associated with holiday and travel. The travel agents act as booking agents for holidays and travel and disseminate information and give advice on such services. This role can be summed up as follows:

(i) to give advice to the potential tourist on the merits of alternative destinations, and

(ii) to make necessary arrangements for a chosen holiday which may involve booking of accommodation, transport or other relevant services associated with his travel.

A travel agent, in order to give an advice to his potential customers on the merits of a destination, must possess knowledge, expertise and up-to-date information about that destination. Besides, a travel agent has close contacts with providers of services, i.e., their principals from whom they purchase services for their customers. In other words, a retail travel agent is an intermediary providing a direct link between the consumer and the suppliers of tourist services, i.e.., airlines, transport companies, hotels, auto rental companies, etc. The retail agent is the one who acts on behalf of the principal, i.e., the original provider of tourist service such as an airline company, hotel company, shipping company, insurance company, railways or a tour operator. An agent sells the principal's services and is rewarded by a commission.

The Operations

The scope and range of travel agency operations would depend on the size of an agency. If the company is large in size, the range of activities will be more comprehensive. In this case the agency will have specialised departments, each having to perform different functions. To deal with the subject of a travel agency, the best method of approach is, perhaps, to consider its functions. These may be broadly classified as follows:

Information Provision

One of the primary functions of a retail travel agent from the point of view of the tourist or the general public is to provide necessary information about travel. This information is provided at a convenient location where the intending tourist may ask certain questions and seek clarifications about his proposed travel. This is a very specialised job and the person behind the counter should be a specialist having excellent knowledge of various travel alternative plans. He should be in a position to give up-to-date and accurate information regarding various services and general information about travel, etc. The presentation to the potential customer must be forceful, and exciting variations must continually be devised to help sell tours. A good travel agent is something of a personal counsellor who knows all the details about the travel and also the needs and interests of the intending traveller. Communication plays a key role in dissemination of any type of information. This is equally true in the case of dissemination of travel information. The person behind the travel counter should be able to communicate with the customer in his language. The knowledge of foreign languages is an essential prerequisite for personnel working in a travel agency.

The Itineraries

Tourist itinerary is a composition of a series of operations that are a result of the study of the market. A tourist journey is characterised by an itinerary using various means of transport to link one locality with another. Preparation of different types of itineraries is another important function of a travel agency. A travel agent gives advice to intending travellers on the type of programmes which they may choose for their holiday or business travel. The study and the realisation of the itineraries call for perfect organisation (technical and administrative) as also knowledge of the desires of the public for a holiday and the propensity to receive tourists by the receiving localities.

Liaison with Providers of Services : Before any form of travel can be sold over the counter to a customer, contracts have to be entered into with the providers of various services. These include transportation companies, hotel proprietors, the providers of surface transport like motor cars or coaches for transfer to and from hotels and for sightseeing, etc., and also for general servicing requirements. The work carried out under these headings is usually that of the owners or senior employees of agencies concerned. In the case of a large agency with worldwide branches, the liaison work involves a great deal of coordination with the principals.

The Planning

Once the contracts and arrangements have been entered into, there comes the task of planning and costing tours, both for inclusive programmes and to meet individual requirements. This job is intensely interesting and at the same time challenging. It calls for a great deal of initiative and drive, for travel to those places which are to be included in the itineraries. Paradoxically many of those who do this type of work visit comparatively few of the places included in the itineraries they prepare. This is essentially a job for a meticulous person and calls for considerable training and ability. Many agencies, with the cooperation of airlines and other transportation companies, take the opportunity of arranging educational tours for such staff to destinations with which they deal.

Many large agencies have experts who are authorities on particular countries and, in addition to a general programme, many will issue separate programmes dealing with specific territories. Separate programmes, dealing with holiday offers based on specific forms of transportation, e.g., air, rail, road or sea, may also be prepared. Programmes also have to be prepared to cover different seasons of the year.

Publicity is an important part of the programme. Having spent considerable time and money on preparing all that goes into the issue of a programme, publicity must feature considerably in the activities of a travel agency and more so if the agency happens to be a large one. The majority of large travel agencies have their own publicity departments under the management of an expert in the publicity field.

Ticketing : Selling tickets to clients using different modes of transport like air, rail and sea is yet another important function of a travel agency. This calls for a thorough knowledge of schedules of various modes of transport. Air carriers, railways and steamship companies have hundreds of schedules and the person behind the counter should be conversant with all these. Ticketing is, however, not an easy job as the range and diversity of international airfares is very complex and varied. There are several different types of fare combinations on the North Atlantic route alone. Changes in international as also in the local air schedules and additions of new flights from time to time makes the job of the travel agent one of constant challenge. An up-to-date knowledge about various schedules of air companies, steamship companies and railways is very essential.

Computerised reservation system has in recent years rather revolutionised the reservation system, both for air and rail seats, and also a room in a hotel. Many large travel agencies are using this system. This system comprises a computer network that can be used by the travel agent to reserve an air or rail accommodation as also accommodation in a hotel. Through a wide network, confirmation of reservations are available in a matter of seconds.

Settlement of Accounts : Linked with the function of ticketing and reservation of accommodation in a hotel is the settlement of accounts of the clients. Accountancy plays an important part and is one of the major duties to be performed by the travel agency. Dealing with the settlement of accounts in all parts of the world calls for a thorough knowledge of foreign currencies, their cross-values and, above all, the intricacies of exchange control regulations, which vary from country to country.

Provision of Foreign Currencies : Provision of foreign currencies to intending travellers is another specialised activity of a travel agency. Some of the larger travel agencies deal exclusively in the provision of foreign currencies, travellers' cheques, etc. This is an important facility to intending travellers as it saves them a lot of time and energy in avoiding visits to regular banking channels.

Insurance : Insurance, both for personal accident risks and of baggage, is yet another important activity of the travel agency. Some of the larger travel agents maintain sizeable shipping and forwarding departments, aimed at assisting the traveller, to transport personal effects and baggage to any part of the world, with a minimum of inconvenience.

The multifarious activities mentioned in the above paragraphs show that the travel agency's range of services in modern times has expanded a great deal. The field of expertise is quite large and is constantly growing with the fast changing travel needs of the people. The job description of a modern travel agency can be summed up as follows :

(i) Preparation of individual pre-planned itineraries, personally escorted tours and group tours and sale of pre-paid package tours.

(ii) Making arrangements for hotels, motels, resort accommodation, meals, car rentals, sightseeing, transfer of passengers and luggage between terminals and hotels, and special features such as music festivals and theatre tickets.

(iii) Handling of and giving advice on the many details involved in modern day travel, e.g., travel and baggage insurance, language study material, travellers' cheques, foreign currency exchange, documentary requirements (visas and passport) and health requirements (immunisation and inoculations).

(iv) Possession of professional knowledge and experience, as for instance, schedules of air and train connections, rates of hotels, their quality, whether rooms have baths, etc. All of this is information on which the traveller, but for the travel agent, will spend days or weeks of endless phone calls, letters and personal visits.

(v) Arrangement of reservations for special interest activities such as conventions, conferences, and business meetings and sports events, etc.

Travel Organisation

There are various activities which a travel agency has to perform in order that an intending traveller undertakes his proposed journey and enjoys a holiday of his choice. There are various steps involved from the time a traveller visits a travel agent to buy a ticket until he returns home after visiting a place of his choice.

Organised travel by a travel agency can be of two types, i.e. (i) single client, and (ii) group client. In order to effect the journey, the following main elements (in both types of travel) need to be considered:

(a) Study of the journey,

(b) Estimate of expenditure,

(c) Execution of the journey, and

(d) Presentation of accounts.

Individual or Ordinary Trips : The following steps are involved in organising individual or ordinary trips:

(i) The client turns to the travel agent to organise for him a particular journey (cultural, natural, business, religious, etc.).

(ii) The agency from this angle will examine as to what will be involved, e.g., scope of journey, when the journey is to take place, various services needed and the accessories required.

(iii) Based on the above evaluation and other elements in his possession, the travel agent will suggest an itinerary and will then communicate to the client the estimated maximum cost for the client's approval.

(iv) The travel agent will then compile the definite estimates, a total of a series of various costs added up, e.g., transport, accommodation, the services such as those of guides, operative costs such as (postage, telex, telefax, E-Mail, telephones, etc.).

(v) The travel agent then will present a document of the amount of money to be paid in duplicate to the customer.

The client returns one of the debit copies signed on acceptance accompanied with a deposit (in anticipation). The deposit normally is about 25 per cent of the total cost.

(vi) Once the client's approval has been obtained, the travel agent's operation department then executes the journey.

(vii) The 'operation' department's task now is to book for the established dates the transport and various other services. After the booking confirmation has been received, the travel agent issues the vouchers.

(viii) The travel agent prepares the 'tourist itinerary' which will accompany the client through the entire journey. It will indicate the tickets to be used, the hotels and other services booked and will include vouchers, etc. Normally the itinerary is made in triplicate: one for the client, another for the agency and the third for the hotelier or those who will provide the required services paid by means of vouchers.

(ix) The last formality is the delivery to the client of the vouchers, confirmed tickets, the technical itinerary.

(x) When the group is particularly large, e.g., for sports, etc., the travel agent needs to take extra care by way of informing public authorities for purposes of security, etc.

Travel agents in a highly developed market cover all the above activities and range of services which depends upon the extent of the economic development of that country. The travel patterns of the population in advanced countries are different as compared to those in developing countries. The services of travel agents are increasingly utilised in developed countries. In some of the advanced countries like the USA, Canada, Germany and Japan a very large percentage of tourists are utilising the services of travel agents.

Role of Tour Operator

The dramatic growth of tourist traffic to the Mediterranean countries of Europe is a principal feature of the history of mass tourism in the last forty years. A major contributing factor in this growth of air travel holiday tourism has been the development of 'inclusive tour', a method of packaging a holiday. The idea of buying a package of travel, accommodation and perhaps some ancillary services such as entertainment etc., became established in Western Europe in the 1960s. Essentially an 'inclusive tour' is a package of transport and accommodation and perhaps some other service which is sold as a single holiday for an all inclusive price. This inclusive price is usually significantly lower than could be obtained by conventional methods of booking transport and accommodation separately from individual hotel and transport tariffs. The principal feature of the inclusive tour is that the tourist may buy, for a single price, a holiday which is much cheaper than would be possible for the holiday maker if he bought the components of his holiday separately and directly from individual hotels and from transport companies or from a retail travel agent.

The chief functionary or the principal in this system is the tour operator. It is the tour operator who buys aircraft seats and hotel beds and certain other facilities such as surface transport or entertainment and makes up the package. Historically, the tour operator has mostly emerged from retail travel agency. However, today a clear distinction must be made between tour operator and a travel agent. The latter, the retail travel agent, undertakes to sell the travel services of his principal, who will be airline companies and other transport undertakings, hotel groups, shipping lines and the providers of such ancillary services as traveller's cheques, etc. Unlike the travel agent who is the retailer of the tourism product, the tour operator is a manufacturer of a tourism product. He plans, organises and sells tours. The tour operator makes all the necessary arrangements - transport, accommodation, sight-seeing, insurance, entertainment and other matters and sells this package for an all-inclusive price. A package tour is designed to fit a particular group of travellers. These may be special interest tours, i.e., mountain tours and can be escorted. Escorted tour normally includes transportation, meals, sightseeing, accommodation, guide services, etc. It is the escort or the group leader who is responsible for maintaining the schedule of the tour and for looking after all the arrangements.

Group Inclusive Tour (GIT) : This is the most popular form of tour in this category where people travel in groups of 15 or more persons. These tours are available for any destination. The terms and conditions for group inclusive tours are laid down by IATA. The escort for such groups normally travels free as the airline provides him with free passage and accommodation. "Foreign Inclusive Tours' (FIT) on the other hand are unescorted package tours. These tours are comparatively more flexible. The traveller can buy a predetermined package with arrangements for sightseeing, hotels and certain meals, where necessary. He does not tour with a group. He can make his own arrangements and programmes according to his liking. The inclusive tour is one of the several devices which enable tourists to enjoy the lower prices.

How does the tour operator manage to sell the package to the traveller at such a low price? The low price of the package holiday or inclusive tour is made possible by reason of the lower unit costs obtainable both for the air travel and for the hotel accommodation. The tour operator enters into long-term contracts for aircraft seats and similar contracts with hotels for booking rooms. By mass-producing holidays in the form of package tours, the tour operators are able to procure substantial discounts from carriers, hoteliers, etc. and offer their package deals at much lower rates. The profits of the tour operators and the success of his operations, however, depend on achieving of very high load factors for the aircraft and very high occupancy rates for the hotel. In this way, unit costs can be maintained sufficiently low to enable the tour operator to offer his package at a price which is often less than the cheapest available fare alone. A breakthrough in the business of tour operation came when airlines recognised that tour operation can fill the empty seats and introduced special fares for use exclusively by tour operators for combining into an inclusive tour.

The tour operator has thus emerged as the true manufacturer of the inclusive tour product packaged, standardised and mass-produced. The tour operator may sell this product directly to the public or through the channels of the retail travel agencies. It can be marketed successfully in the tourist generating countries to a mass market just because it is standardised, packaged and quality controlled. The product is therefore susceptible to the similar marketing techniques that are applied to the marketing of consumer goods.

The Guidelines

The agent's role in handling a client is very important. Once a client enters the agency it becomes necessary for an agent to properly anticipate his needs and requirements. The client also has come with a predetermined notion about a destination he is visiting. WATA, the World Association of Travel Agencies, has prepared comprehensive guidelines for handling a client. These guidelines are based on the WATA Master-Key, an annual publication of the World Association of Travel Agencies. Updated and published yearly, the WATA Master-Key is a selectively comprehensive source of travel information. Individual agency tariffs given in the publication, represent the selling tool for members, incoming and outgoing services. Along with the tariffs the Master-Key gives a country description sheet containing a wealth of useful background information of a destination. In addition, the Master-Key also gives detailed information about some hotels located in important cities and tourist centres together with prevalent confidential tariffs and other relevant information for travel agencies.

The WATA Master-Key is a valuable reference material for travel agents. Its presentation makes it easy for the users to extract the information they need. The guidelines as enumerated in the Master-Key are as follows:

Sale of Tour : It should first be determined whether the client who wants to book a tour prefers to:

a. Join an escorted tour, or
b. Choose a FIT, combining leisure and activity according to his individual tastes and interests.

FIT/Your Relations with Client : If your client wants a "tailor made" tour, let him make the suggestions, without imposing your own views, on the following points:

Itinerary

1. Determine the cities to be visited.
2. Number of days (overnights) in each place.
3. Mode of transportation between cities.

4. Establish a rough time schedule, taking into consideration the time at his disposal.

Transportation

1. Air transport should be used when time is limited and for long distances.
2. Surface transportation should be recommended for shorter distances.
3. For trains, determine whether advanced reservation is necessary. Indicate stations where trains are to be changed.
4. Bus should be recommended in some countries, as it usually allows additional sightseeing.
5. When arranging timetables, remember that your client is on vacation, and therefore avoid early departures.

Hotel Accommodation

Category of Hotels : Examine with your client which category of hotel he wants to stay at-Deluxe, First Class, Standard or Economy class. It is preferable that he is accommodated in a maximum rate room; however, if he must consider the cost, then rather suggest a lower grade hotel with best available room.

Type of Rooms : Examine whether your client wishes a special room on a special floor, with or without bath/ shower, sea view, outside or inside, etc. Draw his attention to the fact that in high season a room with a bath may be difficult to obtain in some places. In some cases a double room for single occupancy can be suggested, a single room being often small or not well situated. If your client insists on having a particular room, he may have to pay a supplement.

Meals : Ask your client whether he wants to have accommodation on bed and breakfast, demi-pension or full pension basis. If accommodation is on bed and breakfast basis, keep in mind that in certain resorts, demi or full pension is compulsory.

Check-in Time: Remind your client that check-in time at hotels is usually after 12 noon. Immediate occupancy on early morning arrivals can only be secured if the room is reserved for the previous night. If your client leaves late in the evening you may propose to him to pay for an additional night.

During periods of festivals, fairs or congresses, hotel space may not be available, rendering it necessary for your client to change the dates in those places; cabled hotel confirmation should, therefore, be suggested.

During periods, such as important festivals and events, a minimum stay of 5-7 days may be required. The same is applicable to some winter resorts, where a minimum stay of two weeks is required at Christmas and New Year.

Transfers

1. The need of transfers upon arrival or departure results from the fact that it is often difficult to find one's way at airport, piers or stations with which one is not familiar.
2. Transfers by agencies include interpreter meeting and assistance, accompanying clients (unless otherwise specified), porterage and transportation of 2 pieces of hand luggage per person between airport, station, bus or air terminal and hotels or vice versa, as well as tip to driver, but it does not include tip to hotel porter.
3. Type of vehicle varies according to cities, generally by private car or taxi/cab.
4. Airport transfers are naturally more expensive, but also the most convenient ones.
5. When opting for transfer from city air terminal, your client must know that there will be no assistance at the airport, that he will have to tip for baggage at the airport and pay for bus between the airport and the city terminal.
6. Bus Arrivals: Certain bus companies stop at the major hotels to drop or collect clients, the disadvantage of this being the clients' dependence on time schedules and waiting for his turn to be dropped off. In addition, it will be necessary for the client to contact the local agency if other services are not to be provided in that city.

Sightseeing/Excursions/Tours

1. The advantage of arranging sightseeing in advance is that your client does not have to waste his time, queuing up in the local agency. Also, a balance can be established in

advance between leisure time and sightseeing, as well as for tours of the city and countryside.

2. Motor Coach Tours : Apart from the economic viewpoint, there is the advantage of meeting other travellers, but clients have to arrange their own transportation to meeting points, as pick-up is very seldom done on motorcoach tours.
3. Private Car Tours : Your client is picked up at the hotel, has the choice of time of departure and can stop wherever he likes, but this is the most expensive solution. In some places there are regular private car tours, or else sightseeing can be done on a seat-in-car basis.
4. Hire of Private Car with Chauffeur
   (a) City hire-must be recommended to deluxe clients, whose time is limited between trains, boats or planes, or who already know the city and want to see only special places or go shopping. Since very often the chauffeur cannot act as a guide, a private guide will be needed for sightseeing.
   (b) Touring hire-if a private car is used for travelling from one city to another, local guides in each place will be sufficient. Distance covered daily should not exceed 250 km. Client's attention has to be drawn to the fact that he will have to pay for empty run of car (return to point of departure). The full daily basic charge is due, even if the vehicle is picked up in the evening.
5. Motor Launch Tours/Boats Trips : The same applies here as for motor coach tours. Deluxe clients will be picked up at the hotel by private car and driven to embarkation pier.
6. Self-driven cars can also be provided when clients fill the necessary conditions and, if wanted, a local guide can be placed at their disposal.

Music Festival, Theatre and Concert Tickets

Clients must be told that advance reservation is necessary. Confirmation of requested tickets cannot be guaranteed and tickets are not refundable unless they can be resold.

Land Arrangements : On the basis of all details furnished by your clients, it will enable you to make an estimate of the land arrangements.

Transatlantic/Pacific Transportation : To the land arrangements, the cost of flight/boat tickets for Transatlantic/ Pacific transportation has to be added.

Cost Price : Items a and b above give you the cost price.

Selling Price : In order to obtain the selling price you have to add your handling fees or mark-up, as well as a margin safeguarding any possible increase.

Suggested Itinerary

(a) A suggested itinerary should be drafted of what has been agreed with your client and submitted to him, together with the final price. The accompanying letter should clearly specify what is included in the price:

   1. Price and type of land arrangements.
   2. Price and class of air/sea/rail tickets, indicating that they are subject to change without notice.
   3. The agency's conditions regarding handling charge , cancellation fees, possible deposit request, etc.

(b) It should also point out what is NOT included, such as cost of passport, visa, gratuities, tips to hotel porters, beverages, laundry, taxes (government, landing, embarkation), etc.

(c) Acceptance of suggested itinerary should be requested to enable you to proceed with reservation, and a deposit should be asked.

Your Relation with Service Suppliers : Reservation Procedures

(a) Once you are in possession of the client's agreement you can start reservations with carriers and hotels.

(b) In case your client requests only hotel reservations in a few places, it is advisable to make the reservations directly with the hotels.

(c) However, if transfer, sightseeing or other services are also requested, then it is preferable to go through the local agent, who is in a better position to replace a hotel by a similar one, in case of full occupancy.

Transfers : Due to frequent changes in time schedules and/or due to changes your client may require, it is NOT advisable to send transfer requests earlier than one month prior to final documentation. An exception can be made if a special service is required and rate confirmation is needed.

Transfers should be requested by vouchers, indicating the following items:

(a) Full name of client(s) and number of passengers (for a child or an aged person give their age also).

(b) Date of transfer.

(c) Full description (indicate type of car, name of airport, city air terminal or station, exact flight or train number and arrival/ departure time).

(d) Name of hotel the client is staying at.

(e) Town and date of issue.

(f) If you do not have the rate of a service, request the rate of confirmation on the voucher copies.

Transportation : Whenever possible, obtain all tickets for rail, bus, boat, cruise, sleeping cars, etc., that may be required locally from agencies of foreign railroads, bus companies, steamship lines, etc.

Hotel Accommodation

1. Depending on the time you have, hotel reservations can be made by reservation requests, by telex or cable (give paid reply), through hotel representatives, or through a WATA office. If you reserve through a a hotel representative or WATA office, their conditions should be respected.

2. Once you have a hotel confirmation, issue a voucher for re- confirmation, indicating the following items:

   (a) Full name of client(s) and number of persons (for a child or an aged person give their age also).

   (b) Type of room.

(c) Arrival and departure date, time of arrival and flight/train number.

(d) Meal conditions - clearly indicate whether rooms only, bed and breakfast (Continental or American/English), half or full pension.

(e) Always mention on hotel vouchers: "All taxes and service charges included".

(f) Method of payment-indicate who will pay the bill. If the client settles the bill directly with the hotel, even when a deposit has been sent, hotels do not always pay a commission.

(g) Always ask for a re-confirmation of the rate on the voucher copies.

3. If the best room is required, it should be determined as DELUXE, and a 10 per cent supplement foreseen.
4. If a suite is required, it can be estimated a 2½ times the normal tariff.
5. Whenever necessary, an extra night is to be foreseen for early arrival or late departure. Indicate on voucher early a.m. arrival the following day or request additional night or day use, advising the exact departure time.
6. In case of split stays at the same hotel, a separate voucher should be issued for each day.

Sightseeing/Excursions/Tours

The same applies as for transfers - regular sightseeing tours should not be requested earlier than one month prior to the final documentation, except when a special service is required (e.g., sightseeing starting at airport) or for excursions/tours of two or more days' duration.

1. Sightseeing/Excursions/Tours should be requested for WATA affiliates by vouchers, indicating the following items:

(a) Full name of client(s) and number of persons (for a child or an aged person give their age also).

(b) Date of sightseeing/excursions/tours.

(c) Reference number of tour (if given), tour designation and title.

(d) By private car or by regular scheduled motor coach.

(e) For regular tours, give time and place of departure for private car tours, indicate "pick-up at hotel".

(f) Name of hotel client is staying at.

(g) Town and date of issue.

(h) In case a complete description does not appear in the agent's tariff, ask for additional information and rate confirmation.

2. If your client wants to start a sightseeing tour from airport or station, add transfer-rate to sightseeing rate.

Chauffeur Driven Car Hire

1. If private car hire with chauffeur is required, it has to be reserved in advance on the basis of rates quoted in the Master-Key. If rates are not given, apply to the agency for rates and details.

2. For requests, issue voucher, indicating the following details:

   (a) Full name of client(s) and number of passengers.

   (b) Type of car (year of construction if available).

   (c) For city hire : Date and time of beginning of hire, length of hire or time of termination.

   (d) For touring hire: Date of beginning and termination of hire, starting time of hire and termination point, as well as stopovers.

   (e) Special requests, such as automatic cars, air conditioning, luggage, rack, etc.

   (f) Name of hotel client is staying at.

3. City and Touring hire must be issued on separate vouchers, as tariffs and minimum daily averages are not the same. Also, if more than one day city hire is required issue one voucher for each day.

4. Touring rate is established on the basis of a reliable map. Ten per cent of total mileage should be added for detours.

If there are overnight stops, an additional 20 miles should be foreseen for possible use of car during the stay in city.

5. For empty runs, it should be noted that the law does not authorise chauffeurs to drive more than 310 miles/500 km per day, therefore, the total distance should be divided by this authorised maximum to reckon the number of chauffeur's overnights to be added to the touring rate.
6. For chauffeur's accommodation, the rate appearing in the tariff has to be multiplied by the number of days the car has been used (special rates if outside the country).

Self-Driven Cars : If given, use rates appearing in the WATA Master-Key, otherwise, apply to the agency or consult Hertz, Avis, etc., for details and rates, whenever so indicated.

WATA Master-Key is a valuable document for a travel agent. The guidelines given in 'key' make the job of a travel agent a lot easier. As a comprehensive source of travel information it facilitates the work of a travel agent. The destination profiles provide a wealth of background information not only for a travel agent but also for a traveller. The 'key' is updated every year making it a valuable reference material.

IATA Accredition : Travel agents are the marketplace intermediaries responsible for selling the services of airlines worldwide. Considering the role and importance of air transport which is at the heart of travel and tourism selling, its services becomes the key motivation for engaging in travel agency business. Therefore, the importance of IATA approval for a travel agency is essential to enable it to sell the services of airlines.

For setting up a travel agency business there are no legal requirements. In some countries, however, governments exercise some kind of a licensing control over agencies. Most principals license the sale of their services through the issue of an agency contract, or agency agreement. In the absence of such a contract or an agreement, a travel agency will not get any commission from selling the services on behalf of the principal. The income of a travel agent is derived only from a commission which he receives from the principal after selling their services.

A licence is required by a travel agency for a commission to be payable on the sale of services of air carriers who are members of the International Air Transport Association. Domestic air services are, however, exempted from this. Most airlines want to sell their services worldwide but cannot do so on their own as it is not economically viable for them to set up extensive network of sales offices in every city of the world. It is the travel agents who are the marketplace intermediaries who make the sale of the services of the airlines possible worldwide through their own network.

As IATA travel makes up a substantial proportion of a total sale of a travel agency turnover, it is important for the travel agent who wishes to offer his clients the full range of travel services to obtain the necessary IATA approval or appointment.

IATA-Controlled Approval : The travel agency approval of IATA is controlled by its Agency Administration Board. This Board is made up of a number of IATA members operating from a particular country. Before approval is granted by IATA, a travel agency has to fulfil certain conditions. The most important condition is the demonstration by an agency of its financial soundness or financial standing. It has to prove that it has sufficient finances to settle the accounts of various airlines whose business it is handling. Another condition which an agency has to fulfil is to ensure the suitability and security of its premises. The premises of a travel agency are to be centrally located preferably in the centre of the town in a commercial district having proper security. The security aspect is very important as the agency has to keep the ticket stock of various airlines and this is quite expensive.

Proficiency of the staff of a travel agency is another important aspect which is considered by IATA before giving an approval. The staff has to be professionally trained in the handling of airlines business. IATA in association with UFTAA conducts the International Travel Agents Training Programme to meet the growing demand for a professionally trained manpower for the travel industry. The IATA-UFTAA training programme operates under the authority of the Passenger Agency Training Board. IATA's Agency Training Services (ATS) located in Geneva

(Switzerland) is responsible for the general administration of the programme.

In the field, the training programme is administered by a Local Coordinator who is responsible for the promotion of the training courses, the distribution of the training materials and the organisation of the examinations. The Local Coordinator is provided by the local IATA Agency Services, the National Airlines or the National Travel Agents Association in a particular country.

The IATA-UFTAA training courses have been designed primarily for travel professionals who work in IATA accredited travel agencies and whose main task is to sell international air transportation on behalf of IATA member airlines. The agents' staff can demonstrate proficiency by completing an IATA/ UFTAA (passenger) training course.

The applicant's ability to generate new business is another requirement to be taken into consideration by IATA before considering an application for approval. This is to ensure that an agent is capable of generating new business in the market and has sufficient contacts to do so. To sum up, any travel agency, in order to get IATA approval for selling the services of IATA airlines worldwide, has to ensure the following:

(i) Financial standing
(ii) Suitability of the premises
(iii) Security for control of ticket stock
(iv) Proficiency of the staff
(v) Ability to generate new business

After considering the above aspects and if the IATAs Agency Administration Board is satisfied, necessary IATA approval is accorded to an agency. Once approved, a Passenger Sales Agreement is issued and a numeric ticket validation code is provided which will be stamped on all tickets issued by that IATA-approved agent. IATA approval enables the agent to do business on behalf of all IATA members. It enables the agent to sell the services of all IATA member airlines throughout the world. The entire process of getting IATA approval can be quite time-consuming and lengthy and in the meantime agents applying for

IATA approval are expected to generate business without getting any commissions.

Additional Approvals : In addition to the IATA approval which is basic for a travel agency, there are certain other approvals/ recognitions required for running a travel agency. These approvals, however, will depend on the extent of activities and range of services which a particular agency would like to offer to its clients. For instance, in order to make commissionable sales on the services of railways, domestic airlines services and other principals such as car hire companies, shipping and cruise services, necessary approval is to be obtained. These approvals will enable travel agents to sell services on behalf of these principals with remuneration. In case a travel agency is an IATA-approved agent, or a member of the National Travel Agents Association, obtaining approvals for most of other principals becomes largely a formality.

Associations of Travel and Trade

Formation of associations by independent firms in a particular trade or a group of industries is primarily done with a view to protecting the interests of its members. Trade Organisations are voluntary bodies formed by individual firms belonging to a particular trade not only to protect but also to advance the common interests of their members. The main objective of forming an association by independent firms is to get strong representations which act as channels of communication with the government and other organised groups to further the interests of their members. In almost all disciplines, members sharing similar interests or complementing each other's interests in some way or other have formed organisations/associations.

The ever-increasing importance of the tourism sector and the increase in the growth in its volume over the years have resulted in the formation of associations in this sector. Secondly, the ever-increasing international character of the modern day tourism and the growing influence of international agencies in various fields have also influenced the growth of international cooperations in the field of tourism. All these developments in turn have brought together members of the travel associations at national, regional and international levels collectively to further their trade interests.

Different producers and sellers of various tourist services like tour operators, travel agents, hotel companies, airline companies, ground operators, etc., have formed associations of their members.

The scope of discussion in this chapter is limited to the associations of travel agents and tour operators. These associations today have assumed great importance and provide a platform to their members where ideas are exchanged and topics of mutual interest discussed and solutions arrived at. They provide services like information, assistance and advice in the conduct of their business to their members. The various associations in the field of tourism can take different forms. Broadly, the following five forms can be identified:

(i) Those based on the education and training needs of the industry. These may include professional bodies like Hotel and Catering Management Association, Travel and Tourism Management Association which are primarily concerned with the training and educational standards of personnel working in hotel and travel agencies.

(ii) Those which are concerned with the sectoral interests of their members. They include the National Associations of Travel Agents and Tour Operators. Each country has such associations. For instance, the American Society of Travel Agents (ASTA), the Australian Federation of Travel Agents (AFTA), the Association of British Travel Agents (ABTA), the Japan Association of Travel Agents (JATA), the Indian Association of Travel Agents (IATA), the Swiss Travel Agents Association, the German Travel Agencies' Association, etc.

(iii) Those which are responsible for developing, promoting and facilitating tourism among a particular region. These regional organisations draw their membership from public or private sector organisations dealing with tourism and sharing a common interest in the promotion and development or marketing of a specific tourism geographical area or a region. This area may represent a region, a state, a country or a resort. The membership is opened to groups or organisations, both in public and private sectors, rather than individuals, such as Pacific Area Travel Association (PATA), etc.

(iv) Those which are concerned with the promotion and development of tourism globally. These organisations deal with all the aspects of tourism. The rapid expansion in tourism activity globally was responsible for creating a need for world bodies to deal with tourism issues at the government level. The World Tourism Organisation (WTO) is one such global tourism organisation representing public sector tourism from most countries of the world.

(v) Those which are responsible for promoting and furthering interests of specific trade groups in the travel industry, like travel agents, and tour operators at the global level. Unlike the sectoral trade association of travel agents and tour operators, these have international impact. They play an important role in representing the common interests of travel agents and tour operators worldwide in crucial international issues like negotiation of travel agency commission rates with International Air Transport Association (IATA). Universal Federation of Travel Agents Association (UFTAA) and the World Association of Travel Agencies (WATA) are such associations. Both UFTAA and WATA play an important role in representing the interests of travel agents worldwide. The following pages will discuss in detail the roles and functions of these two international organisations of travel agents.

Universal Federation of Travel Agents Association (UFTAA) : Universal Federation of Travel Agents Association (UFTAA), an important organisation of travel agents on a worldwide basis, was founded in Rome in November, 1966 by the merger of the International Federation of Travel Agencies (IFTA) and the Universal Organisation of Travel Agents' Associations (UOTAA). The General Secretariat of UFTAA is located in Monaco.

The membership of the Federation consists of the National, Travel Agents' Associations from most of the countries in the world. Today it represents over 33,000 travel agencies globally. National Travel Agents Associations are the full members of UFTAA. The membership of the Federation is split into nine regions each covering a group of countries.

List of Countries of which the National Association is a Member of UFTAA

Algeria	Guatemala	Norway
Argentina	Hungary	Pakistan
Australia	Hong Kong	Paraguay
Austria	India	Peru
Barbados	Indonesia	Philippines
Belgium	Iraq	Poland
Bolivia	Ireland	Portugal
Brazil	Israel	Fuerto Rico
Bulgaria	Italy	Senegal
Canada	Ivory Coast	Singapore
Chile	Japan	South Africa
Colombia	Jordan	South Korea
Costa Rica	Kenya	Spain
Cuba	Kuwait	Sri Lanka
Cyprus	Lebanon	Sweden
Czech Republic	Malaysia	Sudan
Dominican	Malawi	Syria
Denmark	Malta	Thailand
Egypt	Mexico	Trinidad & Tobago
Ecuador	Mauritius	Tunisia
El Salvador	Monaco	Turkey
Finland	Morocco	Uruguay
France	Nepal	Venezuela
Germany	Netherlands	Zaire
Ghana	New Zealand	Zambia
Greece	Nigeria	Zimbabwe

The Aims of the Federation : The following are the main aims of the federation :

(i) To act as the negotiating body with the various branches of tourism and travel industry on behalf of its members and also in the interest of the public;

(ii) To ensure for all travel agents through their national associations the maximum degree of cohesion and understanding, prestige and public recognition, advancement of the member's interest and protection from legislation and legal points of view; and

(iii) To offer to its member all the necessary professional and technical advice and assistance in matters concerning their trade.

UFTAA provides several advantages to its members which include the right to reproduce the symbol on the stationery, information service on all matters of legal or professional nature, free of charge assistance by its Legal Department for the recovery of outstanding debts, arbitration services for litigations between a member agency and a hotel company in different countries, etc.

The Annual General Assembly of UFTAA is the policymaking body. The Assembly decides on the general policy of the Federation and makes recommendations on any matter within its competence. The Board of Directors, consisting of Directors elected from candidates proposed by National Member Associations handle the routine business of the Federation. The Executive Committee is responsible for handling day-to-day activities and also urgent matters. The UFTAA world congress which normally takes place annually is the advisory body of the Federation. The world congress is open to UFTAA registered agents and enterprises, UFTAA individual members, suppliers of services and regional, national and international public authorities.

UFTAA claims to have a series of achievements since its inception in the year 1966. Prominent among its achievements is its collaboration with the International Rail Union resulting in obtaining increased commission on several railway networks, creation of professional training courses and introduction of Rail inclusive Tours. With regard to air transport, the cooperation between the Federation and IATA over a number of years has resulted in the raising of commission, introduction of an overriding commission, 50 per cent reduction for the spouses of travel agents and creation of international correspondence courses for the training of agency sales staff. In the sphere of hotel industry, the federation, following negotiations with the International Hotel Association has created an international convention, setting down regulations for booking, and cancellation fees. A court of arbitration to settle disputes between hotels and travel agents located in different countries has also been created.

World Association of Travel Agencies (WATA) : WATA, the World Association of Travel Agencies, is another important worldwide association representing travel agencies. Founded in the year 1949, WATA is a non-profit organisation created by independent travel agents for the benefit of all travel agencies around the world. The Association has over 200 members from 175 cities in 80 countries. The headquarters of WATA are located in Geneva, Switzerland.

The basic idea of WATA is to bring together local travel agencies into an international network, so that every member is offered all the facilities and advantages of being associated with an international body in addition to enjoying local prominence. WATA is registered as an association under Swiss Civil Law, and is essentially a non-profit making organisation. Under its statutes, WATA and its members are required to assist one another.

The General Assembly of WATA held every year provides a forum for discussion of the Association's business and an opportunity to talk with fellow members. It enables members to have an exposure to new business and ideas applied successfully elsewhere. One day, before the General Assembly, the meetings of the Regional Assemblies are held which provide a chance to its members to discuss regional travel problems as well as the implementation on the regional level of the decisions taken by WATA governing bodies. The regions also have the possibility to submit to the General Assembly ideas and suggestions.

Advantages of a WATA Membership : The advantages of WATA membership include :

Guaranteed Payment of IHA Invoices : WATA headquarters guarantees payment of all invoices for services rendered by the International Hotel Association (IHA) hotel members to WATA members, up to a certain amount. In return, the IHA has requested its members to accept vouchers for individual clients issued by WATA members to be billed after the client's departure.

Internal Guarantee : Subject to certain conditions, unsettled services rendered by one WATA member agency to another, are paid by WATA headquarters.

WATA Standard Exchange Voucher : An agency's own exchange voucher bearing the WATA logo and the reference to the IHA/ WATA agreement or the standard WATA exchange voucher printed by the headquarters with the name of agency, are widely accepted by hotels worldwide. In the majority of the cases, hotels accepting these vouchers will agree to bill the services after the departure of the clients without prepayment or deposit.

Membership List and Introduction Card : A small booklet listing all WATA members and their addresses is available for agencies to give to clients who go on extended trips, in case they need assistance and service en route. For specially important clients, a special introduction card is available for the members.

WATA Master-Key : Updated and published yearly, the WATA Master-Key is a comprehensive source of travel information. Individual WATA agency tariffs represent an invaluable selling tool for members' incoming and outgoing services. Master-Key carries the tariffs of WATA members offering incoming services. A standard presentation makes it easy for users to extract the information they need. Along with the tariffs is a country description sheet provided by the respective National Tourist Offices containing a wealth of background information.

WATA Circular Letters for Latest Developments : This internal newsletter keeps members abreast of new developments in WATA. It also gives members an opportunity to describe special activities of their own.

WATA's Overriding Commission : A supplementary commission of 5 per cent is allowed between members, on prices published in WATA Master-Key for transfers, sightseeing, excursions, tours and chauffeur-driven car hire.

WATA Membership Categories

Full Members : Membership in WATA is open to any travel agency, preferably privately-owned, which can prove a sound financial structure, adheres to the highest professional ethics expected in the industry and enjoys prominent standing in the local community.

All WATA members have the same rights, privileges and obligations within the association. Individual members are grouped into three sub-categories depending on the scope of their activities, as follows:

(1) Agencies offering both outgoing and incoming services.

(2) Agencies offering outgoing activities only.

(3) Agencies offering incoming service only.

Associate Members : A travel agency may apply to become an associate member. This category offers the possibility to become a WATA associate member for a trial period of 2 years. The associate members have the same rights and obligations as the full members but the fees are generally reduced.

Allied Members : A category open to hotels, airlines, shipping lines and car hire companies. The aim of this category is to develop the business relations between the members and their partners. Allied members may attend the WATA General Assembly, they will be listed in the WATA publications, receive all WATA publications and circulate letters and have the right to display on all their printed matter, the WATA logo created for this category. They have no voting right nor can they be elected to the WATA governing bodies. Both UFTAA and WATA are playing a valuable role in representing the interests of travel agents worldwide. In addition to the above two international travel associations representing travel agents, there are some important national travel agents organisations like the American Society of Travel Agents (ASTA) which has influence beyond the confines of USA. The American Society of Travel Agents draws its membership not only from travel agents and principals within the country but also from principals throughout the world who have interest in promoting overseas tourism from United States to their country.

The American Society of Travel Agents (ASTA) : American Society of Travel Agents (ASTA) is the leading professional society of travel agents in the USA. The world's largest professional travel trade association, ASTA was established in New York in the year 1931. Originally named the American Steamship and Tourist Agent's Association, the present name was adopted in the year 1944. The Society was established to foster programmes for the advancement of the travel agency industry, promote ethical practices and provide a public forum for travel agents. It has now over 25,000 members and is the only organisation representing all segments of the travel industry. The membership consists of travel agents, carriers, hotels, etc.

Purpose : The purpose of ASTA is the promotion and advancement of the interests of the travel agency industry and the safeguarding of the travelling public against fraud, misrepresentation and other unethical practices. The Society maintains legal representation and also a Government Affairs office in Washington, D.C. to provide direct contact with the Federal Government and the regulatory agencies in the travel and transportation field, and to protect the legitimate interests of travel agents.

Services : ASTA's services to travel agents also benefit the general public. Such activities include sponsorship of frequent conferences on travel matters, involving airlines, steamship companies, agents, municipal and government officials, and other interested parties; discussions with airlines on fare structures and travel destinations; research studies into traveller preferences; close cooperation with various city, state and government agencies across the country in travel-oriented matters, assistance to all agencies across the country in travel-oriented matters; assistance to all levels of government consumerism departments in upgrading standards of service to travellers.

The American Society of Travel Agents is primarily the trade association of the travel agency industry. There are more than 25,000 members in the Society covering all segments of the travel industry. Out of the total membership of 25,000 over 14,000 are travel agents in the United States of America and Canada. In addition to travel agents, there are allied members representing airlines, railways, hotels, government tourist offices, etc. The Society has a membership in over 140 countries all over the world. In order to qualify for the membership of the Society, an applicant must be in the business of travel under its present ownership or control for a minimum period of three years.

Membership : There are two basic classifications of membership-Active and Allied. Active members are year-round travel agents or tour operators. Allied members include airlines and steamship companies, railroad, bus lines, car rental firms, hotels, resorts, government tourist offices and other organisations regularly engaged in the travel industry or associated industries.

ASTA has over 2,500 travel agency members outside the USA and Canada. All are engaged in travel agency operations on a year-round basis and have been in business for at least three consecutive years. The international roster has its own elected governors and actively participates in all phases of Society meetings. International members come from Algeria, Bolivia, Sri Lanka, Denmark, Ethiopia, Fiji Island, Ghana, India, Iran, Japan, the Netherlands, Portugal, South Africa and Sweden.

ASTA World Travel Congress : The year's foremost meeting place is the ASTA World Travel Congress. The Congress is the single most important meeting held annually in the travel industry and the programme includes workshops, seminars, business meetings, film presentations, and social events. Members from throughout the world travel industry participate, give talks, lead discussion groups and conduct sessions. The ASTA World Travel Congress has been the platform for launching many important and beneficial education programmes for agents. The Congress grants Travel Hall of Fame awards, an honour given to those whose careers have made long standing impacts on the development and expansion of the travel industry and tourism. The awards are given every year to outstanding members. ASTA consists of the following departments:

(a) policy implementation

(b) administration

(c) Industry relations

(d) Membership relations

(e) Communication

The members of the society derive various advantages which include education and training. ASTA has a comprehensive list of travel courses and seminars which are attended by its members. The society also offers professional training courses to senior travel agency personnel. Various research papers and newsletters are brought out from the Society's headquarters for use of its members.

ASTA Chapters : The society has 28 chapters in the United States of America and Canada and another 28 chapters overseas. Each chapter has elected officers and appointed committees. There is a National Board of Directors which establishes policies of the Society. Every two years a new President and Chairman of the Board are elected by Active Members. Day-to-day activities of the Society are looked after by a professional staff which works under the guidance of an Executive Vice-President who, in fact, is the Chief Operating Officer of the society and makes recommendations on policy matters to the Board and Executive Board. The Vice-President directs the headquarters staff in providing a broad programme of services and facilities to ASTA's membership and carrying on the day-to-day business of the Society. ASTA world headquarters are located in New York City, USA.

Scene in India

As long back as in the year 1954, the Government of India was aware of the important role which the travel agents were to play in the development of tourism. It was recognised by the Government that tourists who visit a foreign country often prefer to secure the services of travel agents who assist them in order to make best use of time and money at their disposal. The government felt that many a time unauthorised persons offer themselves as agents and in return fail to render satisfactory services, and even exploit the ignorance of the tourists for their personal benefit. With a view to curb this the government evolved a system of granting recognition to travel agents. The rules for recognition were as follows:

(i) No firm shall be granted recognition unless it has been engaged actively in handling tourist traffic for at least one year before the date of the application.

(ii) Firms granted recognition shall be entitled to such right and privileges as may be granted by the government from time to time and shall abide by several terms and conditions of recognition.

(iii) Firms granted recognition shall undertake to maintain an office under the charge of full time members of their staff who should, apart from issuing rail tickets, be in a position to give up to date and accurate information regarding transport and accommodation facilities, currency and customs regulations and general information about travel, etc.

(iv) The recognition may be extended for the whole of the country or be limited to a particular region.

(v) Firms granted recognition shall undertake to employ only guides approved by the Ministry of Tourism.

(vi) All recognised firms shall furnish yearly statement of their activities and such other information in regard to the volume of tourist traffic actually handled and other relevant matters.

(vii) The decision of the government in the matter of recognition shall be final and it reserves the right to cancel or withdraw it at any time.

Subsequently, following clauses were also added:

(i) The recognition to be granted by Ministry of Tourism shall not automatically entitle the firm to be appointed agents for the sale of rail tickets by the Ministry of Railways (Railway Board). The agencies thus recognised shall apply separately to the Railway Board.

(ii) Firms seeking recognition as travel agents should have a minimum paid-up capital of rupees one hundred thousand.

(iii) Applications for grant of recognition by the Ministry of Tourism will be considered only if the firm:

(a) is approved by the IATA;

(b) has licence to book foreign passages issued by the Reserve Bank of India;

(c) has the approval of the Ministry of External Affairs to handle travel documents and to deal with passport offices;

(d) is registered under the Local Shops and Establishment Act.

The recognition is now granted by the Ministry of Tourism in the Ministry of Tourism and Culture. The application for grant of recognition is to be made in the prescribed form and is to be addressed to the Director General, Ministry of Tourism who is the authority empowered to grant such recognition.

Travel Agents Association of India (TAAI) : The travel agents decided to form an association on all-India basis as long back as in the year 1952, when an All India Travel Agents Association was established. The main objective of the association is to safeguard and protect the interests of its members by way of having a constant dialogue with the concerned government agencies. The annual convention of the association is attended by a large number of representatives from travel trade both government as well as non-government. Important matters related with the promotion of product are discussed in these conventions. The Travel Agents Association of India has its registered office in Mumbai and regional offices in Kolkata, Delhi and Chennai. The association publishes a monthly magazine *Travel News* for of its members.

The vital role played by the travel agents in the growth and development of tourism in the country and its promotion is recognised by all segments of the travel industry. The government works in close collaboration with them not only in India but abroad as well, encouraging them to plan and organize package tours for various destinations in India. In suitable cases, the Ministry of Tourism recommends the foreign exchange to travel agents to enable them to open their branch offices abroad. The ministry has also instituted a special tourism award which is given every year to the agency earning the maximum amount of foreign exchange.

11

Exhibitions and Fairs

Travel Industry fairs and exhibitions are the major marketing vehicles in today's highly competitive market place. In the rapidly changing world and with a view to keeping pace with new innovation in products, travel fairs and exhibitions have a special significance and importance. Today, no country, howsoever advanced and developed in technology, can afford to keep itself aloof from participating in travel fairs and exhibitions. These are considered an effective way to facilitate contacts, for exchange of information and ideas and to initiate sales in many industries.

In the present day world, no country can be self-sufficient in any field inspite of technological advancements. Rapid innovations in various fields make it difficult for any country to keep pace unless the knowledge and experience is shared together on a common platform. Almost all the countries in the world organise travel fairs and exhibitions of one kind or another in small, medium or a large scale. Several countries have put up permanent exhibition grounds, complexes equipped with state-of-art facilities to accommodate as many exhibitors as possible or just to participate. The scale of participation is constantly on the rise especially in well known travel fairs. Some times it is not possible for several exhibitors to get the space because of increase in the numbers of participating countries wanting to display their products. In several cases the space booking is to be done well in advance of the event dates.

Advantages of Participation

International trade fairs and exhibitions give an opportunity to the exhibitors of participating countries to meet a large number of buyers and exhibitors from different countries at one place, to study the market trends and to compare the price and quality of similar products. In addition, participation in trade fairs open up avenues for locating new markets. The trade fairs and exhibitions also provide a common platform to participating countries to come together under one roof and exchange technical know how and personnel as well as help promote joint ventures between two countries. Apart from the presentation of exhibits, the fairs also provide a platform for exchange of knowledge and information through a medium of seminars, workshops, symposia on related exhibition, by experts from participating countries.

Participation in trade fairs also provide an opportunity to the exhibitors from participating countries to assess their own progress *vis-a-vis* that of the exhibitors from other countries and the steps necessary to achieve better performance and results. The importance of the fairs can also be assessed by the fact that they are organised not only by different trade bodies or chambers, but also by semi-government and government bodies which assist in organising such fairs send their official representatives to participate directly or indirectly. Following are the advantages to the exhibitors:

(a) transfer of technology and know-how between countries;

(b) exchange of information and technical know-how under one roof;

(c) assessing the progress *vis-a-vis* that of the other country and steps necessary to achieve better performance;

(d) creating better conditions for two-way communications among international partners in the market;

(e) creating proper surroundings or encounters and dialogues between suppliers and customers.

Certain important action areas, which are to be taken care of by the prospective participants in order to get maximum mileage from the fair, need particular mention. The following observations are considered to be of practical importance for those who are planning to participate in the trade fairs and exhibitions:

(a) Visitors to trade fairs are normally senior and high-ranking executives with decision-making power;

(b) Transaction of actual business may not come through and this should not disappoint the exhibitor. It is not unusual for some period of time to lapse before business deals are concluded. The participation in the fair should primarily be utilised to establish as many contacts as possible and to initiate discussion with prospective business partners;

(c) Systematic collection of data on visitors is very important as it will help in follow-up action. A business opportunity should not be missed on account of a delayed follow-up or due to failure to give the required information immediately on the spot;

(d) No opportunity should be missed to cultivate the media. Through this contact, the product will receive the required publicity;

(e) The importance of the type of publicity material prepared for the fair can hardly be overemphasised. This gives an opportunity to the visitors to go through the contents at his leisure;

(f) Use of audio-visual media with emphasis on the product will greatly help the visitor identify the product;

(g) The representation at the stand needs to be high level so that discussion with the visitors are meaningful. First impressions are extremely crucial and help a great deal in transacting the business;

(h) Opportunities to hold business discussion with the customers should not be missed. In addition to transacting business with existing clients, it is necessary to contact the new clients;

(i) Competing products should be examined with a view to updating one's own product. Trends in pricing, design, packaging, distribution, etc., should always be studied with a view to achieving better results in the competitive market; and

(j) Exhibition authorities bring out comprehensive catalogues of all the exhibitors. It is necessary that the exhibitor gives complete information to fair authorities about the firm and its products for inclusion in the catalogue. The catalogue is used quite often as a reference book even after the fair is over.

The Background

It was in the late 1950s that the first attempts were made to establish and organise fairs. The main objective of fairs for the tourist industry from the very beginning was two-fold:

1. As "public fairs" the purpose is to enable travel agents and tour operators, hoteliers, carriers and National Tourist Offices to establish contact with their markets, especially with the travelling public, and thus to promote their programmes and services.
2. As "trade fairs" in the more specific sense, their aim is to create opportunities for contact and business discussion, contract negotiations and exchange information within the industry itself.

In relation with the first of these two objectives, tourist fairs are often combined with exhibitions organised by manufacturers of sports equipments, both water and winter, camping and caravan equipments or by leisure industries. Since the emphasis here is on the consumer, the fair gives greater emphasis on their requirements. In many of these exhibitions there is a direct sale. On the trade side, the trade fairs are mostly for professionals and the emphasis here is on purely transacting business. During the trade fairs, conventions and annual assemblies of trade associations are sometimes held in conjunction with the fair. In major travel generating as well as receiving countries, the organisation of travel trade fairs has become a regular annual event.

The first such travel trade fair known as the International Tourism Borse (ITB) was held in the year 1967 in Berlin. Since then, there have been a number of other countries which organise travel trade fairs regularly. The enthusiastic participation in these travel trade fairs is a result of the ever - expanding travel trade

Travel Industry Fairs : A large number of exhibitors participate in these fairs representing all segments of travel industry and include travel agents, tour operators, hoteliers, airline companies, shipping companies, national tourist organisations, etc. In addition, travel trade media is also present.

Over the years there has been a steady growth in the number as well as participation in the travel trade fairs. Not only this, the organisers have been increasing the number of participants. New exhibition complexes are being constructed to give the travel trade fairs a modern look. The reason for the spurt in the travel trade fairs can be attributed to the involvement of tourism organisations in the marketing of tourism, particularly international tourism. It has been increasingly felt in the travel trade circles, especially those responsible for marketing, that the medium of travel trade fairs is a cost - effective way of communicating. Exhibitions by their very nature enjoy economies and advantages of lower costs because of the scale. The sheer size of the exhibition also makes it to be the great attraction, both for buyers and sellers of a tourist product.

Participation in travel trade fairs have several inherent advantages which are responsible for the growth in their numbers over the years as also the participation. Some of these advantages of participating in the travel trade fairs are as follows:

(a) Opportunity to both buyers and sellers of tourism services to meet under one roof and transact business;

(b) Lower cost of participation because of the advantage of scale;

(c) Effective vehicle of communication with clients;

(d) Better quality of attendance;

(e) Single platform to introduce the product (in the form of a brochure);

(f) Easy access to travel trade media;

(g) Cultivating new business contacts;

(h) Acquiring new information about the travel product;

(i) Opportunity to see the competitors' product; and

(j) Opportunity for effective public relations.

There has been an appreciable growth, both in the number of people looking for convenient places to display their products as well as consumers, to inspect and get an opportunity to buy these products. The travel trade fairs are the most convenient places for this to happen.

Every organisation which has to do something or other with tourism business feels it necessary to participate in these fairs either as an exhibitor or just a visitor. Participation in the travel trade fairs in fact has been a very important issue. The advantages of such a participation have been amply recognised. However, the question arises as to where to participate. Each travel firm would like to get maximum advantage with minimum cost from participation in a trade fair. Because of the multiplicity of events, making a choice has become rather difficult. Besides, there are various types of fairs available in different countries where participation is possible. There are the international fairs, both trade and consumer, the regional fairs and the national fairs.

Although international fairs like World Trade Mart (WTM), International Tourism Borse (ITB), International Tourism Exchange (ITE), International Brussels Trade Fair (BTF) are very popular with the travel trade, there are some other fairs also where participation is quite significant. The two most popular international trade fairs, however, are WTM in London and ITB in Berlin. Almost everybody who is somebody in the travel business likes to be seen in these two prestigious travel marts. Attendance as well as interest in these two fairs have been extremely high ever since these fairs have been organised.

UFTTAA Survey : Market Research Section of the Universal Federation of Travel Agents' Association (UFTAA) conducted surveys with the objective of determining as to who are the people who attend several of these fairs and what they hope to gain by participating. The UFTAA Survey was first used at the annual congress of UFTAA in Vienna and then at the International Brussels Trade Fair (BTF) in Brussels and the World Travel Market (WTM) in London. The sample of the survey consisted of over 100 participants at each of the above events. Each participant was asked 70 questions, of which 15 allowed an "open response". The major findings of the survey showed that travel industry trade fairs, though competitive, attract many of the same travel professionals and that an overwhelming percentage of those attending participated in the trade fair because they expected to gain business at each of these fairs.

Outcome of the Survey

The UFTAA Survey findings were published in 1986. The following were the main findings of the Survey:

(i) 80-95 per cent of participants at the above three events expected "positive practical benefits" from their attendance;

(ii) Three main motives for attending the trade fair were: forming of new business contacts, acquiring new information and promoting their own services;

(iii) About half the participants at both the fairs were travel agents or tour operators;

(iv) The suppliers of services like hotel companies and airlines were the next largest group;

(v) The average age of participants at BTF in Brussels was over 40 years in case of 70 per cent of the participants as compared to under 40 in case of 64 percent at WTM in London;

(vi) More than half of the participants at the two trade fairs were from outside the country where the fair was located (58% in the case of WTM). Most of the foreign visitors, however, were from receiving countries rather than from buying countries;

(vii) Advanced publicity for BTF was received largely through direct mailing (42%) and only through trade press (24%) and national associations (17%); on the other hand publicity on WTM was received largely through the trade press (49%) rather than direct mail (29%) or national associations (16%);

(viii) Regarding importance of press coverage for the event, 43 per cent of those interviewed at BTF said that the same was important as compared to 96 percent at WTM who believed that the fair was an important event;

(ix) ITB and WTM in that order are the most important trade fairs in the industry according to participants at both trade fairs;

(x) Comparative attendance at other trade fairs shows that many participants at WTM also go to ITB (43%), but few attend any other trade fairs (11% go to ASTA, but fewer attend all the others). Participants at BTF, on the other hand, participate extensively in other trade fairs;

(xi) The most stimulating themes for seminars and workshops according to the participants were topics on travel agents versus direct sale, automation, incentive travel, licence regulation, insurance issues, marketing, commissions, and sales through videotex.

Advantages : In addition to ceremonial and official events, the programme at trade fairs includes a series of seminars and workshops, discussion panels and presentations by private firms and official organisations including National Tourist Organisations active in tourism. The seminar programmes include half/full day sessions on important subjects such as International Conference and Conventions, marketing and promotion, modern information techniques, prospects and forecasts for international tourism.

Travel Trade fairs provide an opportunity to travel agents and tour operators of acquainting themselves with latest trends in the travel and tourism world under one roof with every sector of the industry represented, Each contact made during the fairs gives a certain return on the company's marketing investment to travel agents and tour operators. Trade fairs provide an efficient and cost effective international business environment where new products and services can be presented and negotiations on future contracts made.

Travel trade shows provide an opportunity to a tour operator to introduce his products in the form of a travel brochure and put the same in front of a buyer as travel show networking proves more valuable for individual operators because many buyers go to travel trade shows already holding established contracts with other sellers. Travel agents look forward to these shows to receive new products and negotiate future deals.

Worldwide, there are several travel industry fairs held at regular intervals which are frequented by the members of travel trade. These are held throughout the year. Some of them like ITB, WTM have however become quite popular with the trade and attract very large attendance as compared to others. In fact, these two events claim to be the largest, attracting a large number of both buyers and sellers from around the world and can be called international events of the travel industry.

International Tourism Borse (ITB) : The ITB as it is popularly known in the travel trade world was held for the first time in the year 1967. The ITB's story commenced way back in the sixties. In the year 1966-Messe Berlin provided space for nine exhibitors from the world of tourism at the Overseas Imports Fair and also staged a two-day convention in the Berlin Congress Hall. It was these two events that gave birth to the world's largest travel and tourism trade fair.

The publicity and the marketing of the fair by the organisers made it very popular in the subsequent years. In the year 1972 the fair attracted over 1,30,000 visitors from over 60 countries. The ITB organisers in the year 1973 included annual convention of the Active Members of the ASTA, the American Society of the Travel Agents. The ASTA subsequently held its 1975 full convention in Berlin coinciding with ITB of that year.

From its inception in the year 1967, ITB today claims to be the world's largest travel trade fair. In the year 1995, about 5,250 exhibitors representing 172 regions and countries of the world attended the fair. More than 52,000 trade visitors and over 60,000 private travellers transacted business. The trade visitors attending ITB '95 included 29 per cent from outside Germany.

Survey Findings : Based on a survey conducted by an independent trade fair market research institute and reported in Messe Berlin Press Release in March 1995,42 per cent of exhibitors were able to finalise deals at the ITB 1995. They reported signing contracts in the following sectors of the market: holiday and recreational travel (64%), business travel (32%), incentive travel (26%), educational and study trips (23%), conferences and congress travel (19%), sports travel (15%), adventure tours (13%), travel to health resorts and for health reasons (7%) and other contracts signed (18%). Based on their numerous contacts with the international tourism industry, 34 per cent expect follow-up business to be good, and further 48 per cent think it will be satisfactory.

Among the general public visiting the fair, 89 per cent intend to take at least one holiday and 70 per cent of them have already decided on their destination. Among those who have made their decision, more than half have already made their bookings. Altogether 81 per cent of general interest visitors stated that they would be booking a trip based on information and ideas obtained at the ITB '95.

One in four trade visitors (24%) was able to sign contracts during ITB '95. The sector in which the most business was conducted was that of holiday and recreational travel, with 52 per cent. Other contracts were signed in the following sectors: business travel (18%), adventure tours (14%), incentive travel (12%), educational and study trips (12%), conference and congress travel (11%), sports travel (9%), travel to health resorts and for health reasons (5%), and travel for other purposes (8%). Trade visitors signed contracts with exhibitors from the following countries/regions: Germany (43%), European Union (26%), Central and Eastern Europe (18%), North America (18%), Central America/Caribbean (15%), South America (14%), East Asia (14%), Africa (14%), Australia/New Zealand/Oceania (10 per cent) and Western and Central Asia (8%).

Trade visitors in ITB '95 represented the following sectors of the tourism industry: travel agents (24%), tour operators (18%), carrier (15%), hotel companies (14%), institutes (11%), tourism offices and associations (8%) and national tourism organisations (7%). Twenty-nine per cent of the trade visitors attending the ITB'95 came from outside Germany, the majority of them from

Austria, Poland, Italy, Switzerland, France, Spain, the United Kingdom, Belgium, Greece and Russia.

The International Tourism Exchange also includes a series of extensive supporting programmes. These include seminars and workshops, discussion panels, and presentations by private firms and official organisations including National Tourist Organisations active in tourism promotions. The seminar programmes include sessions on international conference and conventions, marketing and promotion, modern information techniques, prospects and forecasts for international tourism and a host of other important topics. Over the years the scope of the fair is being widened to incorporate more areas of interest in the field of tourism. For instance, the congress "Electronics in Tourism" has been introduced with a view to updating the travel trade in the latest technology concerning use of electronics in various tourist trade fields. ITB has also become an annual venue for several regional meetings of travel agents and hotel chains.

Originally being held for a period of seven days, it is now held for period of six days. During ITB '95 a Travel Visitor's day was devoted entirely to business contacts. No general public is allowed on the exclusive trade visitors' day. The travel fair is normally held in the month of March each year. The total available space for exhibitors is around 163,000 square metres.

World Travel Market (WTM) : Like ITB, World Travel Market is another, important event meant exclusively for travel and tourism professionals. Popularly known as WTM, The world Travel Market is an annual event held in London (England) every year in the month of November. WTM was first organised in the year 1980, as an international forum where the world's travel industry members meet to exchange ideas, establish new contacts, launch new products, and develop new business.

WTM attracts several thousand industry professionals every year from a number of countries. Similarly number of industry visitors is also increasing each year. According to organisers, WTM was attended by over 29,000 industry visitors in the year 1998 from over 138 countries. The industry visitors included tour operators, retail travel agents, hotel companies, inclusive organisers, group travel organisers, business travel agents and tourist transport companies. Almost 50 per cent of the total industry visitors, however, were tour operators and travel agents.

WTM has evolved a unique feature since the last few years whereby the exhibitors can meet the leading buyers with prior arranged appointments. This feature is the membership of the Meridian Club. Meridian Club is a business club for industry buyers open only to those buyers nominated by the exhibitors. Main stand holders (exhibitors) are entitled to nominate four buyers per square meter of contracted stand space. For example an exhibitor with 25 square meter stand can nominate 100 buyers. The companies which are sharing space with main exhibitors are each able to nominate 20 buyers. Meridian Club benefits to the exhibitors include an exclusive two Meridian Days during the Mart to meet only the industry's leading buyers, access to Meridian Club and pre-arranged appointments. The club membership gives a range of other advantages which include:

1. Pre-registration and advanced event information.
2. Advance exhibitor list to enable members to pre-arrange business appointments.
3. Express entry and a complimentary welcome business pack which includes event catalogue.

Meridian Club membership includes senior managers of the companies having decision - making powers to transact business deals on behalf to their companies.

World Travel Market has recently launched a new high-tech "database driven" web-site that delivers personalised information and various services designed to make participation more effective. The most interesting new feature is the "meeting scheduler" a tailor made appointment booking service which enables Meridian Club members to request meetings with main or space sharing exhibitors. Meridian Club members select who they wish to meet, view their available time slots and request a meeting. A summary e-mail is sent to each exhibitor each week detailing any new accepted or declined meetings. This new technology at WTM according to the organisers will help buyers and sellers to make the most of their time at World Travel Market.

World Travel Market provides an opportunity to the exhibitors to present their products and services and negotiate future business contracts. By providing a system of prearranged appointments with prospective new clients as well as existing ones, the forum provides an opportunity for generating additional sales. It also helps maintain high visibility among the international travel media.

International Brussels Travel Fair (BTF) : Popularly known as BTF the International Brussels Travel Fair is held every year in the month of November in the city of Brussels in Belgium. The city of Brussels has a unique advantage of being the capital of the European Community and its geographical location in the centre of Western Europe gives it an advantage over other cities in organising the travel trade fair, with increasing international participation. The three-day event is held between Thursday and Saturday. Started in the year 1975, the fair was being held in four halls having an exhibition space of 12,000 square metres (gross) and 8,000 square metres (net). Since the last two years that fair venue has been moved to Hysel exhibition complex with more exhibition space and modern facilities.

The BTF is more a technical than a promotional event. It may be described as a workshop. All the three days of the duration of the fair are for the professionals and they are, therefore, of great interest to operators, hoteliers and travel agents. The Brussels event is said to have proved consistently profitable for its organisers during its 25 years of operation.

Salon Mondial Du Tourism Et Voyages (SMTV) : Popularly known as SMTV, the Salon Mondial du Tourism et Voyages is held in Paris every year in the month of February. The fair is held for a period of six days of which the first two days are kept exclusively for the trade visitors. Travel mart is planned for subsequent days. Trade attendance at the mart is quite impressive. The fair organisers organise a buyer's and seller's mart during the trade days.

The SMTV had its first fair in Paris in the year 1975, in a spacious exhibition complex covering a gross area of 24,000 square metres (net 12,000 square metres). The venue of the fair has since been shifted to a most modern exhibition complex in La Defense, located at the west end of the city of Paris.

Feria International Tourismo (FITUR) : Spain has a special significance in the field of tourism. Few other countries in the world receive as many tourists as Spain in one year. The total tourist arrivals even outnumber the total population of the country. Spain also holds the key to the Spanish-speaking markets. Tourism being a major industry, the holding of a trade fair in the country was therefore considered to be crucial. Spain's international tourism fair (FITUR) was first started in the year 1980. The fair is organised each year in the month of January in a spacious exhibition complex of Madrid's 1,800 hectare Casa de Campo. The total exhibition area consists of about 15,000 square metres. The fair is held for a period of six days out of which the first three days are exclusively devoted to trade. The fair in Madrid places major emphasis on the Spanish speaking markets. This is because participation in the fair boosts tour programmes in Latin America as well as in Spain itself.

Travel Trade Workshop (TTW) : A travel trade fair on a smaller scale but with a stronger orientation towards the public in general is the Tourism Trade Fair 'Salon International Tourism' held regularly in early spring each year in Montreux, Switzerland.

The Swiss lakeside resort of Montreux provides an excellent picturesque setting for the first of the season's major travel events. The trade fair is held for a duration of three days in the month of 'October each year. The event is meant for professionals only.

Started in the year 1975, the Tourism Trade Fair is a leading event of its kind in Switzerland. Special trains and buses are utilised to bring in professionals from other parts of the country. The total exhibition space covers 10,200 square metres of the Montreux Congress Centre.

The exhibition stands include the official tourist offices of various countries, travel agencies and tour operators, regional tourist offices from different parts of Switzerland, companies promoting the sale of vacation homes like caravans, etc. A large portion of the exhibition surface is allocated to companies manufacturing camping equipment, photo and cinema equipment, mobile homes, pleasure boats and launches, etc.

European Incentive and Business Travel and Meetings (EIBTM): The Geneva meeting and incentives exhibition, known as the European Incentive and Business Travel and Meetings Exhibition, is a buyer-seller meet in the area of incentive and business travel. The major objective of the EIBTM is to encourage the expansion and development of the incentive travel industry through a programme. Carefully selected international buyers travel to the event and stay free, a concept pioneered by EIBTM as a major initiative to guarantee attendance by leading buyers. Held for the first time in the year 1988 at Palexpo Exhibition Centre, Geneva, EIBTM is classed as 'World Ranking' event in the area of incentives and conferences. A new visitor promotion campaign for the exhibition includes:

(i) Increased target for hosting quality buyers;

(ii) New meeting and incentives consultancy service to offer free service to participating buyers-

(iii) Regular market bulletins to keep industry contacts uptodate with what buyers perceive to be business trends;

(iv) A computerised 'World Who's Who in Business Tourism' is prepared for the exclusive use of buyers which enables them to pinpoint key suppliers from over 100 countries.

The EIBTM is held every year for a period of three days in the month of May. The display area is over 12,500 square metres.

In addition to the major travel trade fairs, there are, however, some more important events drawing a good number of exhibitors and professional visitors. Some of these are as follows:

International Tourism Exchange (ITE) : Started in the year 1979, the fair is held every year in the month of February. It covers a gross area of 65,000 square metres. The fair is held in the Milan fair-grounds.

Swedish International Tourism and Travel Fair (TUR) : Started in the year 1982, the fair is held every year in the month of March in Gottenburg, Sweden. The gross area of the TUR is 20,000 square metres (14,200) square metres net. A separate area is set aside for camping.

Dutch Travel Trade Exhibition (TOUR) : Started in the year 1981, the fair is held every year in the month of December. It covers a gross area of 14,850 square metres. The fair is held in a spacious RAI Exhibition Centre in Amsterdam and is a very well organised fair.

Among the trade fairs discussed it is recognised by travel trade that only two, i.e., the ITB and WTM, are truly of international character. The global character of these two trade fairs can be judged by the fact that a large percentage of exhibitors as well as visitors are from overseas. Although organisers of most of the other fairs also claim these to be of international character, these are the only national exhibitions with the participation of some overseas clients.

In between the few international exhibitions and scores of national exhibitions, another interesting range of regional exhibitions have also surfaced. These regional exhibitions are normally organised by one or the other of the regional tourism organisations such as Pacific Asia Travel Association, etc. These associations specialise in setting up regional shows in prime target markets abroad.

Pata Travel Mart : Pata Travel Mart organised by Pacific Asia Travel Association needs special mention. The Travel Mart is geared to bring worldwide buyers of Pacific Asia Travel product services to meet with PATA member supplier organisations. The core of the Travel Mart concept is the appointments system whereby meetings are held during private scheduled business appointments. This enables buyers and sellers of Asia/Pacific travel products and services to meet in pre-scheduled, private business sessions to discuss and contract business for the coming years.

PATA makes efforts to secure the participation of tour wholesalers, conference and incentive planners, tour operators, corporate travel buyers and leading travel agents from around the world to meet with representatives from member hotels, airlines; cruise lines, government tourist offices, auto rental companies, ground operators and other suppliers. The names and business profiles of these participating buyers are furnished in an "Advance Guide to Buyers" and mailed to all registered booth contacts. The contacts are then requested to review the Appointment Guide and discuss with their staff the types of buyers they would like to meet during the Travel Mart. This information is then passed on to PATA via the Appointments Request Form. Buyers are also asked to review the Appointment Guide of Sellers and advise PATA of sellers' representatives with whom they would like to have appointments during the Mart. The information is put into a computer and schedules appointments are made for both contacts and buyers according to the following priority system:

(1) Buyer and seller wish to meet each other.

(2) Buyer wishes to meet seller.

Appointments are not scheduled based on requests by sellers only. An on site appointment scheduling session is held immediately prior to the start of the Mart to enable the sellers to book additional meetings during unscheduled periods of the Travel Mart schedules. Seller requests are provided to the buyers to inform them of the sellers' interest in seeing them during the Travel Mart.

After the computer scheduling has been completed, one receives a copy of his appointment schedule approximately two weeks prior to the Mart. Every buyer receives a copy of his organisation and forward copies to all his Travel Mart delegates. A secondary appointment schedule, reflecting cancellation that occurred subsequent to the appointment scheduling, are given to all delegates during registration at the Travel Mart site.

The participation in the Travel Mart is, however, limited. Among the buyers, the eligibility is restricted to only the delegates whose organisation has received an invitation to participate. The buyers are to be from organisations which are either doing business in the Asia/Pacific or have the ability to develop programmes and send their clients to PATA areas. Among the sellers, only delegates from PATA member organisations, that have registered as a booth-holder or co-exhibitor for the PATA Travel Mart, are eligible. The delegate category includes sales and marketing representatives of carriers, hotels, ground transport companies, auto rental companies, and destination promotion organisations.

The number of travel industry fairs have increased since the first travel trade fair known as the International Tourism Borse

(ITB) was held in the year 1967 in Berlin. Many countries now regularly organise such fairs. This is a result of the ever expanding travel trade industry. More and more industry fairs are being added in the list of existing events. Earlier in the chapter some important established travel trade fairs have been discussed; some recent additions include the following :

1. International Tourism Trade Fair (ITTF) Zagreb, Croatia.
2. British Travel Trade Fair (BTTF), Birmingham, England.
3. Moscow International Travel and Tourism Exhibition (MITT) Moscow, Russian Federation.
4. International Travel Expo (ITE) Hong Kong.
5. International Tourism Asia, (ITA) Hong Kong.
6. Feira International de Lisboa (BTL) Lisbon, Portugal.
7. International Mediterranean Tourism' Market (IMTM) Tel Aviv, Israel.
8. Swedish International Travel and Tourism Trade Fair, (TUR), Gothenburg, Sweden.
9. International Travel Exhibition, Copenhagen, Denmark.
10. Arabian Travel Mart, (ATM) Dubai, UAE.
11. India International Tourism Expo and Mart (IITEM), New Delhi, India.

Participation in travel industry fairs is a costly affair for the exhibitors because of the rising cost of renting a space. In addition, to the high cost of stand, the exhibitor has to spend a considerable amount of money on decorating the stand, travel publicity material, receptions etc. Any exhibitor, therefore, has to take into account the relevant advantages which will be available to him *vis-a-vis* the cost of participating. In order to achieve maximum benefits from the participation, certain basic norms are to be taken into consideration with a view to achieving maximum mileage. These would include the status of the fair, whether it is of international or national status, expectations from each fair, in order to determine its value, type of competing exhibitors, quality and the attendance of buyers, timings of the fair, etc . Careful planning will go a long way in obtaining the best results from the participation in the travel trade fairs and exhibitions.

12

Business Routine

The American Express Company, Thomas Cook and Wagon Lits were the only big names in travel business till 1920. In 1928, another big company, Exprinter Travel-Service, appeared on the scene in Los Angeles. It started the wholesale business of selling tours to small travel agents.

As long as travel was by rail and sea, tickets could be sold at railway stations or at the offices of the steamship companies. When airlines and coach operators appeared on the scene, their tickets could not be sold through these outlets. They offered direct competition to railways and shipping companies. The airlines, therefore, looked for sales outlets and that started the business of retail travel agencies. In the thirties, Pan Am Airways was so small that they could not afford a ticket counter. They borrowed three square feet of counter space from a Cooks office in New York. In return for this facility, Cooks got a commission of ten per cent from Pan Am while other agents received only five per cent. After World War II, a number of people set themselves up as travel agents, some of them while working as teachers and clerks and operating from their homes.

Travel Agency Business

There were an estimated 67,000 travel agency locations throughout the world in 1995. The fact that almost fifty per cent of the travel agencies are in the US is not surprising when we realise that US airlines earn over forty per cent of the world's airline passenger revenue. According to a study conducted by Louis Harris Survey in association with the Travel Weekly of New York, travel agency sales in the US soared to 85.9 billion dollars in 1991—up from 30 billion in 1980, and only US $ 5 billion in 1970. The airline revenue constituted 56 per cent of the average agency's total dollar turnover. The number of travel agency locations in USA in 1995 was about 40,000.

While airlines in US have been incurring massive losses during the last four years, the travel agencies have had a field day.

Airlines' Distress

The travel agents, it appears have prospered through airlines' distress. To boost their business, the airlines have been offering higher commissions to travel agents in USA. In the wake of deregulation, a plethora of new and confusing air fares brought the customers to the doors of travel agents to get the best deal instead of approaching the airlines direct for purchase of tickets. The commissions of travel agencies soared to over US $ 3 billion in 1995 — an all time record. The growth of commission has outpassed the growth of sales. The average domestic commission rate — was record 9.99 per cent and the average international rate 14.39 per cent — also a record. These commissions do not include any overriding commission which travel agents may have received directly from airlines.

Travel agencies have expanded their market. According to the US Bureau of Labour Statistics, travel agencies employed 152,200 persons as of June 1990. The average hourly wage was US $ 9.14 — a good wage by national standards in USA.

Travel agencies in USA are also changing their profile. This male-dominated business is slowly passing into the hands of women. In 1992,81 per cent of the management position in travel agencies were held by women, 60 per cent were owned by women.

How Travel Agencies Influence Business Are travel agents only order takers or do they play an important role in shaping the consumer's vacation plans? To get answer to the question, Travel Agent magazine of USA sponsored a survey in 1990.

Some 97 per cent of the travellers polled in the survey said that they visited a travel agency after having already decided to travel by air. However, 67 per cent among them had not decided on the airline. Among the buyers of cruise holiday, 37 per cent had not decided which cruise line to take. Of the people buying a tour package, 28 per cent had no particular preference for a destination and sought the advice of the travel agent.

The travel agent apparently has tremendous influence in the choice of an airline. Among the customers who had no preference for an airline, 83 per cent accepted his advice. That explains why airlines try to outdo each other to prove that they care for the travel agent or they are travel agents' best friends.

Of the 37 per cent clients who come with their own choice of an airline, if the travel agent made a recommendation, 13 per cent switched to the airline recommended by travel agents.

Among those who stayed in a hotel, 44 per cent used a property recommended by the travel agent. Of those who had a preferred hotel, 21 per cent switched to the property suggested by the travel agent.

The survey proves that a travel agent is no more an order taker—he does influence the choice of the clients in favour of airlines, hotels and destinations.

In the United Kingdom, the number of full service travel agencies in 1995 was 7,300.

In India, the number of IATA approved travel agents was a little about 1100 in 1996. Besides, there are over 1,000 ticket shops which are kind of sub-agents for IATA — approved travel agencies or for the General Sales Agents (GSAs) of Airlines. They buy tickets for their clients from IATA agencies or GSA's splitting commissions two-way, with the authorised agency as well as with the purchaser of ticket. They work on very low margins as their overheads are insignificant.

Chain of Distribution

Before going into the role of travel agencies in distribution of travel services, let us first examine how tourism demand is met by the concentrated efforts of a wide range of tourist services — where travel agency is an important cog in the wheel.

The term 'chain of distribution' is used to describe the method by which a travel product or service is distributed — from the point of manufacture to the point of sale to the eventual consumers. Normally, it is achieved through a number of intermediaries. They buy the products and sell it to other links in the chain. Among them are wholesalers, retailers, etc. Producers, however, need not sell the product through the intermediaries — they are free to sell it direct to the consumer. And some do it in a limited way, though not very successfully.

The tourism product, as we know, consists essentially of transport, accommodation and attractions—natural and man-made.

The producers of tourism services include air, rail, road and sea carriers; hotels and other forms of accommodations, and various man-made attractions designed to attract the visitors.

Brokers are closely involved in the distribution chain, specially in the field of air transportation and hotels. They make bulk purchase from the producers with an advantage in price and then resell it to retailers at nominal profits for themselves. Tour operators are also directly involved in the chain. They buy a range of tourist products in bulk—airline's seats, hotel rooms, coach services. They 'package' them for subsequent sale to retailers or consumers. Their product is called Inclusive Tour Packages.

Travel agents, normally belong to the retail sector of the distribution chain. They buy travel services for their clients, providing a useful service to the travellers without any significant cost to them. Their income comes from the principals—the producers of travel product — airlines, hotels, car rental company, etc. The principals offer them commission on the sale of their products.

There are a variety of support services which interact with the central distribution system to make it work. A government, for instance, provides support services to the development of good tourist product — the product in this case being the destination. The private sector joins hands with the government to make sure that the product is saleable.

Among the government controlled support services, are the National Tourist Administrations (NTAs) and local level tourist organisations, etc. The private sector support services include training institutes for tourism personnel, travel trade media, marketing support organisations, guide services, etc. We can add to the list by adding the private sector trade organisations. In India, these would be the Travel Agents Association of India (TAAI) and the Federation of Hotels and Restaurants Association of India (FH & RAI), etc. Internationally, the World Tourism Organisation (WTO), the Pacific Asia Travel Association (PATA) etc.

Travel Agency and The Distribution Chain

Support Services (Private Sector) ↔		*Producers of Tourist Products* ↔		*Support Services Government*
↓	↓	↓	↓	↓
Travel Trade press ↓ Financial Services	Carriers Airlines ↓ Shipping Services	Accommodation Hotel Motel Guest Houses	Man-made Attractions Palace Hotels	National Tourist Administrations State and Local Tourist Organisations
↓	↓			
Guide Services ↓	Railways ↓	Villas Apartments	Ancient Monuments	Visa and Passport Organisations
Tourism Training Institutes ↓ Marketing Support Services	Roads (Coach, Car, Taxi Hire)	Camps Caravan Sites, etc.	Theme Parks (Like Disneyland)	

(Roads, Camps and Theme Parks columns joined) → Tour Operators and Brokers
↓
Travel Agents
↓
The Tourist

The following chart provides the framework within which the distribution chain functions — supported by public and private sector organisations:

The Operation

In order to understand the economics of the travel industry, it is important to have a basic understanding of the structure and working of the distribution system in the travel industry including the middlemen who form part of the system. The term "sales distribution system" implies the method by which a firm sells its products and/or services to the customer.

If we analyse the current business practices in the travel industry, we notice the following four types of sales distribution systems: one stage system, two-stage system, three-stage system and the four-stage system.

TRAVELLER
↓
MIDDLEMEN
Travel Agents, Wholesaler, Tour Operators, Speciality Channellers
↓
PRIMARY SUPPLIERS
Airlines, Shipping Companies, Hotel, Restaurants, Bus Companies, Resorts, etc.
↓
SECONDARY SUPPLIERS
Chauffeurs, guides, caterers, Musicians and other specialists

The one-stage system provides sales from primary suppliers of travel services. For instance, an airline selling tickets directly to customers through its own sales and reservation department or a hotel chain selling its rooms through the reservation office of the chain in the city. The advantages of the system are simplicity, flexibility, greater profitability to supplier, and personal control over the sale. Its negative factors are high cost of maintaining a professional sales department and resultant overheads.

Supplier Dependence

	Estimated Per Cent of Volume Booked by Agents
Airlines	80% (Domestic)
	85% (International)
Hotels	25% (Domestic)
	85% (International)
Cruise Lines	95%
Rail	37%
Bus	Less than 10%
Rental Cars	50%
Packaged Tours	90%

Source: Travel Industry World Yearbook —The Big Picture

The two-stage system involves a single middleman, for example, the travel agent between the supplier and the traveller. This system has several advantages. A traveller, while receiving professional services, can also buy other travel products such as an airline ticket, hotel accommodation, transport and insurance from this office. The client has the advantage of receiving a single bill for all the services instead of different bills from different sources. The traveller can also have some price advantage because a travel agent can obtain better price in the case of group tours, conferences, etc., for his clients. A travel agent's services cost little to the traveller as he receives commission from the principals and also helps the latter in promotion by developing off-season travel packages.

The three-stage system involved two middlemen, usually a retail travel agent and a wholesaler or a tour operator. It provides the traveller and the supplier the same benefits as the two-stage system. An additional advantage is that the wholesaler makes bulk purchase of the travel product for which he gets a sizeable discount, a part of which he may pass on to the traveller by offering a low-priced package.

A four-stage system is like the three-stage distribution system except that it has an additional middleman, generally a speciality channeller involved in the development of a tour package. For instance, if a university decides to send a tour from USA to Europe, their office of overseas studies may also come into the picture.

The middlemen in travel sales, therefore, are travel agents wholesale and retail tour-operators, and speciality channellers. Their respective areas of operation are explained below.

Travel Agent

Louis Harris and Associates have developed the following definition of a travel agent in the Travel Weekly magazine of New York.

> "A travel agent, besides selling prepaid package tours, also prepares individual itenerary. He arranges for hotels, motels, accommodation at resorts, meals, sightseeing, transport of passengers and luggage between terminals and hotels; furthermore, he can provide the traveller with a host of other information (for example, on rates, quality and so on) which would normally be hard to get. The travel agent is paid for his services through commission. For example, if a travel agent reserves an air ticket or makes a reservation in a hotel for his client, he gets paid by the carrier or hotel in the form of a commission. In short, a travel agent saves the customer both time and money."

There are two types of travel agents: wholesale and retail.

A wholesale travel agent, or 'wholesaler' as he is called, specialises in putting together tour offerings, which are marketed to the public through a network of retail agents or airlines. He does not deal directly with the consumer unless he also operates at retail level. Some large wholesalers in the USA and Europe do have retail divisions. Wholesalers may contract with a tour operator for all or only certain land arrangements.

A wholesale travel agent may design tour packages marketed under his agency's name, or he may take land packages already assembled by a ground operator and combine them with air or a surface transportation to form new packages. The later practice is more common in international tourism. It eliminates negotiations directly with individual vendors — hotels, transport operators, and guides. A foreign wholesaler who wishes to offer an India programme may find it more convenient to contract an Indian ground operator for all land arrangements and then add international air transportation between the point of origin and the destination and his own mark-up. The suppliers of such services are called inbound tour operators.

The retail travel agent or 'retailer' sells travel services directly to the consumer. He represents or acts as the agent for airlines, steamship lines, railways, hotels, car rental firms or, sometimes, for the wholesale travel agencies mentioned above. Most reliable travel agents hold appointment from IATA and steamship conferences—it gives them a stamp of credibility.

US Travel Agency Sales

	$ Billions	***Percentage of Total Sales***
Airlines	47.9	56
Cruise Lines	13.6	16
Hotels	10.5	12
Car Rentals	6.7	12
Other Sales	7.2	8
Total	$85.9	100

Source: Louis Harris Survey for Travel Weekly -1992.

The distinction between a wholesaler and a retailer is only theoretical. A retail agent may design custom tours for individual clients by assembling prepaid, prearranged packages, the basic services requested by the prospective traveller. Occasionally, he may develop a package or packages which he may "wholesale" to other retailers. The dividing line is further blurred by the fact that some travel agencies operate both retail and wholesale division. In addition, it is not uncommon in the USA for individual retail agents to unite and form a cooperative that functions as a wholesale agency.

Tour Operator **:** A "tour operator" is responsible for delivering the services. Some tour operators own buses, hotels or other facilities or these may be obtained from contractors such as specific hotels, bus companies, restaurants, resorts, attractions, car rental companies or other tour operators. In some cases, tour operator's offerings are developed for, and marketed directly to, the general public. In others, they are designed as a package tour to the specification of a wholesale travel agent who markets them under his agency's name through his own network of retail agents and/ or through airlines.

A tour operator normally offers a variety of packages which, collectively, are known as "tour programmes". Packages may be for individuals or groups and may be independent (without escort) or escorted (with escort). Services that may be included in a package by a tour operator include transportation to the destination or destinations, transfers, overnight accommodations, certain or all meals, sightseeing and/or admissions, and car rental.

Ground Operators **:** Tour operators referred to as "ground operators" normally provide services at the destination only and do not package or market transportation to or from the destination. The services provided by such operators include overnight accommodations, sightseeing, guides and transfers. These are collectively known as "land arrangements". Ground operators who specialise in services for incoming visitors, particularly tourists from foreign countries, are called the inbound tour operators.

How large is the business of tour operators in the USA and UK? In USA, according to Louis Harris survey, 21 per cent of the US travel agency volume comes from sale of packaged or inclusive tours. This amounted to US $ 20 billion in 1995.

US Travel and Tourism Administration has estimated that of all the US citizens travelling overseas, 27 per cent bought prepaid, packaged or inclusive tours in 1990. In India the percentage is less than 5.

In UK, a survey by the Association of British Travel Agents (ABTA) revealed that inclusive tour formed 54.5 per cent of the total travel agency turnover. The rest of the turnover consisted of air tickets 31 per cent, rail tickets 2.6 per cent, ferry tickets 2.3 per cent, insurance 1.0 per cent, car hire 0.3 per cent, others 8.2 per cent including hotel bookings. The high percentage of package tours in UK is due to the availability of tours by charters.

The principal earnings of travel agencies in India are from airlines commissions that is their bread as well as butter.

Speciality Channellers : Speciality channellers include incentive travel firms, meeting and convention planners, hotel representatives, interline representatives, association executives, corporate travel offices, and travel consultants. These intermediaries may represent either buyers or suppliers and have the power to influence how, where and when the travel product will be distributed. Unlike travel agents or tour operators, speciality channellers do not usually receive commissions. With the exception of incentive travel firms, they are typically salaried employees who contract travel services at efficient costs on behalf of their organisations. An incentive travel company may either sell its professional services of designing, promoting and executing an incentive travel programme for a buyer or act as a middleman for both buyers and suppliers. Incentive tours are a new US $ 3 billion business now and the companies promoting such tours wield considerable influence in bargaining with principals, especially the airlines and hotels.

In India, there are some specialised travel agencies dealing with special kind of travels, i.e., incentives, conferences, senior citizens, etc. Most of them fall in the category of general business. Most travel agents are willing to take up anything which comes their way as the speciality market is not very large.

Functions of a Travel Agent : A travel agent provides complex and varied services to his clients. Some of these may be classified as under:

Valuable Information

A travel agent provides information relating to the destination, climate, modes of travel, prices, timetable, visa, currency, health, etc., to people who wish to travel. A good travel agent is something of a personal counsellor or psychologist, who knows all the ins and outs of travel. He often adjusts his travel services to the needs of a client. If the client is an affluent old man, he needs better class services with not much consideration to cost, and if he is a young person, on a budget, he may need different advice.

Destination Information

The travel agent provides information to clients on hotels and various other accommodation at the other end of the airline ticket. This includes the location and category of hotel, and prices. He makes the required reservation with the approval of the client and arranges sightseeing tours, excursions, visits to various museums. He reserves seats for theatres, concerts and other places of entertainment. On arrival at the airport, he arranges for the client to be met by a chauffeur-driven car and a guide or by a self-driven car. He also arranges cars on rent.

A sense of geography is part of his equipment. Every year, new destinations appear on the travel horizon where people wish to go. For instance, Seychelles and Male in the Indian Ocean, Kovalam and Laddakh in India, Algarve in southern Portugal and St. Martin in the Caribbean. A travel agent himself is a widely-travelled person. Special familiarisation tours are arranged for travel agents to acquaint them with the facilities in host countries. Often, their tours are co-hosted by an international carrier and the National Tourist Administration (NTA) of the host country. Every year, US Travel Service — the official national tourist organisation of USA — invites over one thousand travel agents from all parts of the world for what they call a "Pow Wow" or face to face discussion with US travel agents.

Every year, the Department of Tourism, Government of India, hosts about three hundred travel agents and travel writers from different areas of the world as part of their familiarisation and promotional programme.

Among the other functions:

(a) A travel agent sells packaged tours and sometimes escorts the group personally.

(b) Arranges for hotels, motels, resort accommodations, meals, car rentals, sightseeing, transfers of passengers and luggage between terminals and hotels, and organises special features such as music festivals and theatre tickets.

(c) Handles and advises on many details involved in modern travel such as baggage, foreign currency exchange, documentary requirements (visas and passports) and health requirements (immunisation and other inoculations).

(d) Uses professional experience to give information on schedules of train connections, rates of hotels, their quality, wherever rates include local taxes and gratuities for which a traveller may spend days or weeks to get information. Arrange reservations for special-interest activities such as religious pilgrimages, conventions and business travel, gourmet tours and sporting events.

Package Tours

A travel agency's function have diversified considerably. The travel agent is no longer an intermediary between the traveller and the supplier of tourist services. Today, a major source of his income, especially in the developed countries, is through development of package tours, tailor-made at the request of the client or sold as a readymade package. The agent can sell a readymade package on behalf of wholesale tour operators, in which case he deducts his own commission (generally ten per cent) and remits the remainder to the tour operator who has marketed this package. The tour operator has his own mark-up for profit. If the travel agent has resources, he can become a wholesaler himself, designing and selling to other retailers.

The organisation of package tours with an advantage of price requires creativity on the part of travel agent, coupled with innovation and good management. Airlines, hotels, and ground transport operators offer special rates to group tours because of bulk business. Travel agents promote areas which sell easily and where the profit margin is high. It is here that the National Tourist Administration come into the picture. At times, the NTA subsidies the tour operator's promotional advertising. They have to convince the travel agent with valid arguments that the destination which they represent will sell well and yield profits. The easiest destination to sell in the United States, for instance, is Hawaii or the Caribbean and perhaps one of the most difficult is India. Hawaii and the Caribbean have the advantage of price and proximity. Similarly, in Japan the most saleable tour packages are Hong Kong, Guam, Hawaii, Taiwan or the Philippines. Sometimes, these packages are even cheaper than a trip to a destination within Japan because of the higher cost of living in the country. Young Japanese find it cheaper to spend their honeymoon in Guam — a small American island in the Pacific — than a week in Osaka or Nagoya.

The types of package tours available as well as Inclusive Tour charters, which have become a way of life in Europe.

The Excursions

As part of their diversification, travel agents operate their own city sightseeing tours and excursions.

Travel agencies offer standard readymade tours or tailor them to the requirements of a group of travellers or an individual. Some travel agencies have their own tourist coaches and cars and offer regular sightseeing tours at fixed prices on a seat in the coach or seat in the car basis.

Excursion tours often include lunches, local entertainment and overnight accommodation where necessary. For instance, there are day-return excursion tour from Delhi to Agra and back, but a typical Delhi-Agra-Jaipur tour requires overnight accommodation either at Jaipur or both at Jaipur and Agra.

In India the government has entered the lucrative business of arranging sightseeing tours through India Tourism Development Corporation (ITDC) offering sightseeing tours and excursions to many cities. Several State Tourism Corporations have emulated the example of ITDC and it is now a big business. Several state corporations have started inter-state tours.

Business Travel : The business travel sector is often the most profitable element of a retail travel agency.

In India, business travel is the mainstay of the travel agency operations. Domestically, air travel is 75 per cent for business which also includes government servants travelling on official work.

Another 15 per cent air travellers in India are foreigners visiting India and the remaining 10 per cent travel by air.

In UK business travel constitutes 50 per cent of the air travel. In USA, business travel is the third largest area of corporate expenditure after salaries and data-processing, according to ABC International—1988 survey.

If retail travel agents want to capture a share of this important market, they have to offer an efficient and cost effective service to their corporate clients. The following principles have to be kept in mind while cultivating the corporate sector.

1. Setting clear-cut guidelines for staff regarding the way the arrangements for the travel of executives of a corporate client are made.
2. Getting them the best value for their money by negotiating special rates with hotels, airlines and car rental companies.
3. Travel agency staff must be well-trained to change a travel itenerary at short notice.
4. There is need to guarantee corporate clients that their travel policy is being scrupulously followed and the company money is used efficiently. A successful travel agent must develop an expense reporting system with details of all expenses, payments, overdue claims, etc., for the business clients. Nothing should remain hidden.
5. From time to time, there should be a review of the existing company procedures to develop effective systems both in the interest of the company as well as the retail travel agent.

The increasing use of computers in travel agencies is changing the way the corporate clients are serviced. An inefficient travel agency will lose its corporate clients, if it does not move with the time.

Setting up a Travel Agency

Setting up a travel agency in India requires a high degree of skill and organisational capacity. A travel agency may be large and not so large. A large travel agency has several members on the staff while a smaller unit is managed by only a few hands. Some travel agencies may offer complete service including airline ticketing, hotel booking, tour packaging, cargo, shipping and rail bookings while others may limit their activities to certain specified areas.

It is necessary to obtain a number of recognitions and approvals to start a travel agency. For getting the recognition easily, the following conditions need to be followed:

(a) The agency is centrally located, preferably in a business area and easily accessible to the general public. A ground floor location is preferred.

(b) Should have been in business for at least one year and must demonstrate its desire and ability to promote travel in a professional manner.

(c) Have competent and experienced staff to quote fares and schedules, make reservations and issue tickets.

(d) Have adequate finance.

(e) Maintain ethical standards of business in its dealings with passengers or/and the principals.

(f) Be able to obtain the required government licences where applicable. The travel agents in India offering documentation services, like passport and visa, have to be on the approved list of the Regional Passport Office of the Ministry of External Affairs as well as on the Reserve Bank of India for release of foreign exchange and for eligibility of passengers to travel.

(g) Have the approval of International Air Transport Association to represent member airlines. Separate recognition is required for passenger and cargo sales. This recognition is granted only after satisfactory functioning of a travel agency for at least one year. The airlines insist on certain minimum financial guarantees for IATA approval. Similarly, Indian Airlines demands separate bonding for its approval. Private Airlines in India accept IATA approved travel agents for their sales distribution.

(h) Have the approval of Indian Airlines to sell Indian Airlines tickets. Here again, separate recognition is needed for selling passenger tickets and booking air cargo on Indian Airlines.

(i) Have the approval of the Department of Tourism to claim publicity and promotional benefits for tour operators handling inbound tourists. This approval is not necessary for travel agents who do not deal with inbound tourist traffic.

Business from Overseas

A travel agent need not have all the appointments if he limits his business to areas more profitable to him. In the Indian context, there are tour operators who thrive only on handling and servicing inbound tourist business from overseas. An inbound tour operator gets his approval from the Department of Tourism if he has been in business for at least one year, has a good office, and has a paid-up capital of at least one hundred thousand rupees in the company.

Tour operators in India have set up their own representative body, the Indian Association of Tour Operators (IATO). It has been successfully functioning since 1982.

Travel agents specialising in handling inbound foreign tourists often publish their confidential tariffs providing details of services offered and prices for making travel arrangements. Confidential tariffs are mailed or given in person to travel agents in countries from where tour-operators seek tourist business. The tariffs are useful to foreign agents as they can pre-cost their services and offer it to clients in their own countries without making reference to the agent in India.

Special tourism awards are given by the Department of Tourism every year to travel agencies earning maximum foreign exchange through servicing of foreign tourists in India.

The number of IATA approved travel agents in India is about 1100. Only 100 travel agents and tour operators were on the approved list of Department of Tourism for inbound business in 1995. The government approved agents are entitled to concessions and incentives against their foreign exchange earnings.

Under the new incentive scheme, the government have exempted from income tax, 50 per cent of the profit of travel agencies on inbound tourism received in foreign exchange. The remaining 50 per cent is also tax exempted, if reinvested in tourism projects.

Different countries have different regulations for starting a new travel agency. But IATA approval is necessary in all countries except in USA where they have their own set-up. The travel agents in USA need the appointment to Air Transportation Conference (ATC) which is recognised by IATA. All agents appointed by ATC are endorsed by IATA. The other two appointments needed in USA are Railway Travel Promotion Agency for issuing of railway tickets and Trans-Atlantic Passenger Steamship Conference for shipping services. On getting these appointments, travel agents are entitled to claim commissions. Minimum financial bonding is required to get the appointments mentioned above.

Problems of Inbound Tourism : The new consumer movement in Europe and USA has made handling of inbound tourism from these countries very risky. The laws of these countries are biased in favour of consumers without realising the problems and ground realities in the host countries. IATA Travel News (August, 1994) has given some examples of cases awarding compensation to travellers on flimsy grounds:

1. The wife of a German on their honeymoon got pregnant because the suitcase which contained birth control pills was delayed during travel. The airline was asked to pay child support till the child was 18.
2. A group booked at a beach hotel had another group staying in the same hotel which consisted of handicapped persons. So they could not enjoy the holiday. The group sued the tour operator and was awarded compensation.
3. A tourist fell off the balcony in a hotel in Spain and he sued the tour operator. He was awarded compensation.
4. A client of a travel agent who opted for sharing accommodation, got an alcoholic as the room partner as a result of which he too became alcoholic. The agent was sued and the client got compensation.

5. A client got a room which he claimed was smaller than the size advertised. Management gave him 30% discount and he stayed happily. On return he sued the travel agent for US $ 10,000, the case was settled out of court for US$ 2000.

There are a numbers of similar examples. The travel agents in India will have to buy adequate insurance to meet such exigencies if they want to remain in business.

Legislation to Regulate Travel Agencies : Many governments including those of USA, UK, Japan and Singapore have enacted a legislation to regulate working of travel agencies and to protect the consumers. The regulations stipulate that licensed travel agency establishments must have trained staff, have minimum capitalisation and buy insurance for consumer protection. The laws to regulate travel agencies were enacted in recent years as several large agencies in these countries declared bankruptcies leaving their clients high and dry in foreign lands.

India has no legislation to regulate and license travel agents. Anybody with an office and a telephone can call himself a travel agent. Often, they buy tickets for their clients from IATA approved travel agencies or the General Sales Agents of Airlines (GSAs) splitting the commission with clients. Splitting commissions is unprofessional and illegal on the part of IATA agencies, yet it is a common practice among the small and medium sized agencies. In the process, the consumer suffers as the fly-by-night travel agent may close shop and disappear.

Size of the Market in India : Overall, the IATA approved travel agents sell more than 60 per cent of domestic and 75 per cent of international tickets in India. The rest of the selling is done either directly by airlines or their General Sales Agents which have mushroomed in many parts of India.

GSAs are normally appointed by an airline exclusively for the sale of its own tickets — technically, only at places where an airline has no office of its own or where there is no IATA agent. But in practice, there are more exceptions to this rule. In Delhi, for instance, where all airlines have their offices, several of them have a GSA too. Air India is one of them.

GSAs normally get 11 per cent commission — 2 per cent more than the IATA agents, 9 per cent for acting as the office of the airline. They are, therefore, in a better position to discount.

It is hard to police a system when everybody is playing an unfair game.

IATA approved agents, specially the members of the Travel Agents Association of India (TAAI), are hostile to the institution of the GSAs. They believe that General Sales Agencies are being set up by airlines to undercut their business and to deny IATA agents their legitimate share in business as selling arms of the Airlines. Some not so popular airlines are reported to illegally discount up to 25 to 50 per cent through their GSAs.

Travel Agency Organisation

Normally a large or medium size travel agency would have two parts: the headquarters and its branch offices. The headquarters, which is the main office, would have several sections—planning, operations, public relations and advertising, outbound sales, incoming tourist handling, accounts, audit, etc.

The planning section would look after the organisational planning of fares and costing. The operation section will run the tours. The promotion and public relations people will look after the marketing. In a smaller agency, all these functions will have to be performed by two or three experienced and trained persons on the staff. Arrangements have to be made and contracts signed with carriers, hotels, bus operators. For overseas tours, arrangements are made with handling agents in the destination areas.

Another important section in a travel agency is the one dealing with information, rates and documentation. This section collects and analyses a mass of literature coming from different parts of the world, and keeps the sales staff informed of the latest facts and figures, both at the headquarters and in the branch offices. The accounts sections deal with problems relating to foreign currencies, rates of exchange, exchange control regulations, payments, collections and receipts. In India, some leading travel agencies have sections dealing with railways. Selling railway tickets is not a profitable business as railways do not pay any commission. But it is done to provide complete service to regular clients. Travel agents levy service charge on the purchase of tickets.

India is one of the few countries in the world where customers are provided home delivery service for air and rail tickets. It is possible to provide these services in India free because of relatively cheap labour and intense competition among travel agencies. In Western countries, the client either picks up his own ticket, or pays extra delivery charges.

Following is a suggested organisation and chart for a medium size travel agency.

Travel Agency Managing Director

↓

↓	↓	↓	↓
Sales Division	Research & Planning Division	Destination & Service Division	Finance & Control Division
↓	↓	↓	
Advertising	Market Research	Contact with One's Agents	
↓	↓	↓	
Sales Promotion	Reservation & Contracts	Tourist Promotion	
↓	↓	↓	
Public Relations	Cost& Pricing	Technical Help	
↓			
Branch Offices.			

India to other Countries

It is ironic that till November 1977 Government of India kept Indian nationals tied down to their Indian homes. No holiday travel abroad was allowed in the interest of saving foreign exchange. People who wanted to travel abroad were given only US $ 20. Despite these restrictions, Indians managed to travel, dishonestly manipulating foreign currency regulations.

A little liberalisation followed in December 1977 when Indian citizens were allowed US $ 100 for travel abroad on Air India only once in three years. The law was later modified to include all airlines and the foreign exchange allowance was increased to US $ 500. The malpractices in foreign currency continued as US $ 500 did not go very far in overseas travel, especially as the dollar too lost its shine.

The new government at the centre under Prime Minister Narasimha Rao realised the folly of restricting foreign travel through currency controls. The foreign exchange issued to Indian citizens going abroad has since been increased from US $ 500 once in three years to US $ 2,000 per person every year. The business travellers can get US $ 300 per day plus entertainment expenses upto US $ 2,000 per trip. There are signs that even these restrictions may be lifted in the near future.

This should have given tremendous boost to outbound travel but the impact is not yet evident. The devaluation of Indian rupee has made outbound travel for holiday astronomically expensive, especially with the increase in the price of international air fares by 50 to 70 per cent in rupee terms in just three years.

Outbound travel is up, especially business and FIT, but not many groups are going as yet. In 1996, it is estimated that over 4 million Indians travelled abroad—more than the tourist arrivals.

In the next five years, outbound traffic is likely to double.

No wonder, some foreign countries have already set up their tourist offices in India to promote traffic.

How to Develop a Marketing Plan for Small or Medium Travel Agencies : In today's competitive environments, a travel agency which wants to survive and succeed must have its own marketing plan. A travel agent does not need the services of experts to develop a marketing plan, though experts can make a difference. An intelligent travel agent can develop his own plan on the basis of the suggestions made in the following paragraphs.

To assist you in this respect, let us develop a marketing plan for a small travel agency called Worldwide Travel, a one-office agency located in the city of Mumbai.

An important point to remember is that the plan must be for

one year, but the goals and objectives must be determined for three to five years.

To simplify the formulation of the marketing plan, it is necessary to define the product that we sell through the Worldwide Travel — we must know clearly what we are selling and where we are selling.

The Worldwide Travel is a small travel agency with an office in the heart of Mumbai. But, the turnover of the company has never exceeded Rs. two crores making it an agency which barely meets its expenses. The agency has no other branch in the city or in any other part of the country.

The company has not progressed because the management is largely dependent on in-house business from a business house with which it is linked. The manager is kind of an accountant who does not believe in investment for promotion. However, the company is in a position to augment its resources as the business house is in a position to provide resources.

How to go About it : Any marketing plan requires to clearly set its objectives and goals. It is the first step. The goals are set on the basis of proper market feedback which we call research.

Goals should be based on realistic assessment of travel agency's current market profile and how the management wants to change it.

When the plan is put into action, there is need for regular monitoring and follow-up with corrective measures.

Aims and Objectives

The chairman decides that the objectives is to make Worldwide Travel a leading single office travel agency in Mumbai. The time frame is 5 years.

Goals

1. Increase sales by 50 per cent in the current one-year period over the last year.
2. Increase income from commissions by 25 per cent.
3. Solicit up-market business from corporations and business houses — increase it by 50 per cent.

4. Diversify into inbound tourism business, concentrating on two new markets — Singapore and Malaysia.
5. Start up-market domestic tourism business to hills and beach resorts.

Case Study

Success of TCI : The Travel Corporation (India) with its headquarters in Mumbai is India's largest travel agency in terms of financial turnover, offices in India and abroad, and the staff employed.

July 1961 was a watershed year for the travel trade in India. It marked the merger of 3 leading Indian travel agencies—Jeena & Co., Lee & Muirhead (India) Pvt. Ltd. and N. Jamnadas & Co.—to form one company called the Travel Corporation (India) Limited.

Since then TCI have pioneered new areas in tourism and helped thousands to discover India and other parts of the world. Along the way, they have earned the Indian exchequer millions of dollars in foreign exchange, collected many prestigious tourism awards and secured a global reputation as successful tour operators in India.

TCI's Progress in First Four Decades

Rupees in Thousands

	1961-62 (Rs.)	*1970-71 (Rs.)*	*1980-81 (Rs.)*	*1985-86 (Rs.)*	*1989-90 (Rs.)*	*1992-93 (Rs.)*
Turnover	4,500	69,651	2,51,434	4,81,018	7,50,000	11,70,000
No. of Staff	100	350	700	923	1,060	1,100
Foreign Exchange Earning	5,204	1,3,610	72,407	1,20,386	2,80,000	5,20,000
No. of Offices in India	5	13	23	25	27	28
No. of Offices Abroad	—	3	6	8	10	10

Complete Travel Shop : TCIs services range from international and domestic ticketing to travel documentation and hotel reservations. Their exclusive "SPEEDOTEL" service assures instant room reservations at over 100 hotels all over India. TCI has its own fleet of air-conditioned and non-airconditioned deluxe coaches and limousines. TCIs are agents for India's extensive rail network Indrail. They are also special representatives of Eurail, Brit Rail and Greyhound of the USA in India.

Other companies which TCI represent in India are: KD River Cruises of Europe, Carnival Cruise Lines, Epirotiki. Lines, Princess Cruises and Holland America Lines.

TCI has an annual turnover of Rs. 1,170 million. It has over a thousand professionals in its 27 offices in India and has 10 sales offices in London, Paris, Frankfurt, Milan, Barcelona, New York, Los Angeles, Seoul, Sydney and Tokyo. Two more offices will be added soon in Toronto and Brussels.

TCI is a member of almost all major international travel trade associations. It represents more than 1,000 international tour operators.

TCI has achieved distinction through its innovative efforts, was often the first with new travel ideas, like exploring and developing new areas for tourism such as Sikkim, Bhutan, Lakshadweep Islands, Ladakh and the Andaman Islands, promoting India as a conference destination and pioneering cruises in the Indian Ocean; introducing air charters and in developing incentive and special interest tours to India. TCI was the first to offer scuba diving facilities in India at its Andaman Beach Resort.

Inbound Business : In promoting inbound business, TCI has been very innovative. For instance, it was one of the first agencies to introduce special interest tours. A fantastic variety of special interest tours in India is offered. Among these are:

Anthropology	Yoga
Archaeology	Angling
Architecture	Biking
Astrology	Desert Safari
Buddhism	Golf
Cuisines	Hang Gliding

Fairs and Festivals
Horticulture
India by rail
Museums
Ornithology
Palaces
Photography
Shopping
Gems & Jewellery
Heli-skiing
Rock Climbing
Scuba Diving
Skiing
Trekking and Mountaineering
Water Sports
White-water Rafting
Wildlife

Another area of their specialisation is incentive travel to India. Incentive travel tours are luxurious travel programmes offered by major international companies as rewards to their best workers. TCI designs its programmes in India with great care and imagination adding special touches like the flowers and sandalwood welcome, elephant and camel rides, mock Indian weddings, folk and classical dances, palmistry, magic shows, juggling and folk entertainment. Lavish banquet and theme parties are organised in chandelier-lit ballrooms of Maharajas' palaces and royal gardens. Sometimes, desert camps are organised for guests. Hospitality for each group is different. Bazars and fashion shows are organised. Special souvenirs, video films and photo albums pertaining to their visit are gifted to clients.

International conferences is an area where TCI has done a good job. They have set up a special conference management cell to undertake the handling of international and national conferences with precision. Their services include selection of conference venues, hotel and airline reservations, local transportation, sightseeing, pre- and post-conference tours and the supporting services required for the smooth operation of an international conference.

Air Charters : TCI pioneered the development of tourist air charters to India. With the liberalisation of government regulations on charter movement, TCI is now handling the charter travel from UK, Germany, France, Italy and Scandinavia.

Similarly, TCI handles ground arrangements for many luxury liners calling on Indian ports, looking after their tour and travel arrangements while these ships berth in Mumbai, Madras, Cochin or Goa ports.

Discovering New Areas : Discovering new areas for tourism has been a tradition with TCI. They were the first agency to discover the potential of Andaman and Lakshadweep islands. TCI built the Andaman Beach Resort, the first deluxe resort in Port Blair in 1978, opening up the area for international tourism. They introduced a wide variety of water sports in the resort. Andaman now receives over 5,000 foreign guests annually. TCI was the first to introduce cruises in the Indian Ocean in 1975. They also have ambitious plans to operate their own cruises in the Indian Ocean.

Ladakh was yet another area which TCI promoted and brought it on the international tourist map.

India Outbound : TCI is a major promoter of overseas holidays tailored for Indians and is the largest outbound tour operator of the country.

TCI's "Funtours" are carefully planned and include accommodation at first class hotels offering Indian vegetarian and non-vegetarian meals, transportation by deluxe coaches and sightseeing with knowledgeable local guides. Every tour is accompanied by an experienced TCI tour escort.

Destinations include Europe and UK, USA, South-East Asia, East Africa, Mauritius, the Maldives, Nepal, Turkey, Greece, Egypt, Dubai and Australia. Every year more than 5,000 Indians make use of TCI services for overseas holidays.

Domestic Tourism : TCI is active in domestic tourism, though it is not its strongest area.

Specially designed for the up market Indian holiday market, TCI's "24 Carat Indian holidays" are flexible and economical packages to popular holidays destinations like Goa, Shimla, Kulu-Manali, Darjeeling, Bangalore, Mysore, Ooty, Kodaikanal, Cochin, Thiruvananthapuram, Periyar, Andaman and Lakshadweep Islands, Mahabalipuram and Delhi-Agra-Jaipur.

During more than three decades of its existence, TCI has grown in strength due to its creative marketing approach. In promoting international tourism to India, TCI has several firsts to its credit. It was the first Indian travel agency to open offices overseas. It responded to the needs of the market and wherever it found potential, it opened an office despite high costs. For instance, it opened its office in Tokyo immediately after the Japanese started travelling overseas in the mid-sixties. Now, it has opened an office in Seoul as South Korea is fast opening up for foreign Travel, adding also this year two more overseas offices — Brussels and Toronto.

TCI is one of the first to introduce automation in its operations.

To look after the training of its own staff, TCI has opened an In-house Training School. Soon, the facilities will be open to other members of travel industry.

The success of any modern travel agency depends upon its ability to respond to the needs of customers. TCI seems to follow that golden rule.

Success of SITA

India's leading travel company, SITA World Travel, has grown into its present giant profile due to the untiring efforts of one man, Inder Sharma. Inder Sharma started as a transfer assistant with another travel agency which he has left far behind in business. He moved to SITA, an American company in the late fifties as manager of a 3-member office. In 1963, SITA became an Indian company and Inder Sharma became a partner. Soon, he was joined by another stalwart of the travel industry, Gulam Nagshband, and together, they made a formidable team. In 1970, Inder Sharma bought the foreign equity of the company and became its Chairman.

There has been no looking back since then. Service backed by experience, network and reputation are the most important essentials behind SITA's growth and strength. A staff of over 750 trained travel personnel offer quick and personalised service at 22 offices throughout India. Plus an overseas network of 8 marketing offices, and an excellent rapport with international and domestic airlines, hotels and tour operators, have made SITA one of India's leading travel agencies and tour operators.

Growth in all spheres has been the highlight of SITA's progress. Between 1970 and 1993-94 the company achieved a spectacular growth rate of 3,062 per cent. The foreign exchange earned during the same period, increased from Rs. 6.8 million to Rs. 417.6 million — an impressive record.

SITA and Inbound Tourism : As one of the foremost tour operators SITA offers a host of tourism services to the foreign tourist visiting India, Nepal and Sri Lanka. Carefully planned tours of the Indian subcontinent for both groups and individuals are prepared and executed. These tours include all facilities, choicest hotel accommodation, varied cuisine, well informed guides and escorts, and air and surface transportation.

SITA has been winning Tourism Awards instituted by Government of India since their inception in 1975.

Incentive and Special Interest Tours : Travel as an incentive has increasingly become an important marketing tool. SITA arranges incentive tours to exotic and luxurious spots that India offers. From a ceremonial welcome with colourful rituals, caparisoned elephants and camels, classical and folk dance programme to traditional Indian banquets in fairytale palaces and fun-filled cocktails and theme parties in plush hotels or outdoor locations, the arrangements are executed with utmost details.

SITA and the Business Traveller : The importance of a wide network becomes evident, when SITA takes charge of complete travel requirements. As an IATA approved agent it makes air reservations through computerised reservation systems, delivers tickets of the business traveller with confirmation of hotel accommodation and car hire. Being one of the largest business travel agencies, SITA negotiates special advantageous tariffs from hotels and car hire companies for its clients while offering preferential rates for its own fleet of cars.

For the globe-trotter, it is SITA's wide experience that counts. Apart from passport, visas, bank clearances, International Air Transport Association (IATA) approved Agent, SITA arranges air tickets of all international airlines.

As a member of World Association of Travel Agencies, (WATA), SITA has a worldwide network of correspondents in 179 cities in 81 countries.

Trade Fairs and Holiday Tours : In order to cover all the important international trade fairs for the business travellers, SITA offers specially designed tours that combine both business and pleasure. Years of experience has given SITA an edge over others.

If it's a vacation abroad, SITA Select Holidays open up a world of excitement through attractive package tours to the USA, Europe and the exotic East and Australia.

SITA and Air Cargo : For exporters, SITA offers at most of its offices air cargo facilities — customs clearance, advice on the best air cargo routes, favourable freight rates, insurance covers and of course, expeditious and safe air freighting.

Transport : SITA maintains a Transport Department with an impressive fleet of airconditioned cars and coaches at Delhi and few other important tourist centres.

Conferences and Conventions : As a member of the International Congress and Convention Association (ICCA), SITA is well equipped to offer services for conferences and conventions — selection of suitable convenient sites, reservation of hotels, transport and pre- and post-conferences tours.

Aside from travel related services, SITA provides complete conference management services on turn-key basis.

Membership of International Organisations : SITA has achieved international standing and is a member of the following national and international organisations:

TAAI, IATA, ASTA, AFTA, COTAL, JATA, PATA, UFTAA, USTOA, WATA and WTO.

The growth of SITA over the years has crossed the borders of India and has taken the company into the neighbouring countries of Sri Lanka and Nepal. This makes SITA the only Indian company to have its presence in the three countries of SAARC.

Training Programmes : Recognising the growing need of the travel industry for well trained professionals, SITA Travel & Tourism Academy was set up which organises specialised courses in the field of travel, tourism and in ticketing.

Future Programmes : SITA ranks amongst the leading destination management companies in the country. With multifaceted structures and activities, SITA is now poised to enter the 21st century in a multidimensional manner to represent and market in India the services and products of foreign government tourist offices and international airlines, hotel chains and other travel-related organisations. A new company—called TRAC Representations (India) Pvt. Ltd. has been started.

In the direction of diversification, SITA has opened its first 84-room ethnic holiday resort under the name "The Heritage Village", 44 kms outside Delhi on the national highway to Jaipur. They plan to add another in Goa. SITA's goal is to have at least one office in every state of India.

13

The Automation

Addressing the 41st Annual Convention of the Pacific-Asia Travel Association (PATA) in 1992 at Hongkong, Ronald Underwood of AT&T Communications revealed some interesting facts about phone services. He said, "When we first opened the Trans-Atlantic Phone Service between London and New York in 1927, a telephone call between the two cities cost more than US $ 700 of today. Now, the same 3 minute call to London costs $ 1.7 only."

He attributed this drastic reduction in telephone rates due to the amazing world of telephone wires, wrapped in glass. Each year, telephone companies send millions of international calls across the world oceans on beams of light that travel through a few strands of glass, each thinner than the human hair, but capable of carrying tens and thousands of calls at once with great clarity and economy.

Since 1927, when AT&T pioneered international calls, technological revolution in communications has brought travel within the easy reach of a good percentage of population in the world.

Telephone was followed by telex, and telex by fax. Now, fax which stands for facsimile is being further refined. The next generation of machines will bring about more changes. The new machines will transmit images as sharp as photographs taken from a Nikon-35 millimetre camera. They will transmit a page in just five seconds compared to 30 seconds today. And not the least, they will print on regular paper.

Another significant development is a new service which will multiply the strength of fax machines by several powers of ten. Enhanced fax uses the computer intelligence in the network to provide features that are useful to business of every size and type. For example, with automated broadcast feature, one may feed four papers through the machine only once. The enhanced fax service can then broadcast them to tens, hundreds or thousands of destinations on a mailing list at virtually the same time.

For travel industry, it means, we can send our message across all parts of the world in less than a minute.

Mr. Underwood revealed how travellers on the road will be able to move their office along. He said, "We will be seeing more laptop computers and public phones. AT&T's Public Phone 2000 is currently being tested at New York and Kennedy Airports at New York. The public phone is virtually a portable office for travellers on the road. The travellers can plug in their laptops, access electronic mail, or dial any home or business data base. It has speed dial access to travel reservations, voice message and translation service." Interestingly, it is hearing-aid compatible, its keyboard can be used as a telecommunication device for the deaf.

Mr. Underwood also disclosed how AT&T was overcoming the language barrier for the travellers. "AT&T has a great way of helping travel industry's present and future customers break the language barriers. It is called AT&T Language Line, and helps visitors to communicate with everyone from the hotel staff to travel agents to emergency medical personnel. Our Language Line is an interpretation and document translation service that gives any subscribing member, say a resort or an airline, access to interpreters fluent in more than 140 languages. It is open for 24 hours a day and 365 days a year."

There are other developments in the area of communications revolution. The facility given by the telephone departments in many countries to hold international or national tele-conferences with their executives has opened new horizons but, to some extent, reduced the need for business travel. In years of recession, business travel is the first casualty of the economy drive of any company.

However, researchers have discovered that despite these technological developments in communications overall business travel in the world is up. The reason apparently, is that business, trade and industry are growing worldwide, again due to technological revolution provided by fast communications.

Therefore, it is difficult to say what hurts what. In this new environment of global economy, the travel industry can never look back — it is bound to grow faster than other industries.

Computer Reservation System (CRS) : By far the most significant development in automation of travel industry is the emergence of a very powerful, comprehensive and sophisticated Computer Reservation System (CRS).

How CRS Started? Old-timers will recall checking in at the counter of Air India and Indian Airlines only 10 years ago when the check-in staff used to spread on the table large sheets of papers to locate the name of confirmed passenger to allot him a seat. It could take one, two or even more minutes to give a boarding pass to a passenger. But, now, it just takes a few seconds and the boarding pass comes out of a machine, duly printed. No manual writing is involved. The system simply started as an automatic reservation process. In the fifties, a few airlines had begun to use computers to keep track of the number of seats available on some of their busy flights. The travel agents who called those airlines discovered that they could get the seat confirmed promptly. Initially, the computers simply kept track of the number of seats sold on a 'flight'. Later, an important breakthrough came when computers developed the ability to match a seat sold with the passenger's name and thus were able to create a record. However, each airline had a different system. So, when one airline wanted to make reservation on another, their computers could not talk and they had to send teletype messages.

As the airlines industry continued to grow in the 1960s and the 1970s, it was realised that both carriers and travel agents could benefit if agents could communicate directly with the airline's computer than with a reservation agent. Calling in for reservations, changes or cancellations was a time-consuming and costly effort for airlines as well as their agents. Since travel agents sold all airlines tickets, they could not afford to keep the computers of all the airlines in their office. They neither had space nor the resources to do it. Therefore, need arose for a Computer Reservation System which could show the flight availability of all the airlines, or at least many of them.

An attempt was made to develop a Central Reservation System (CRS) which could serve the needs of all airlines without having a bias for or against any airlines. But, the efforts could not succeed in the absence of a consensus.

Now, a few major airlines have developed their CRSs on their own or in partnership with others. Travel agencies have also discarded the tele-ticketing machines in favour of airline systems that permit acquisition of more hardware and two-way automated communications. As a result, a travel agency now spends less time calling airlines and waiting on hold and even much less time in typing and writing. Agents put information directly into the system using their keyboards and by entering special formats.

The airlines can communicate with individual travel agents by using a queue format. The reservation systems have printers that produce tickets, invoices, and itineraries. The printers differ from earlier tele-ticketing machines in that an agent and not the airline gives instructions to the computer to print the tickets.

In the USA and Europe, 96 per cent of travel agencies now purchase or lease hardware from one, and occasionally from two carriers. In India. "The 4% of travel agencies that were not linked to a system were 'technological dinosaurs' or focused on niche market that are not well represented on CRS" (Collier D 1993). Air India and Indian Airlines have recently gone into automated computer reservation system and the computer their terminal are available in offices of leading travel agencies. Others are still depending on the telephone system to get reservations which are given by the airlines promptly. In the next 5 years, all IATA approved travel agencies are likely to have their own terminals. It is becoming affordable and small by medium sized travel agencies.

CRS as a Marketing Tool : The development in computing and telecommunication technology have radically changed the way in which multinational organisations like airlines and hotel chains do their business. New methods of storage, organisation, distribution, exploitation and analysis of the product and consumer data have changed the marketing techniques and investment priorities of airlines.

CRS, today, is unmistakably the most important marketing tool of airlines. No need to hire an army of salesmen to talk to travel agents, individually explain to them the product and price and to buy them free lunch to get more business. Now, the objective can be achieved by a fax message.

The CRSs originated in the USA. The first and also the largest is SABRE, owned by USA's leading carrier American Airlines.

American Airlines' Sabre, began operation in early 1960's (Collier, 1989). At this time sale seats on a flight usually involved a transaction between an airline reservation agent who would consult his internal CRS, and a remote travel agent. Travel Agents searched through printed guides and tariff for flights and fare information before calling the airline to determine availability and confirm other pertinent information.

The labour intensive nature of this process did not change till the late 1970s when the CRS began to make the leap from 'in house systems' to remote, networked terminals (Balfet, 1993). The change was driven by several factors like increase in the number of airlines as a result of deregulation of airlines in the USA and resultant increase in the range of fares and flights available to the general public. Another motivating factor was that the travel agencies could use their CRS terminals for several other labour saving purposes like accounting, issuing reminders to customers who had not paid etc.

Presently, Sabre and three others owned by US Airlines dominate the market not only in the USA but also in the rest of the world through alliances. Each member airline pays a fee when the computer makes a reservation for it. The other three leading US

CRSs are Apollo (United Airlines), System One owned by Eastern Airlines and Worldspan - jointly owned by TWA, Delta and North-Western Airlines.

A brief description of Sabre's organisation and capabilities will illustrate the sophistication of the modern CRSs. Sabre is one of the largest privately owned computer networks of the world. Its hardware is situated in Tulsa, USA, in a building specifically designed to make it virtually impregnable to terrorist and/or criminal attack and safe from natural disasters. It is difficult not to be impressed by Sabre's size and capacity.

1. It uses six of the largest IBM computers, connected by 70,000 miles of network data circuits to well over 100,000 terminals.
2. It contains flight and fare data on over 35,000 city pairs throughout the world with the schedules of over 700 airlines.
3. Its database has more than 50 million domestic and international fares, with the ability to construct many more, updated every business day at the rate of up to one million per day.
4. It can be used to book rooms in over 17,500 hotels, properties, rental cars from over 50 companies and seats on six railways. It contains detailed information on more than 65,000 vacation and recreation activities.

In July 1994, Air India and Indian Airlines signed an agreement with American Airlines to distribute Sabre Reservation System to travel agents in India.

Air India and Indian Airlines have decided to brand the Sabre product as Sitar or the System Interface for Travel Agents Reservation. Sitar is a customised version of Sabre to be marketed by Air India and Indian Airlines in India.

At present, there are 350 travel agents on the Air India/ Indian Airlines reservation network with terminals of their own. They will have access to Sabre product also.

Sitar provides travel agents with flight schedules, fares, seat availability and instantaneous reservation on 360 airlines in the world. Hitherto, Indian travel agents could only access the reservation system of one airline at a time and not all airlines of the world on a single screen as available through Sitar.

The new Sitar system also gives them access to information on rail journeys, car rentals, 27,000 hotels and 36 tour wholesalers.

It is interesting to note that SABRE system, now Sitar in India, connects 29,000 travel agents in 70 countries and in six continents representing 1,10,000 video terminals. (Canedy - 1996)

Developments in Europe : As the American carriers developed the CRSs, the European and Asian Airlines felt discriminated. The owning airline would naturally have a Trias' in its favour or what is termed as 'HALO EFFECT'. The 'Halo Effect' is the additional business which an airlines may derive from ownership of a CRS. The agents who subscribe to that CRS are likely to be more familiar with the services of the host airline. One way of producing the Trias' is that the owning airline invariably includes its own service on top of the flights available between one city and another. Since the computer screen can accommodate on first screening, only six to eight flights, the flights of the host airline may get a preferential treatment. Although the agent can seek the display of second or third set of flights on his computer screen, researches have confirmed that 75 per cent of the booking are done by travel agents on the first display itself. Agents do not have patience to go for second or third displays unless the client has already given his choice of the airline.

Some systems claim that they do not have bias while others admit and plead that the computerised reservation system is after all, a marketing tool and the Owning airlines have made massive investments in developing these CRSs.

The business from the 'Halo Effect' could be substantial. So, some European and Asian carriers did not want to be sidelined. They developed their own CRSs. British Airways, Swissair, KLM, Alitalia, Austrian Airways, Olympic of Greece and TAP of Portugal now own the GALILEO, and Air France, Lufthansa, Iberia and SAS have jointly developed AMADEUS. The name Amadeus came from the restaurant, where the executives of these airlines met and chalked out a programme to develop their own CRS.

Asian Airlines have not remained far behind. And the Cathay Pacific of Hongkong (CPA), and Singapore Airlines (SIA) have their own CRS—ABACUS.

The following chart will give the readers an idea of how the CRSs are being used. The number of agencies using the CRSs is estimated to have gone up by 25 per cent since this information was compiled in 1991.

CRS in Different Regions

Region	*Company*	*Agencies*	*Terminals*
USA	Sabre	14,000	69,000
	Apollo	11,500	44,000
	Worldspan	8,500	38,000
	System One	7,120	30,000
Canada	Gemini	3,500	10,500
	Sabre	1,600	5,400

Source: US Travel Weekly,Oct.91.

Europe	Amadeus	12,000	60,000
	Galileo	n/a	27,000
	Sabre	2,600	n/a
	Worldspan	3,500	n/a

Source: Companies' Estimates, Nov. 91.

Asia/Pacific	Sabre 2,900
	Apollo 1,000 (inc. 900 Japan)
	Worldspan Abacus 1,600 (SE Asia)
	Worldspan Infini 1,500 (Japan)
	Galileo S. Cross 1,300 (Australia)

Source: US Travel Weekly, New York, Oct. 91)

Rest of the World	GETS	2,000+00,000 Terminals)
	Sabre	2,000 (750 Latin America/ Caribbean)
	Apollo	1,300
	Worldspan	1,200
	System One	800 (mostly Latin America/ Caribbean)

Source: US Travel Weekly, New York, Oct. 91 & Companies' Estimates, Nov. 91.

In order to remain competitive, Air India decided to participate in several of them. Beside Sabre they include Apollo, System One, Data II (Delta), Gemini (Air Canada), Galileo, Amadeus and Abacus.

All CRSs are not the same. There are two basic types of CRSs which differ both in terms of operation and information offered.

Single Access : Single CRSs are the most common. The advantage of a single access CRS is that for any given city pair it will show the services of all participating airlines operating on the route, including many who do so by means of connecting services. The passenger is, therefore, able to choose the service he wants.

Multi-access : Multi-access CRSs are different. They provide travel agents/ subscribers with access to the individual CRSs of several airlines, without the need to have more than one computer terminal. Essentially, a multi-access CRS is just a switch which directs an agent's enquiry to the CRS of one of its participating airlines.

For owners of major CRSs, the systems have become an important source of revenue. When asked if it came to a crunch, whether he would sell his airlines or his company's CRS, Sabre, Robert Crandell, Chief Executive of the American Airlines said, "The Airline". He is also reported to have stated that if the company wanted to make more profit on each dollar invested, it should give up flying aeroplanes and just concentrate on CRS.

Computers and Travel Industry : The travel industry needs computers for the following resons:

1. Direct access to an airline's reservation system (CRS) enables an agent to see the schedules and fares of airlines worldwide and make reservation immediately.
2. The same CRS has access to data on hotels, car rental companies, trains, cruises, buses, destinations, climate, currency, exchange rate, etc. With the push of a button, all arrangements are confirmed.
3. Besides reservation, the computer can perform routine tasks at lightning speed, i.e., changes in reservations, cancellation, etc.
4. When linked to a printer, the computer can print complete airline tickets, itineraries and invoices.
5. A computer with appropriate software can summarise sales and commission income. Such information permits the manager of a travel agency to monitor the performance of his company.
6. Through sophisticated backroom system, an agency can print invoices, record of payments made by clients, keep track of receivable accounts, write cheques on date specified by the agency, keep an inventory of tour and group programmes, track commissions from hotels and car rental companies, maintain the agency's payrolls, produce financial statements, compile employee's productivity reports, store mailing list of special clients, print address labels and undertake many other functions. There is hardly any function of the travel agency which your computer cannot do.

What CRS Can do for Travel Agents : Automation allows the agent to:

(a) Check flight availability on any of the world's major carriers nearly a year in advance.

(b) Display schedules and connecting services between city pairs.

(c) Display the schedules of hundreds of airlines.

(d) Quote domestic fares, international fares, and many specially constructed fares.

(e) Book the reservation and automatically price most itineraries.

(f) Assign reservations to queue for ticketing on the appropriate date.

(g) Print the ticket, provide an invoice, and prepare the passenger's itinerary.

The system also can

(a) Check availability and confirm reservation for hotels.

(b) Confirm car rental reservations.

(c) Make Reservations and book tickets for some railway journeys.

(d) Provide international rail information.

(e) Access cruise information.

(f) Provide such information as weather conditions, theatre offerings, ski conditions, and availability of convention facilities.

(g) Keep files on frequent travellers and their preferences.

CRS and Airlines : An airline reservation can be made in either of the two ways:

(a) By requesting availability display and choosing flights from the display.

(b) By requesting space directly if the flight number and the airline to be booked is already determined.

After choosing the flight, the complete record of the passengers — Passenger Name Record (PNR)—appears on the display. It contains the following mandatory bits of informations:

(a) Name of the airline

(b) Right number

(c) Class of service

(d) Date of departure

(e) Departure city

(f) Destination city

(g) Desired number of seats

When the necessary segments are confirmed, the following information is added:

(a) Passenger's family name, initials and titles.

(b) Passenger's home/business telephone number.

(c) Travel agency—name, phone and agent's identification code.

(d) Ticketing information, the date by which the passenger must pay for and pick up the ticket or lose the reservation (option data) and the form of payment.

Additional fields (hotels, cars, cruise, etc.) could also become part of the record — if necessary.

To complete the PNR, the user must press a key on his CRT to end the transaction. This key indicates that the transaction is complete, and that the message should now be sent to suppliers concerned. If the booking agent does not press the key, the entire PNR will disappear and no record will be left.

Computers rarely lose messages — that can happen only if the computer is malfunctioning. The message, however, can be delayed as other messages may be waiting in the queue.

Future Trends : Four main trends can be seen in the international CRS world:

Commercial and Regulatory Pressures : Increased competition between CRSs, the rising costs of system maintenance and development, as well as the poor financial position of many airlines and travel agencies are squeezing CRS revenues.

The Globalisation

Operationally, there are many inter-CRS marketing and technical agreements. These alliances reflect not only a realistic appraisal by the CRSs that they have to expand to survive, but also an honest attempt to provide a global service for both product vendors and their travel agency subscribers.

Expansion of Travel-Related Sales : To be profitable, the CRSs have to expand their market. An increased focus on travel related or leisure product sales is common to all CRS systems. The development of leisure sales, therefore, has become an essential activity and CRSs are looking to develop leisure-related databases alone or in conjunction with other parties.

Development of New Applications at the Point of Sale This would involve the development of additional services at the point-of-sale or throughout the major CRS systems. Some of these applications are device-related and some are complex PC software applications. Apart from the CRSs themselves other service providers as well as third-party software suppliers are developing new applications.

Tourism Marketing

CRSs provides an excellent tool for tourism marketing. But there are some constraints too.

1. Almost everyone's requirements for information are unique and separate from the decision to travel and process of purchase. It is hard to develop standard replies to different questions.
2. CRSs have only recently started to enhance their range of ancillary services to subscribing agencies. Information technology development now allow organisations to combine a range of their existing assets and activities (products database, customer data base and the reservation system) to offer it to leisure travel organisers.

However, the performance of their new special products is constrained by the archaic basic system architecture from which they have been developed. CRSs as multi-national organisations were developed essentially to serve the requirements of the business travel market. Their role in the service of leisure travel market is, at present, limited by both technical and commercial constraints. But, it is likely to expand in the coming years.

Since the existing travel market is virtually saturated, the CRSs need new sources of revenue from tourism marketeers. The National Tourism Administrations, as yet, are not sure as to what their role is in the new technological developments or CRS systems.

A lot of effort is needed to restructure them to serve the needs of leisure travellers. And, it is bound to succeed in course of time.

A possibility is that Airline's CRSs will soon include information on tour packages and permit agents to book directly from an inventory. Instead of using the same brochures as the client, agents may receive diskettes compatible with back-office systems. The diskettes would enable agents to display pages of special version of the brochure on the CRT as well as additional information on hotels, sightseeing and other optional features. In fact, any agent with ability, time and the right backroom system could enter this data from brochure, reference books, guidebooks and the national tourist offices and could write programmes to aid people who do the selling at the counters. The screen may show to the client a 14-day programme of an Indian holiday starting in October or any other month of the year, or, for that matter, any other destination in the world. It may also include comments from clients who have undertaken similar tours earlier.

Frequent Flying Programmes : Another major marketing tool, besides the CRSs described above developed by airlines, is the Frequent Flying Programme.

The intense competition among airlines in the United States led to an innovative concept of marketing to foster brand loyalty among people who travel most frequently. A few years ago, most of the American carriers in North America introduced what they called Frequent Flying Programmes (FFP) directed largely to people who travel often on business. Passengers gained points for travelling, say every 1,000 kilometres. The more they travelled with a particular airline the more points they earned. At various levels, these points could be turned in for upgrading in the plane to a higher class or for a free ticket for the traveller or his spouse, or even a free fly-cruise package. The airlines which could not create their own Frequent Flying Programmes, joined other airlines to keep pace with the competition. For instance, Air India had once a tie-up with TWA on certain sectors in this programme.

Frequent Flying Programmes have tended to create brand loyalty to specific airlines and have acted as disincentives for regular fliers to try different airlines.

To retain or improve their market share, leading airlines of the world are outdoing each other to offer these incentives to people who can surely pay for their or their spouse's travel.

The Frequent Flying Programme has now wider dimensions, since hotel chains and car rental companies have agreements with one or more airlines whereby participants are credited with air mileage for using a particular hotel chain or car rental services.

All plans work about the same way with minor variations. First, a participant has to sign up with an airline offering a Frequent Flying Programme as a participant. Once enrolled, the flyer must make sure the mileage of each flight is recorded. The mechanics vary. With some plans, you put a sticker supplied by the participating airline on each flight coupon, with others you fill in a certificate and submit it at the gate with your ticket. And with some others, you simply show a membership card or provide your number when you check in for a flight. You automatically get the credit for the new mileage.

Again, frequent flying programmes have their origin in Computer Technology. Computers can keep track of the mileage and points earned by a passenger.

Air India and Indian Airlines Frequent Flying Programme : Air India and Indian Airlines which till recently had no such scheme have introduced their own brand of Frequent Flying

Programme in the face of new challenge from international airlines and the private domestic carriers in India. The system was introduced in mid-1994.

Passengers on Air India and Indian Airlines can now look forward to flying free of cost to over 100 destinations in India and abroad if they join this programme.

Branded "FLYING RETURNS", it is the only Frequent Flyer programme from India to offer the facility of accrual and redemption of mileage points on a combination of domestic and international level and that too to the largest number of destinations within India and from this country. It will, therefore, offer to India-based flyers the maximum flight options and the maximum opportunity to accrue mileage.

Members of the joint AI/IA Frequent Flyer Programme, the most attractive FFP for the Indian travellers, can accrue mileage points on either or both the airlines and redeem them for award of free tickets on either Air India or Indian Airlines or on both airlines. The required mileage points for both international or domestic travel can be accrued with international or domestic travel in any class of service on any sector of Air India and Indian Airlines or both airlines.

Tickets bought and paid for in India against all published fares, including excursion, group fare and night fare tickets, will qualify for accrual of mileage points. Members travelling in First Class will accrue higher mileage points than members travelling in the Executive Class, who in turn will be able to accrue more mileage points than members travelling in the Economy Class. Thus, passengers travelling in Air India's First Class would be able to claim rewards after making a lesser number of trips than if they were to travel in Executive Class (offered on AI/IA Airbus A300/A310 flights). Similarly, an Executive Class (known as Business Class on Indian Airlines' A320 services) passenger would have to make lesser number of trips than an Economy Class passenger.

Members will be able to redeem the mileage accrued by them in the form of award tickets on condition they complete 30,000 mileage points within 12 months of joining. Redemption award tickets will be freely endorseable between Air India and Indian Airlines.

Private airlines have introduced their own special programme for frequent flyers.

The Internet

A new dimension in information technology has been added by the Internet network which is likely to totally change the travel industry distribution in the world. The system is very simple—anyone owning a personal computer (P.C.) will be in a position to book his entire itinerary from airline booking to hotels at the destination by the touch of a button. He will also be able to see on the screen how his hotel looks like and could also see on the screen the lawns of the Taj Mahal or the banks of the Niagara Falls.

Dr. Negorponte — the 'Guru' of the system—in 1995 at the annual convention of Pacific Area Travel Association at Auckland predicted that direct bookings of travel through internet system will be available in the United States in three years and by the year A.D. 2000, it will be commonplace happening in the country. He predicts that by A.D. 2000 there will be 50 million computers in the US and that the price of computers will tumble down from the current US $ 1,500 to only $ 100. Worldwide the number of personal computers will exceed one billion by A.D. 2000.

The system may be operational in USA in 1997 while it will come a little later in Europe and Japan. India, a technology conscious country, will not be far behind.

This will have a tremendous impact on the travel agency distribution system all over the world. Agents depending entirely on commissions from airlines may be phased out — only those agents will survive who add value to their services. It may be interesting to note that of late there has been a stagnancy in the growth of travel agencies in USA — it may as well be the beginning of the decline.

The internet system will accept payment for travel booking through 'CYBER CASH', making the transaction complete. The airline ticket will be waiting for the passenger at the check-in counter at the airport.

Internet Challenge to CRS : Internet is the largest and the fastest growing information network in the world — and represents an important new challenge to the CRS. Not only is the network registering 25 per cent annual growth in users — it represents also a very lucrative market of potentially high spending travellers with an average annual income of US $ 60,000. Of the users 64 per cent have at least one college degree and are classified among the professional or managerial class (Cyberatlas-1996).

The ease and low cost with which its users (consumers and travel retailers) can access it has forced many CRS operators to establish worldwide Web Sites. *Sabre,* for instance, has introduced on-line *EssySabre* for consumers and commercial *Sabre* for corporate use. At present, the cunsumer *Sabre* generates about 2 per cent and commercial *Sabre* only 5 per cent of the Sabre revenue.

Sabre has recently announced that it will launch Internet version of its full CRS system — replacing its traditional hard-wared format. By moving its CRS customers to a web-based system, *Sabre* argues that travel agencies will save time and expense of installing *Sabre* hardware, wiring and dedicated phone lines (Rosen - 1997).

It is not yet clear whether *Sabre* and other existing CRS will continue to dominate the on-line reservations in the 21st century.

Automation in Hotel Operations : Computerised Reservation Systems in hotel industry were first centralised by Sheraton Group in 1956. These were further developed and refined by Holiday Inn in 1960s and since then have gone through generations of refinement. Every hotel chain has its own Computerised Reservation System or one based on readily available software.

From computerised check-in to automatic wake-up call systems; electronic locks to closed-circuit TV; fire and security protection systems to tele-conferencing; nothing is more systemised than today's hotels and resorts. One wonders how a modern hotel operates so efficiently.

The various integrated systems that tie several operational requirements together include a reservation system which checks the availability of rooms for individuals or for groups, assigns room types, tracks deposits, and prints management reports.

A front desk system handles registration and checkout; automatically posts guest accounts; provides telephone operators with room directory; updates accounts receivable and tracks housekeeping staff.

An accounting system handles guest accounting, night auditing and all back-office accounting functions. With available, options, the same system supports energy management, monitors life safety systems and controls telecommunication equipment.

Processing Information

An area in which technology has already advanced rapidly is information processing, including the use of company-wide reservation network, and at individual hotels, room management systems, point-of-sale charging, accounting, word-processing and personal computing. The hotel industry has moved dramatically from non-electronic equipment such as cash registers and accounting machines replacing them with computerised and electronic equipment that integrate conventional data-processing application with other hotel systems like energy control and communication systems.

A second major category of information processing is the broad area of property management systems. Over the past decade, according to a survey of American Hotel and Motel Association, as the technology matured, the number of systems that perform a host of management tasks at property level has increased twenty times. They ably and reliably perform not only reservation functions but also room management, front and back office accounting and operational reporting. That includes among others guest reservation, guest registration and folio accounting (the record of guest charges for room, food, beverage and telephone), accounting including night audit, city ledger, accounts payable, and general ledger, travel agency accounting including record of the commission to be paid, guest history and related marketing reports, daily and monthly operating reports, payrolls and the inventory.

Various vendors are now competing to satisfy the needs of each hotel or resorts. They not only satisfy their specific requirements but go out of the way to modify the systems to meet individual needs. In addition, the vendors will integrate their systems with automated and non-automated parts of the hotel.

For example, the more sophisticated systems are able to interconnect with other equipment that monitors telephone calls, energy consumption, restaurant and bar purchases, and fire and security conditions.

Point-of-sale systems have become commonplace in many food outlets, restaurants, clubs as well as hotels. A restaurant system allows the waiter to place order at a console located in the dining room, which prints it out in the kitchen. The restaurant systems reduce errors in calculating and totalling the final check, immediately post charges to guest's room account and provide a variety of analysis including daily reports and food inventory.

Automation has changed the complexion of travel industry especially airlines industry in less than two decades.

Computer Reservation Systems (CRSs) were perfected during the decade of the eighties. At present, some of the leading airlines own major computer Reservation Systems which can store information on flight schedules of hundreds of airlines and if requested, can confirm the seats on any airline in a matter of seconds. This is not the only thing they do. They store information on thousands of hotels and accommodation establishment, car rental companies, tour packages available and can promptly confirm their availability.

CRSs have, therefore, become a major marketing tool for the airlines, with the owning airline getting some advantage in the matter of display of their flights. The advantage is called 'bias' or 'Halo Effect'.

The Computer Reservation System were first developed in USA in early sixties — their performance improved in the seventies and in the eighties they expanded globally. Since European and Asian airlines did not want to be disadvantaged by the 'bias' of American carriers, some of them joined hands and developed their own CRSs. Airlines like Air India and Indian Airlines who do not have their own CRS, have joined several of the leading CRSs. Their flights are displayed on all of them. They pay a fee to the owning airline for each reservation they receive through them.

The process of airline automation led to travel agency automation. The airline owning the CRSs leased or rented their computer terminals to the agencies. These terminals can do the reservation and printing of tickets instantly as well as perform additional functions through sophisticated backrooms system.

Among these functions are printing invoices, keeping track of receivable accounts, tracking commission payments, maintaining agency payroll, accounts, writing cheques, etc.

Another marketing tool used by several leading airlines is the Frequent Flying Programme. It is a way of developing brand loyalty—clients who travel on the same airline again and again earn points which could get them a free ticket, upgradation to a higher class when one buys an economy ticket, etc. It is a bait which airlines give to business travellers to frequently use their service.

The new technology has similarly changed hotel operations. Most hotel chains have devised their own reservation systems. Others buy the programmes from vendors. Hotel chains also use Airlines CRSs for international and national reservations.

14

Evolution of Demand

Human behaviour can be understood by determining the motives, drives, or concerns which are being satisfied by the action, and secondly by the attitudes and information that the person uses to decide what response he should make in a given situation. A motive can be defined as a person's basic predisposition to reach for or strive towards a particular goal or combination of goals. Attitude, on the other hand, is a more restricted or a confined concept. It can generally be conceived of as an inner factor predisposing one to react positively or negatively towards particular objects, acts or institutions. A person's disposition or attitude towards an object is likely to be depend upon the basic motives with which the object is associated and the degree to which the object is perceived as instrumental in satisfying or blocking these motives.

The question of motivation is basically the question of 'why'. Why does Mr. X go to a temple every day? Why does his brother go on a strike and parade in the picket line four hours a day? Why does Mr X's aunt religiously observe all the cultural taboos? Why has his cousin complained against him to his employers? The answers to all the above questions are usually given in terms of individual motivations. These are because Mr. X seeks social approval, his brother seeks more benefits from his employer, his aunt seeks status and security and his cousin seeks to express his open resistance against the family of Mr. X.

Besides some kind of an active driving force, in any account of the behaviours of people, has an important role. The individual needs, the individual wants, the individual fears, these play a commanding role in deciding individual motivations. The study of the relationships between these two variables, the driving force and the object or condition towards which that driving force is directed, is the study of the dynamics of behaviour and motivation. The basic principles or dynamics accounting for the behaviour of going to a temple, joining a particular association, seeking status and security etc., are the same, no matter how simple or how complex the activity.

In order to make accurate predictions of individual behaviour and in increasing our understanding of social phenomenon, certain questions need to be answered. The questions such as what induces these driving forces of wanting, seeking, fearing in the individuals? What determines for different individuals the specific nature of the objects or conditions towards which these driving forces are directed? What happen, for instance, when an individual, no matter how strong the driving force, fails to achieve his goal? To know the answer to these questions, certain other important questions arise. Does each individual have similar wants, needs and fears? Can an individual's wants, needs and fears be altered or changed? Can one goal be substituted for another goal to satisfy the same want? How can individual conflicting demands be resolved? The answers to all these questions' involve basic principles of perception, thinking and learning as well as that of motivation.

Travel Motivators

Before analysing various travel motivators, it is necessary to recapitulate as to how the evolution of demand for tourism came into being. Tourism and holiday making are only a part of the much wider field of leisure. Increased leisure, however, is an important factor in the growth and development of tourism and is likely to stimulate tourist demand. The implications of the growth of leisure in the twentieth century are manifold. Prior to the industrial revolution, it was only the aristocratic class who were able to afford leisure and had virtually a monopoly of it. The leisure activities of the artisan class were, however, confined to their homes and within the limits of the town. Longer holidays for them were not known. Gradually, as time passed and the working conditions improved, the workers were able to get more leisure time and managed to arrange short holidays. The first significant change, however, came in England in the year 1871 when Sir John Lubbock's Bank Holiday Act came into force. The Bank Holiday Act introduced the "August Bank Holiday" break to give four recognised annual public holidays to the workers.

As the tempo of industrialisation grew, so did the workers' demand for more leisure time. Holidays gradually became an essential part of amenities for the working classes. Various acts were passed by which it became obligatory on the part of the management to grant holidays to its employees. However, it was a gradual introduction of the system of 'holidays with pay' which heralded the era of what is today known as "mass tourism".

Increased leisure alone is not sufficient in the evolution of the demand for tourism. There are, in fact, many socio-economic factors which are important. These factors include: (a) Income; (b) Mobility; (c) Age; (d) Education; (e) Sex; (f) Travel cost.

Income is, therefore, the second important factor in the evolution of demand, after leisure. Level of income forms an important factor in influencing tourism as well as participation in recreational pursuits. The more affluent members of the society are the ones who travel most. *Mobility* is the third important factor in the evolution of demand. With the advancement of modes of transport, the mobility has increased greatly. People are no longer restricted to a particular holiday centre as they tended to be when they mostly travelled by train. The communication systems have advanced tremendously. With the building of the new and fast roadway networks, the mobility has certainly increased manifold. There are also great advances made in air travel, more particularly for overseas holiday-making. Tourists now can reach far off holiday areas in a matter of hours.

Age and sex also affect demand. More and more younger people are taking holidays now. Younger groups participate more in travel because of more income. *Education* is yet another important socio-economic factor which influences the demand for travel. Broadly speaking, the better educated members of the population have higher propensity to travel. Besides, those with better education, travel more often. Cost is another crucial factor which influences the demand for travel. Holidaying abroad is particularly influenced by it. The price levels for various tourist services are specially significant. Countries receiving tourists should be able to compete with the costs of holidays in the generating countries. In Europe, a large number of tourists are attracted to Spain, Italy and France. In fact, these three countries receive the maximum number of tourists. One of the reasons for this is the low cost of Spanish and Italian holidays. Germany and Holland, on the other hand, do not receive as many tourists because of the high cost of food and accommodation. In South-east Asia, Singapore and Bangkok offer low-cost holidays and, therefore, are very popular among tourists.

Socio-economic Factors

Socio-economic factors like income, mobility, age, education and cost are thus crucial in the evolution of demand. Together with leisure, these are responsible for determining the growth of international tourism. The most comprehensive list of factors influencing the growth of tourism, however, comes from Louis Erdi of the Swiss Federal University. The list includes:

(i) Greater affluence and more leisure for an increasing number of people, particularly in the developed countries.

(ii) The emancipation of the young, and the relatively higher wages they possess (when they have no family responsibilities), enabling them to travel.

(iii) Transport facilities, especially air, very much better and cheaper, and there is a high rate of car ownership.

(iv) An enormous growth in international business, necessitating travel.

(v) Package tours allow people, not used to making their own arrangements, to travel with an easy mind, and are good value because of bulk buying of transport and hotel accommodation.

(vi) Relief from adverse climatic conditions in the home country may be found abroad.

(vii) Travel has become a status symbol.

(viii) Conferences and business meetings are proliferating.

(ix) Better education has interested a large section of the public in-cultural tourism.

(x) World exhibitions and trade fairs have become very popular.

(xi) Publicity has become more and more aggressive, whetting the appetite of even those most unwilling to travel.

(xii) Ideological pressure groups (Political, Cultural, Scientific, etc.) organise more and more annual conventions and conferences etc.

Motivation for Travel

Without people's motivation to travel, there would be no tourist industry. The prospective traveller's selection of a destination is sometimes likened to a trip to a travel supermarket, where the shopper walks in and selects the destination from any one of the thousands of choices. Although there are hundreds of thousands of possible destinations, the perspective of the traveller is usually circumscribed by a number of factors. These include time, attitude, family responsibilities, finance, education, physical health and well-being. The basic question of motivation as applicable in different fields can similarly be applied to travel. Why do some people travel and not others? Why one particular member in a family takes to travel while others do not? Why in a particular country or a region, more people engage in tourism activity than in another? The answers to all these questions have been explained in the preceding paragraphs. Several Studies concerning psychology and motivation for tourism have shown that individuals normally travel for more than one reason. Tourism is the outcome of a combination of motives or motivators.

Travel motivators can be defined as those factors that create a person's desire to travel. Motivators are the internal psychological influences affecting individuals choices. Motivations operate on individuals travel purchase choices within the framework already set by the determinants of demand. Several attempts have been made to study as to why people wish to travel or become tourists. McIntosh has stated that basic travel motivators may be grouped into the following three broad categories.

Physical Motivators : These are related to physical relaxation and rest, sporting activities and specific medical treatment. All the above are concerned with the individual's bodily health and well-being.

Interpersonal Motivators : These are related to a desire to visit and meet relatives, friends or forge new friendships, or simply to escape from the routine of everyday life.

Status and Prestige Motivators : These are identified with the needs of personal esteem and personal development. These motivators also relate to travel for business or professional interests, for the purpose of education or pursuit of hobbies.

Motivations for travel cover a broad range of human behaviour and experiences. Breaking down and elaborating these will give reasons as to why more and more people engage in tourism. The breakdown of broad categories would include the following sub categories :

Away from Routine

Getting away from the routine of every day life is perhaps the most important motive of all in recent times. The individuals desire and need for pure pleasure is very strong. An individual likes to have fun excitement and a good time whenever possible. The significance of the pleasure factor is widely utilized by travel agents and tour operators who are astute psychologists when it comes to selling tours. Various brochures and folders particularly emphasise the pleasure aspect of holidays and travel.

Relaxation, Rest and Recreation : Industrialisation and urbanisation has created great pressures on modern living. The stress and strain of modern city life has made it more necessary than ever before for people to get away from all this and relax in an atmosphere which is more peaceful and healthy. Relaxation is very essential to keep the body and mind healthy. There may be various forms of relaxation and rest. To some it is secured by a change in the environment. Others seek relaxation in seeing new places, meeting strangers and seeking new experiences.

Health : The development of spas during the Roman Empire was the result of people's desire to seek good health. The subsequent establishment of many sanatoria in Switzerland was the result of an awareness of the various benefits of good health. These sanatoria laid the foundations for future resort developments. Many travel to spas-and clinics for curative baths and medical treatment. In some countries like Italy, Austria and Germany in Europe, great importance is given to spa treatment. In the Russian rederation along the Black Sea coast and in the foothills of the Caucasus, there are numerous world-famous sanatoria where every year millions of Russian citizens and international tourists come and avail of the facilities.

Participation in Sports : There has been an increasing participation in a wide variety of sporting activities such as mountaineering, walking, skiing, sailing, fishing, sunbathing, trekking, surf-riding, etc. More and more people these days are taking holidays involving physical activities. In recent years there has been a big increase in sporting holidays. The visitors go to places primarily to indulge in a sporting activity to which all their energies are directed.

Curiosity and Culture : An increasing number of people are visiting different lands, especially those places having important historical or cultural associations with the ancient past or those places holding special art festivals, music festivals, theatre and other cultural events of importance. Curiosity has been one of the major reasons for tourism. There has always been curiosity in man about foreign lands, people and places. In the present day world, technological developments in the area of mass media have made it possible for people to read, see and hear about different places. The increasing interest shown by many in architecture, art, music, literature, folklore, dance, paintings and sports, in other people's culture or in archaeological and historical remains and monuments, is but another aspect of man's curiosity to seek more knowledge. This curiosity has been stimulated by more education. International events like Olympic Games, Asian Games, national celebrations, exhibitions, special festivals, etc. attract thousands of tourists.

Ethnic and Family : This includes visiting one's relatives and friends, meeting new people and seeking new friendships. A large number of people make travel for interpersonal reasons. There is considerable travel by people wanting to visit friends and relatives. A large number of Americans visit European countries in order to see their families or because they feel they are visiting their homeland. Every year thousands of people visit India for ethnic reasons. Many friendships have been made as a result of holiday acquaintances.

Spiritual and Religious : Travel for spiritual reasons has been taking place since a long time. Visiting religious places has been one of the earliest motivators of travel. A large number of people have been making pilgrimages to religious or holy places. This practice is widespread in many parts of the world. In the Christian world, for instance, a visit to Jerusalem or the Vatican is considered to be very auspicious. In the Arab-Muslim world, the pilgrimage to Mecca or some other holy centres is considered to be a great act of faith. In India there are many pilgrimage centres and holy places of all the major religions of the world where every year a large number of pilgrims from all over the world congregate.

Status and Prestige : This relates to ego needs and personal development. Many people undertake travel with a view to talk about it to their relatives and friends. They like to impress them by relating their experiences in the various places visited. They also travel because they think it is fashionable to do so and, perhaps, show that they can afford to do it. 'Foreign tour' is a magic word and people like to mention it to their friends and other acquaintances.

Professional or Business : Attending conventions and conferences related to the professions, industry or commerce or to some organisation to which the individual belongs has become very popular. The 'convention travel' has made great strides in recent times. Many countries, in order to attract more tourists, have established grand convention complexes where all kinds of modern facilities are provided for business meetings, seminars and conventions. Large hotels also provide facilities for conventions as a large number of people travel for business and professional reasons. Conventions and conferences associated with education, commerce, industry, politics and various professions are increasingly being held in various parts of the world. Although some people travel strictly for business purposes, the majority link business travel with pleasure.

Professor Krapf cites in his summary to the history of tourism a series of motivations which he considers as the determining impulses of tourism in the past and present. As the *first* motivating factor, Krapf mentions the exploration of the close and distant neighbourhood. If we proceed from the fact that foreign lands and people were originally looked upon as dangerous and even hostile, it is obvious that considerable personal courage was required to visit or confront them. Only a strong man with initiative could dare to forsake the security of the family or the clan and travel to nearby or distant places. The *second* motivation advanced by Krapf is divine service. Originally this also implied an exceptional social position for it was a prerogative reserved for priests to visit places considered as abodes of the deities and it was only gradually that the worldly high-ranking persons were able to approach them. The same held true for the *third* motivation which is participation in events of religious or secular authority. Such participation was again reserved for the selected few, i.e., those of higher social positions. The utilisation of natural medical cures or journeys to watering-places, as the *fourth* motivating factor, is again characterised by being restricted to particular social classes, at first the nobility and later the well-to-do bourgeoisie. Here the restriction flowed from the fact of long distances and the related high costs of travel and sojourn.

The final motive force mentioned by Krapf is the enjoyment of nature which must however be regarded as of relatively late validity at a time when men began to take pleasure in nature and did not look upon it as something to be taken for granted or even, to some extent, dangerous. It was the intellectual call for a "return to Nature" which first exercised the spell and made trips into what is now considered as "magnificent Nature", a favourite social practice. But here again the high costs resulted in this practice being restricted to the well-off, that is the higher social classes. Thus we see that there is no ground for modifying the argument that the spread of the need to travel outside one's habitual place has its roots in the striving for social influence and that the expansion of tourism or the satisfaction of this need is the logical consequence of social progress.

The democratisation of travel, this being formerly a sign of distinction, developed through holiday stays, the travel flow which we encounter at present. Consequently, we must enlarge the test of motivations drawn up by Professor Krapf with a tourist motivation, namely, the enjoyment of travel. It is not the fact of sojourning but of motion, not the destination but the journey, the innumerably multifarious, though often momentary impressions, which account for a part of modern tourism. It is the joy in motion, especially motorised motion, which has become a major motivating force while the landscape which is traversed has become a side-scene. Some of the motivations cited in respect of modern tourism are enumerated as follows:

(a) The exploration of the close and distant neighbourhood, knowing other countries, regions or people, and also travel for studies and cultural ends.

(b) Divine service as a travel motivating force subsists in journeys to sacred religious places and in pilgrimages.

(c) Participation in events of religious or secular authority manifests itself today in the form of travel to political meetings and ceremonies.

(d) The utilisation of natural medical cures comprises in the widest sense all travel undertaken with the object of rest and relaxation, medical care or treatment of diseases.

(e) Travel for the enjoyment of the beauties of the landscape has undergone modifications both in the conception of what is beautiful and in the expression of sentiment.

(f) A further motive force of tourism is constituted by sports travel. This includes travel for the sake of travelling, the joy in motion. In fact, this is only one sports activity projected on the travel scene in addition to the numerous other motive forces connected with sports for which landscape and nature provide the setting for the best possible practice and exercise of sports.

Several reasons as to why people wish to become tourists have been considered. In considering the reasons we are thus dealing with the motivations. After examining the motivations two broad distinguishable groups of travellers emerge. The first group consists of those who have to visit a particular place and includes businessmen and some elements of those who may be described as common interest travellers such as those visiting relatives and friends. The decision to travel, when and where to go, how much to spend, etc., is to a greater or lesser extent outside the control of this group of travellers. They are also less influenced by price or distance factor. Particularly business travel is relatively price-inelastic and is not susceptible to price inducements. The second group consists of tourists in the pure sense who have a freedom of choice. This group decides for themselves whether they should apply a part of their income and a part of their leisure time to participate in tourism. They also decide for themselves where and when to go. The demand for travel for this group as compared to the demand for the former group is highly price-elastic, that is susceptible to price inducements. The reasons for travel away from home in the case of businessmen and others in the first group are self-evident. Each may, indeed, be marginally influenced by those considerations which affect the second group, the pleasure travellers. This may be reflected in the frequency of visits or the consideration of alternatives as, for example, in the choice of venues for conventions and conferences. In pleasure or holiday travel on the other hand, the reasons are varied and not always clearly evident or easily identifiable.

The prime motive to engage in tourism is to be 'elsewhere' and to escape, however temporarily, from the routine and stress and strains of everyday life. From this prime motivation two principal and distinct motivations may be stipulated as dominant. These have been described by Professor Gray as: 1. Wanderlust; 2. Sunlust.

Wanderlust describes the desire to exchange the known for the unknown or familiar with the unfamiliar, to leave things familiar and to go and see different places, people and cultures or architecture of the past, in places famous for their historical monuments and also past associations. This also involves seeing current fashions. *Sunlust* on the other hand generates a type of travel which depends on the existence elsewhere of better amenities and facilities for a specific purpose than are available in the home country of the traveller. It is prominent with particular activities such as sports and with the search for sunshine. Wanderlust calls for facilities geared to short-stay visitors and for means of movement at the destinations. Sunlust on the other hand requires facilities for a longer stay and for recreation.

Tracing the history of travel over the centuries, it is quite evident that the main motives for travel have not changed much. These have remained the same in form. Only the scope and the intensity have changed. The principal motives continue to be the same. While wanderlust in ancient times manifested itself in the exploration and search of the unknown, today it has the same purpose with a different angle. Similarly Sunlust in the past was associated with pleasure travel of the Romans, today it manifests itself in exotic holidays around the beaches and the holiday villages.

Exercises

1. You have been engaged as a consultant for marketing of the tourist product of Goa. Identify the product and develop a marketing plan for Goa Tourism. Also, advise how Goa should be marketed in Europe, USA and Japan. Suggest the communications mix.
2. Define the term 'marketing'. How is marketing different from sales?
3. What are the principal stages of developing a tourism marketing plan for a country?
4. What do you understand by segmentation of market? Why is segmentation essential for tourism sales?
5. How does travel research help the marketing process? What is the role of desk research in tourism marketing?
6. How is a package tour developed? Tell the story of development of package tours through charters from UK to Spain.
7. What are the important components in Communication Mix?
8. Assuming you are appointed as the head of the Indian Tourist Office in UK, suggest a communications mix that you will use to market the Indian tourist product to achieve 25 per cent growth in one year. Start with identifying the Indian tourist product that you wish to market in the United Kingdom.

9. Identify four major market segments in tourism. Write a paragraph on each one of them.
10. What are the four "Ps" in travel marketing? Explain each.
11. Describe the current profile of Indian tourism — the number of visitors, their age groups, mode of travel, season of travel, sex-ratio and the average stay.
12. What is the average expenditure per foreign tourist in India? What are the principal items on which they spend money?
13. Can India become a mass tourism destination? Give your reasons for or against.
14. Why did India's plan to attract 5 million visitors during 1992-1997 not materialise? Give reasons.
15. How has India promoted its tourism? Give a brief summary of marketing approach in the sixties, seventies and the eighties and now in the nineties.
16. Has the travel industry been cooperating with the Government of India in promoting tourism? How do they do it?
17. How would you assess the marketing of Indian tourism during the past four decades? Has it been effective?
18. Develop a Market Plan to increase tourist arrivals in India by 50 per cent in three years.
19. India has a reputation of setting high targets of tourist arrivals and not achieving it. Give some examples.
20. What is a Computer Reservation System (CRS)? What can it do for airlines?
21. What is a 'Halo Effect' in a CRS? How does it help an airline which owns it?
22. Name five major CRSs in the world. Describe two of them.
23. What can a Computer Reservation System do for a travel agency?

24. What are the future possible uses of CRS technology?
25. Explain the Frequent Flying Programmes of airlines. How are these programmes operated?
26. Do Air India and Indian Airlines have a Frequent Flying Programme? How does it operate?
27. Does Air India have its own CRS? If not, how does it manage?
28. What does SITAR stand for? What are its functions?
29. Describe the effect of automation on the operation of hotels.
30. Internet offers a new challenge to CRS. How?

Appendices

The Glossary

Affinity Group : A group bound together by a common interest or affinity. Where charters are concerned, this common bond makes the members eligible for charter flights. One must have been a member of the group for six months or longer. They must travel together, on the departure and return flight, but they can travel independently where ground arrangements are concerned.

Airline : Any air transport enterprise offering or operating a scheduled international air service.

Amenities : Features which enable a visitor to enjoy various attractions and which draw him to a country and for the use of which he normally has to pay. These refer to recreational and entertainment programmes, cultural and art centres, hotels, restaurants, transport services, etc.

Antiquities : Art objects which are more than one hundred years old and which cannot be traded.

Attractions : Natural or man-made features which collectively or singly create the appeal of a country.

Brochure : A pamphlet bound in the form of a booklet.

Bulletin : A news brief periodically issued. A mailing or promotion piece, often devoted to trade news. A painted outdoor display.

Business Travel : Type of travel necessitated by a passengers' professional activities, and possibly requiring special services like conference room, secretariat services, etc.

Campaign : A connected, integrated and organised series of advertising and promotional efforts.

Camping Site : A place providing simple and inexpensive shelter to travellers. The site provides wayside amenities for tourists travelling by long distance coach tours and self-driven cars.

Carrier : A public transportation company such as air or steamship line, railroad, bus, etc.

Conducted Tour : A pre-paid, pre-arranged vacation in which a group of people travel together under the guidance of a touricader who stays with them from the start to the end of the trip. Also referred to as an "escorted tour".

Cruise : An all expense pre-paid, pre-arranged tour by a ship to specific ports.

Cultural Tourism : The form of tourism whose object is, among other things, the discovery of monuments and sites. It contributes to their maintenance and protection and in doing so, brings social, cultural and economic benefits to people.

Destination : The place at which a traveller terminates his journey. The ultimate stopping place according to the contract of carriage.

Destination Facilities : All plant and infrastructure available in a country, an area of local destination.

Destinational Tourist : A tourist who terminates his journey at a particular country for the purpose of making a tour travelling from place to place for pleasure in that country.

Destinational Traffic : Persons (tourist) carried by transportation lines and terminating their journey at one particular place. A tour constructed to meet the specific desire of a client within a single country.

Domestic Tourist : A Agent who makes tour travelling from place to place for pleasure, business, family, mission, meeting, etc., within the country.

Escort Tour : A professional tour escort often called Tour Manager or Courier.

Excursion : A tour outside the limits, but however in the vicinity of the town where the organising agency is located. Such a tour may be for a half day to three days according to the rule adopted in the tariff. It comprises accommodation, meals and transportation from departure to return to the given town or city.

Excursionist : A temporary visitor staying less than twenty four hours in the country visited.

Facilitation : The act of assisting progress or helping to move forward. To make easier or less difficult. Promoting any measure which will facilitate international travel with prime emphasis on achieving minimum entry and exit formalities for temporary visitor.

Facilities : Services which enable tourists to enter and move around the country with the maximum of ease and the minimum of obstacles and to secure maximum enjoyment of their visit.

Folder : One piece of illustrated paper which can be folded. It is usually printed on a single sheet and then folded for easy handling.

Ground Arrangement : All services provided for the traveller by his tour operator after the traveller reaches his first foreign destination. Also referred to as Land Arrangements.

Group Inclusive Tour : A tour which includes group air and ground arrangements for a minimum of 15 persons. They may or may not stay together as a group for both the land and air portion of the trip.

Guaranteed Tour : A tour which is guaranteed to operate unless cancelled 60 days prior to departure. In the event of cancellation within 60 days of departure date, full commission is paid to agents of sold clients.

Guide : A person who is licensed to take paying guests on local sightseeing excursions.

Guided Tour : A tour conducted only by local city guides.

Incentive Travel : A trip offered by a company or any other organisation, to reward or encourage a member of their sales or administrative staff.

Inclusive Tour : A tour which includes all elements of an itinerary, making it unnecessary, for a passenger to spend money for anything except personal extras during the course of the tour.

Infrastructure : The basic public services needed for the successful operation of tourism enterprises and for optimising the comfort of the visitors. It includes such services as roads, electricity, water, security, sanitation and health services, telephone and postal communication, railways and airports.

Interline : Between two or more transportation lines.

Itinerary : Pertaining to a journey. A tourist itinerary as a composition of a series of operations that are a result of the study of the market.

Land Arrangements : All services provided for the traveller by his tour operator after the traveller reaches his first foreign destination. Does not apply to overseas travel. Also referred to as Ground Arrangements.

Market : The totality of actual and/or potential buyers of a given product of service in a specified geographical location at a given point in time or during a given period of time.

Market Segmentation : Process of identifying groups of buyers of the total market with different buying desires or requirements.

Marketing : A total activity which includes an evaluation of market and the requirements of individuals within that market, together with an evaluation of a service, facility or visitor plant, separately or jointly, its cost of accessibility, and the total facilities to provide visitor satisfaction. It includes a merchandising programme aimed at a particular type of customer to convert him to user or purchaser of the service.

Mass Tourism : Large scale movement of travellers and the development of a standardised product.

Multiplier : The numerical coefficient showing how great an increase in income results from each increase in such investment spending.

Multiplier Effect : The money spent by the tourist circulates through the economy and stimulates it, as it changes hands and is spent and respent a number of times. There is a chain reaction of spending, triggered off by the "injection" of the tourist dollar into a destination economy. This constant turnover of tourist expenditure is known as the 'Multiplier Effect'.

National Tourist Organisation : The body responsible for the formulation and implementation of national tourist policy. It is the agency and the instrument for the execution of the national government's responsibilities for the control, direction and promotion of tourism.

Optional : In travel literature the word means that the traveller has a choice of taking or not taking the service mentioned. If he takes it, there is always an additional charge which is not included in the basic tour price.

Package : A travel plan which includes most elements of a vacation, such as transportation, accommodation and sightseeing.

Package Tour : A travel plan including transfers, accommodation and sightseeing in a given city or town.

Passport : A document issued by national governments to their own citizens as verification of their citizenship. It is also a permit to leave one's own country and return.

Poster : A pictorial representation of an idea. It is intended to attract attention rapidly to a single word or idea.

Promotion : All activities in producing and increasing sales, including advertising, publicity and personal selling. The activities that supplement and make advertising and personal selling more effective. Special events individually treated to bring public attention to specific products.

Public Relations : Continuous and consistent representation of an organisation's policies to the public at large and to sections of the public who have a special interest in the organisation's activities.

Resort : A spot which is frequented by the tourists. It is a place which has all the facilities for the comfort of the visitors.

Retail Agent : An agent who sells his individual travel services, e.g., transportation or accommodation to the general public.

Retailing : The sale directed to the ultimate consumer, distinguished from wholesaling—the selling of relatively large quantities of products to those who resell (the retailers).

Sale Promotion : All activities in producing and increasing sales, including advertising, publicity and personal selling. The activities that supplement and make advertising and personal selling more effective.

Sales Letter : A direct mail material through which an attempt is made to gain agreement or favourable action towards a product.

Sample Survey : Study of a given population through only a part or a fraction thereof.

Sightseeing : A tour within the city limits showing to clients the main attractions of the place such as major city centres, archaeological sites, museums, parks, monuments, etc.

Social Tourism : All the relations and phenomena resulting from the accession to tourism of low-income groups made possible or facilitated by specific social measures. It is the type of tourism practised by those who otherwise would not be able to meet the cost without social intervention, i.e., without the assistance of an association to which the individual belongs.

Statistics : That branch of science which deals with the frequency of occurrence of different kinds of things or with the frequency of occurrence of different attributes.

Suggested Itinerary : A preliminary itinerary provided by tour operators for the traveller's consideration. This generally shows routings and approximate times as well as recommended hotels and suggested sightseeing, excursions, and spells out the conditions under which these services will be provided.

Supplier : A company which provides the actual components of travel. It may be a major airlines, a hotel or a local tour operator.

Tour : A long distance circuit of more than 3 days organised by a travel agency in a given town and comprising sightseeing in several other places or towns either within or outside the country of touring.

Tour Conductor : A professional employee of a tour operator who accompanies a group on tour. Not to be compared with Guide.

Tour Inclusive : A tour plan which includes various components such as airfares, hotel and sightseeing.

Tour Manager : One who controls, directs, and manages an enterprise with judicious economy and care.

Tour Operator : A company which specialises in the planning and operation of pre-paid, pre-planned vacations, and which makes these available to the general public through a travel agent.

Tour Organiser : A person who organises a group of passengers to participate in a specially prepared itinerary.

Tour Package : A travel plan which includes most elements of a vacation, such as transportation, accommodation and sightseeing.

Tourism : The practice of touring or travelling for pleasure or recreation and the guidance or management of tourists as a business.

Tourism Facilities : Facilities which include accommodation like hotels, boarding houses, guest houses, youth hostels, etc. They also include recreational and sport facilities of great variety and also all the necessary infrastructure like transportation and utilities.

Tourism Research : Investigation relating to various aspects of tourism. The main objective of tourism research is to find out how people travel, where they travel and why they travel. The areas like travel, demand, domestic and international tourism, accommodation, transport, planning, etc., are covered in the research. The findings of the research become the base for planning and implementation of various programmes connected with tourism.

Tourist : A temporary visitor staying at least twenty four hours in the country visited and the purpose of whose journey can be classified under one of the following headings: (i) leisure (recreation, holiday, health, study, religion and sport); (ii) business, family, mission, meeting.

Tourist Centre : A village or town with a definite concentration of tourist resources, material base and infrastructure of tourism development.

Tourist Complex : A massive architectural installation specifically meant for the infrastructure of tourism.

Tourist, Domestic : A local person who makes a tour, travelling from place to place for pleasure, business, family mission, meeting, etc., within the country.

Tourist Flow : Undisturbed and even movement of tourists from one country to another for the purpose of travelling for pleasure.

Tourist, International : A person who makes a tour travelling from place to place for pleasure to areas foreign to his residence.

Tourist Lodge : A small house providing temporary accommodation to a tourist. The accommodation provided is inexpensive as compared to a conventional hotel. The lodge also offers meals.

Tourist Product : A sum total of a country's tourist attraction, infrastructure and tourist services which hopefully result in consumer satisfaction.

Tourist Region : A branch of economic region with specific high dependence on natural and man-made tourist attractions.

Tourist Visa : A document issued under the authority of the Government to a person visiting a particular country as a tourist.

Travel Agent : A person, firm or corporation qualified to provide tours, cruises, transportation, hotel accommodation, meals, transfers, sightseeing and all other elements of travel to the public as a service.

Travel Kit : A sort of container which contains accessories or tools. A travel kit contains various types of materials like folders, pamphlets, exhibits, presentation items, give-aways, etc., which helps the travel manager in promotional activities. It is an aid which helps in promoting and projecting a product. The contents of a kit, however, vary depending on the area where it is to be used and also on the amount set aside for the purpose.

Travel Magazine : A magazine which contains articles and other reading material devoted to all types of travel and tourism. The main objective of a travel magazine is the promotion of tourism.

Travel Markets : Travel markets are areas which exist in populated localities whose individuals possess leisure, money and desire to visit areas foreign to their residence.

Vacationer : A person staying away from home for at least four nights on any one trip and, in some instances, may include tourists travelling for a combination of business and pleasure.

Visa : An endorsement on the passport issued by the representative of a Government. The endorsement enables a person to travel to a country for which it is issued.

Visa, Entry : An endorsement on passport issued to persons who wish to visit a country for purposes of business, employment, permanent residence, profession, etc. Initially issued for a period of three months.

Visa, Tourist : An endorsement on passport issued to a person who wishes to visit a country as a tourist. The visa is effective for a period of three to six months. Tourists must arrive within six months of the date of the issue of visa. The tourist can extend his stay for a further period of three months if he applies to the concerned authorities.

Visa, Transit : An endorsement on a passport which is issued to a tourist whose destination is somewhere else and is passing across. Such visitors passing through a country en route to some other destination are granted Transit Visa on production of through tickets for the onward journey.

Visitor : Any person visiting a country other than that in which he has his usual place of residence, for any reason other than following an occupation remunerated within the country visited.

Visitor-Plant : All accommodation, transport etc., parks, points of interest in a destination area.

Wholesaler : A travel-oriented organisation that creates and presents ready-made travel package or tailor-made travel programmes exclusively at the request of a travel retailer (travel agent). The travel agent communicates with the prospective traveller, and discusses with him whether he needs a ready-made or tailor-made itinerary.

Wagons-list : Sleeping cars on the European continental railroads, consisting of a private bedroom with accommodation for one two or more persons depending on the class of travel. Items like pillows, blankets, sheets and a sink are included.

Technical Terms

Apex: Advance Purchase Excursion fare. Must be purchased from fourteen days to two months in advance, generally available on return basis only.

First Class: Symbolised by 'F'. Separate compartment, superior seating, a la carte menu, complimentary drinks, extra baggage allowance, no cancellation charges. Unlimited stopovers.

Excursion Fares: Priced midway between Apex and full fare economy class. There are no advance booking requirements but often a minimum stay abroad is mandatory.

Point-to-Point: Relatively a new fare particularly favoured by the Trans-Atlantic carriers and those on the Hong Kong-London and Australia routes. It offers a discount on the full fare in return for the passenger sacrificing his right to stopover and maximum permitted mileage.

ITX: Independent Inclusive Tour Excursion Fare. This was hurried on to the market by the scheduled carriers — mostly to holiday destinations — to counter the loss of business to charter airlines. Ostensibly available to the public only as a component of a holiday package which also include hotel accommodation and/ or car hire, more and more agents have in recent years been selling ITX fares for the flight alone and issuing fictitious hotel vouchers for the customer to produce if challenged at the airport (an extremely rare occurrence).

Economy Class: Symbolised by 'Y'. This is difficult to classify except when used for excursion fares.

IATA: International Air Transport Association. Travellers are most likely to hear of its existence as a travel agent declares a fare to be "illegal under IATA regulations" or as the chief steward apologises over the public address system for being "obliged by IATA regulations" to charge for headsets and alcoholic drinks. The only regulations its bureaucrats try to enforce are those formulated by the airlines themselves.

Budget Fare: Can be booked at least three weeks in advance. Exact travel date not confirmed until seven days before travel. There are cancellation charges too.

GV10: Group ticket for ten people travelling together. A discount fare created for tour operators, it is now widely used by airlines to conceal discounting to individuals from IATA and other investigators. Passengers are consolidated into group on paper without their knowledge — often after the flight has taken off.

Fifth Freedom : Traffic rights of an airline to pick up passengers from one state to another state neither of which is its flag state, is called fifth freedom. Example: Air India carrying traffic from Singapore to Australia and from Australia to Singapore.

MCO: Miscellaneous Charge Orders. A voucher exchangeable with any IATA airline for flights, excess baggage and so on. It is now used as a tax fiddle. Instead of issuing an executive with a first class ticket, a company issues him with an MCO for the equivalent value. He flies to his business appointment economy class and later uses residual value of his voucher to pay for his holiday flights.

Spouse Fares: One spouse flies at full fare, the other receives fifty per cent discount. The husband and wife must travel together on the same flight (s) until reaching their destination. The accompanying spouse may return to the point of origin independently but no stop-over shall be permitted. The airline ticket office staff may require the passport or other documents proving the couple's relationship.

Business Class: Referred to as "C" or "J". Many airlines use their own terminology: Club Class (British Airways); Ambassador Class (TWA); Maharaja Class (Air India); Marco Polo Class (Cathay Pacific); Silver Kris Class (SIA). Most airlines on international routes provide a separate compartment with better seating than economy class, greater menu selection and complimentary drinks.

Legal Fares: These are the fares which licensed and bonded travel agents are allowed to offer their customers. Theoretically enforceable in law, prosecutions of airlines that undercut them, which they often do, are virtually unknown.

MPM: Maximum Permitted Mileage. This refers to the full fare paying passenger's right not to proceed directly from his place of origin to his destination, but to stopover and vary his route by twenty per cent of the maximum mileage without surcharge.

Consolidators: Selected travel agents who receive an allocation of discounted tickets from the airline, then farm them out to other travel agents. A consolidator is, in effect, a wholesaler of discounted tickets.

The Abbreviations

ABTA : Association of British Travel Agents

AIEST : International Association of Scientific Experts in Tourism

AP : American Plan

ASTA : American Society of Travel Agents

BIT : Bulk Inclusive Tour

BTA : British Tourist Authority

CET : Centre d' Etudes du Tourism

DIT : Domestic Independent Tour

ENIT : Ente Nazionale Italiano per il Turismo

EP : European Plan

ETC : European Travel Commission

ETC : Euro-Traveller's Cheque

ETCI : Euro-Traveller's Cheque International

EATA : East Asian Travel Association

FIT : Foreign Individual Tour

FHRAI : Federation of Hotel & Restaurant Association of India

FTT : Foreign Travel Tax

GIT : Group Inclusive Tour

GSA : General Sales Agent

IATA : International Air Transport Authority

IIT : Independent Inclusive Tour

ICAO : International Civil Aviation Organisation

ICCA : International Congress and Convention Association

IATO : Indian Association of Tour Operators

IFTO : International Federation of Tour Operators

IHA : International Hotel Association

ITX : Inclusive Tour Excursion

ITA : International Touring Alliance

IT : Inclusive Tour

ITC : Inclusive Tour Charter

IUOTO : International Union of Official Tourist Organisation

IYHF : International Youth Hostel Federation

MAP : Modified American Plan

MCO : Miscellaneous Ticket Advice

NTB : National Tourism Board

NTO : National Tourism Organisation

OAG : Official Airline Guide

PATA : Pacific Asia Travel Association

PTA : Prepaid Ticket Advice

RTO : Regional Tourist Office

SARTC : South Asia Regional Tourist Council

SATW : Society of American Travel Writers

SST : Supersonic Transport

TA : Travel Agent

TAAI : Travel Agents Association of India

TBRE : Tourist Baggage Re-export

TIM : Travel Information Manual

TGV : Train a Grande Vitesse

TTRA : Travel and Tourism Research Association

UFTAA : Universal Federation of Travel Agents Association

USTOA : United States Tour Operators Association

WATA : World Association of Travel Agents.

Air-Fare Abbrevations

First : First Class

Bus : Business Class

Econ : Economy Class

O/W : One Way

R/T : Round Trip or Return

APOW : Advance Purchase One Way

APEX : Advance Purchase Excursion

Exc : Excursion

OAA : Orient Airlines Association

Spec : Special

Disc : Discounted

BAR : Board of Airlines Representatives

S : Sleeper

P : Point-to-Point

O : Shoulder

N : Non-stop

W : With Stop

I : Low Season

YIP : Yield Improvement Programme

GIT : Group Inclusive Tour

MSP : Minimum Selling Price

Bibliography

Andrew Vladimir : *The Complete Travel Marketing Handbook,* NTC Business Book, Lincolnwood, USA, 1989.

Anand M.M. : *Tourism and Hotel Industry in India: A Study in Management,* Prentice-Hall of India, New Delhi, 1976.

Baker, Machael J. : *The Marketing Book,* Heinmann, London, 1985.

Baron, Raphael Raymond, V.: *Seasonalty in Tourism: A Guide to Seasonality and Trends for Policy-making,* The Economist Intelligence Unit, 1975.

Beaver, Allan : *Retail Travel Practice,* Allan Beaver and Gordon Wharton Landtours Ltd., 1975.

Brian King, Geoff Hyde : *Tourism Marketing in Australia,* Hospitality Press, Melbourne, 1988.

Boniface, Brain G. : *The Geography of Travel and Tourism,* Butterworth-Heinmann, Oxford, 1991.

Burkart & Medlik : *Tourism — Past, Present and Future,* Heinemann Professional, London, 1990.

Bull, Adrian : *The Economics of Travel and Tourism,* Longman, Melbourne, 1991.

Coffmann, C.D. : *Marketing for a Full House — A Complete Guide to Profitable Hotel/Motel Operation Planning,* Cornell University, New York, 1980.

______, *Hospitality for Sale,* The American Hotel and Motel Association, 1984.

Coltman, Michael M. : *Introduction of Travel and Tourism*, Van Nostrand Reinhold, New York, 1989.

Collier, Alan : *Principles of Tourism*, Pitman, New Zealand, 1989.

Chakravorty : *Railways for Developing Countries*, Chetna Publications, New Delhi, 1982.

Chopra, P.N. : *India — An Encyclopaedic Survey*, New Delhi, 1984.

Clare A.J. Gunn : *Taylor and Francis, Tourism Planning*, New York, 1988.

Chib, S.N. : *Perspectives on Indian Tourism*, Sardar Patel Memorial Lectures, New Delhi, 1981.

David, Stewar : *The Theory and Practice of Transport*, Heinmann, London, 1980.

David, R. Yale : *The Publicity Hand Book*, Bantam Books, Toronto, 1992.

Davidson, Rob : *Tourism in Europe*, Pitman Techniplus, London, 1992.

Dale, E. : *Management Theory and Practice*, McGraw Hill, New York, 1983.

Douglas Pearce : *Tourism Today — A Geographical Analysis*, Longman Scientific Technical, 1987.

David Off, Phillips and Doris : *Sales and Marketing for Travel and Tourism*, Blackhill, USA, 1990.

Doswell, Royer : *Case Studies in Tourism*, Berrie and Jenkins, London, 1978.

Elvy, B. Howard : *Marketing Made Simple*, W.H. Allen, London 1982.

Foster, Douglas : *Travel and Tourism Management*, MacMillan, London, 1985.

Gee, Chuck Y., Makens, Choy : *The Travel Industry*, Van Nostrand Reinhold, New York, 1989.

Gidwani B.S. : *History of Air Transport*, Suneja Book Centre, New Delhi, 1954.

Galbraith, John C. : *The New Industrial State*, Signet, New York, 1986.

Godwin, Nadin : *Complete Guide to Travel Agency*, Automation, Albanj, Delmer, 1987.

Holloway, Christopher K. : *The Business of Tourism*, Pitman, London, 1990.

Heynes, Colin : *Guide to Successful Public Relations*, Scots Foresman and Company, Glansview, 1989.

Hawkins, Donald : *Tourism Planning and Development Issues*, George Washington University, 1980.

Jarari, J. : *Role of Tourism in Socio-Economic Transformation of Developing Countries*, 1973.

Kaiser Jr. & Helber : *Tourism Planning and Development*, CBI Publishing Company, Boston, 1977.

Karan Singh : *Indian Tourism — Aspects of a Great Adventure*, Department of Tourism, New Delhi, 1980.

Kotler P. : *Introduction to Marketing Management: Marketing Management Analysis*, Planning and Control, Prentice Hall, 1990.

Krippendorf, Jest : *The Holiday Makers: Understanding the Impact of Leisure and Travel*, 1992.

Lawson : *Teaching Tourism — Education and Training in Tourism in Western Europe : A Comprehensive Study*, Tourism International Press, London, 1980.

Lewis Robert C : *Marketing Leadership in Hospitality*, Van Nostrand, New York, 1989.

Lickorish, L.J. & Kershaw A.G. : *The Travel Trade*, Practical Press Ltd., London, 1988.

Lundberg, Donald E. : *The Hotel and Restaurant Business*, Medalist Publications, New York, 1980.

Mclntosh, R.W. : *Tourism Principles, Practices Philosophies*, John Wily, New York, 1990.

Mathiesor & Geoffreywall : *Tourism—Economic, Physical and Social Impact*, Longman, London, 1982.

Ogilvy, F.W. : *The Tourist Movement—An Economic Study*, Staples Press, London, 1997.

Ogilvy David : *Confessions of an Advertising Man*, Ballantine Books, New York, 1976.

Pearce Douglas G. : *Tourist Organisations*, Longman Technical, London, 1992.

Patric Lavery : *Travel and Tourism*, Elem Publications, London, 1990.

Meredith George : *Incentives in Marketing*, NPSEE Education Fund, New Jersey, 1977.

Morrison James, W. : *Travel Agents and Tourism*, ARCO Publishing, New York, 1980.

Pierson C.G. & Bird, R.G. : *Business Finance*, McGraw Hill, 1972.

Reilly, Robert T : *Hand Book of Professional Tourism Management*, Prentice Hall, 1985.

Richards, G. : *Tourism and the Economy*, Guilford, University of Surrey, 1972.

Rosenow, John E. : *Tourism — the Good, the Bad and the Ugly*, Century Three Press, London, 1979.

Shaffr & Revelshad : *Tourism Planning and Development Issues*, George Washington University, Washington DC, 1980.

Tata J.R.D. : *The Story of Indian Air Transport*, The Sixteenth British Commonwealth Lecture, 1961.

_____, *Travel and Tourism Industry : Strategies for Future*, Pergamon Press, London, 1987.

Urry, John : *The Tourist Gaze — Leisure and Travel in Contemporary Societies*, Sage Publications, New Delhi, 1990.

Wahab, Salah : *Wahab on Tourism Management*, Tourism International Press, London, 1975.

Waters, Somerset R. : *Travel Industry World Year Book*, Child and Waters, New York, 1994.

Yocoumis, John : *Air Inclusive Tour Marketing*, The Economist Intelligence Unit, London 1975.

Young, George : *Tourism—Bliss or Blight?* Penguin Books, London, 1973.

Reports

National Council of Applied Economic Research India, Cost Benefit Study of Tourism, 1975.

PATA, Tourism Heritage and Conservation Conference, Kathmandu, 1983.

PATA, South Asia Communicators Conference, New Delhi, 1983.

PATA India Chapter, Survey on Marketing and Tourism Infrastructure, IIPO, New Delhi, 1982.

PATA, Story Editors, Chuck Gee and Matt Lurie, 1992.

STPB, Strategic Plan for Growth — 1993-1995.

Government of India, Ministry of Tourism, Foreign Tourists Survey -1988-89, J.K. Associates, New Delhi, 1990.

Government of India, Report on National Committee on Tourism, Planning Commission, New Delhi, 1988.

Government of India, Department of Tourism, Report on Manpower Development—Needs of Various Sectors of Travel Industry—1990-1995 & 2000 A.D. New Delhi, 1987.

Government of India, Ministry of Tourism and Civil Aviation, Foreign Tourist Survey 1976-77 by Administrative Staff College of India.

Government of India, Economic Benefits of Tourism, 1987.

Govt. of India, Department of Tourism, Performance Appraisal — 1985-86.

Government of India, Report of the Hotel Review and Survey Committee, 1968.

Government of India, Report of the Hotel Review Committee, 1970.

IIPO, An Updated Report on Indian Tourism, Performance and Potential, 1981-1991.

IATA, Annual Report —1994.

ICAO, Annual Report of the Council —1993.

WTO, Compendium of Tourism Statistics, 1993.

Government of India, Foreign Tourist Survey—1989-90.

